The Culturally Complex Individual

The Culturally Complex Individual

Franz Werfel's Reflections on Minority
Identity and Historical Depiction in
The Forty Days of Musa Dagh

Rachel Kirby

Lewisburg
Bucknell University Press
London: Associated University Presses

© 1999 by Associated University Presses, Inc.

All rights reserved. Authorization to photocopy items for internal or personal use, or the internal or personal use of specific clients, is granted by the copyright owner, provided that a base fee of $10.00, plus eight cents per page, per copy is paid directly to the Copyright Clearance Center, 222 Rosewood Drive, Danvers, Massachusetts 01923. [0-8387-5393-0/99 $10.00 + 8¢ pp, pc.]

Associated University Presses
440 Forsgate Drive
Cranbury, NJ 08512

Associated University Presses
16 Barter Street
London WC1A 2AH, England

Associated University Presses
P.O. Box 338, Port Credit
Mississauga, Ontario
Canada L5G 4L8

The paper used in this publication meets the requirements
of the American National Standard for Permanence of Paper
for Printed Library Materials Z39.48-1984.

Library of Congress Cataloging-in-Publication Data

Kirby, Rachel, 1965–
    The culturally complex individual : Franz Werfel's reflections on minority identity and historical depiction in The forty days of Musa Dagh / Rachel Kirby.
    p. cm.
    Includes bibliographical references and index.
    ISBN 0-8387-5393-0 (alk. paper)
    1. Werfel, Franz, 1890–1945. Vierzig Tage des Musa Dagh. 2. Turkey—In literature. 3. History in literature. 4. Minorities in literature. 5. Identity (Psychology) in literature. I. Title.
PT2647.E77V555   1999
833'.912—dc21   99-19399
                                                                     CIP

PRINTED IN THE UNITED STATES OF AMERICA

To my family

Contents

Preface	9
1. The Theme of Identity in the Works of Franz Werfel	13
2. Identity and the Historical Community in *The Forty Days of Musa Dagh*	53
3. Franz Werfel, the Historical Novel, and *The Forty Days of Musa Dagh*	76
4. *Musa Dagh* as a Participant in Dominant Discourses	111
5. Reception and Literary Response	150
Notes	181
Bibliography	195
Index	201

Preface

THE FORTY DAYS OF MUSA DAGH STRUCK ME ALREADY AT THE FIRST reading as Franz Werfel's most compelling novel, and what I perceived to be its main theme—minority identity—seemed to be handled in convincing fashion. The topic of minorities and minority identity is a natural extension of my personal experience and interests, having been raised in a well-integrated—and what would now be referred to as multicultural—environment: a suburb of Los Angeles. It was in Los Angeles that the archival work on *Musa Dagh* began. The extensive Franz Werfel holdings housed in Special Collections at UCLA include a notebook in which he outlined plot and characters, noted secondary sources, and sketched maps for his own quick reference while planning the 700-page novel. There are also many letters written both by and to Werfel dating to the time during which he was writing the novel. Further work was undertaken at the Austrian National Library, studying a handwritten manuscript of *Musa Dagh*, much of which is identical to the final published version, but substantial portions of which are dramatically different from the finished product. Finally, a collection of newspaper articles from the 1920s and 1930s held at the Archivní Správa in Prague provided a useful resource for contemporary politics in Austria and Czechoslovakia.

As I indicate more than once, I think that Werfel has been, in academic circles, a victim of his popularity in the 1930s and 1940s. I refer to this briefly in the final chapter on reception in the discussion about the commemoration of the one hundredth anniversary of Werfel's birth in 1990. By far the most unabashed utter rejection of Werfel I have ever heard came from a German scholar who, when I told him what I was working on, responded with the quote, "All pigs are equal," a characterization of Werfel that I feel is grossly unfair, but which surprised me only in its degree of directness.

Clearly, I consider some of Werfel's works to be worthy of more serious attention, and indeed, since the one hundredth anniversary there has been some increased activity surrounding Werfel: a major biography, several essay collections, an International Werfel Society, and a journal devoted to Werfel studies. This book attempts to supplement this new scholarship in offering an in-depth treatment of *Musa Dagh;* by bringing in and analyzing new materials from the mentioned archival sources and relating *Musa Dagh* to today's concerns in the areas of identity, multiculturalism, postcolonialism, and minority issues. The connection is not a forced one; rather, I have tried to stress the lasting—if changing—relevance of this 1933 work to late-twentieth-century readers from several different perspectives.

Thanks are due to the staffs of the Austrian National Library (Handschriften- und Inkunabelsammlung), the Archivní Správa in Prague, and the Special Collections at UCLA for their assistance during my research at their respective facilities.

I would also like to thank Princeton University Press for permission to quote Edith Abercrombie Snow's translation of Werfel's *Poems;* S. Fischer Verlag, Frankfurt am Main for permission to quote *Die Vierzig Tage des Musa Dagh;* and the Department of Special Collections, Charles E. Young Research Library, UCLA, for permission to quote from Werfel's letters and notes.

The Culturally Complex Individual

1
The Theme of Identity in the Works of Franz Werfel

IN A PROLIFIC LITERARY CAREER SPANNING THIRTY-FOUR YEARS, Franz Werfel produced works covering a broad spectrum of genres and styles. He achieved early prestige as a leading representative of expressionistic poetry, then gained a wide audience for his dramas, which gradually moved away from the expressionistic themes and style. It was Werfel's realistic novels that launched him to enduring international fame in his thirties and forties. Throughout all these phases, however, there are observable constants in his works. All his works bear traces, in lesser or greater quantity, of his early poetry's pathos and humanism. Although he was best known as a novelist, and indeed owed his financial security to the popularity of his novels, Werfel continued to write poetry his entire life and considered himself above all a poet.[1] A thematic constant to be examined here is the topic of identity. The following chapter will trace the interlocking themes of identity and community as a central problem in several exemplary works up to his forced exile in 1938, leading into the chapter 2 analysis of this topic as it applies to his 1933 novel *The Forty Days of Musa Dagh,* which will be the focus of this book.

Werfel touches on all of the main considerations addressed by scholars of identity since it became a focus of scholarly attention—primarily in the fields of psychology and sociology—at around midcentury.[2] Erik H. Erikson, who was largely responsible for putting the term *identity crisis* into circulation,[3] described identity as "a process 'located' in the core of the individual and yet also in the core of his communal culture, a process which establishes, in fact, the identity of those two identities."[4] This definition contains in condensed form the fundamental elements of identity study. Of foremost importance is that identity is considered to exist only in the context of a society. It is a dynamic, ongoing evolution, a product of a dialectic relationship between society and individual. Peter Berger formulates the process as follows: "Identity ... is always identity within a specific, socially constructed world. Or, as seen from the viewpoint of the individual: One identifies oneself, as one is identified by others, by being located in a common world."[5] An individual's sense of identity is only possible when she or he is a member of some societal entity (or, as will be referred to here, a community).

Being a member of a community involves identifying with its historical legacy. Central to knowing "who one is," is having a sense of "who one was." Alex Haley highlighted this aspect of identity with his *Roots*.[6] He showed that African-Americans, long denied a historical legacy with which to identify, could trace much of their personal insecurity to this very problem. The history of one's society is of great consequence to an individual's identity. When knowledge of it is intentionally discouraged or neglected due to circumstances, individual identity suffers a potentially crippling blow.

The current debate on multiculturalism has returned broad-based public attention to identity issues on a societal scale. The link between society and individual was described by Erikson as a "process." Writing on multiculturalism, Charles Taylor similarly sees the relationship as "dialogical": identity is "negotiated" between the individual and society.

> We become full human agents, capable of understanding ourselves, and hence of defining our identity, through our acquisition of rich human languages of expression. [... But we learn these modes of expression through exchanges with others. People do not acquire the languages needed for self-definition on their own. Rather, we are introduced to them through interaction with others who matter to us—what George Herbert Mead called "significant others."[7]

Multiculturalism holds that these negotiations have been lopsided: the parties involved have not been dealing from positions of equal influence. As a result, our shared language reflects a bias, and terms describing otherness are not neutral but rather tinged with negativity; thus, "female" = "compassionate" (read: weak), "black" = "simple" (unintelligent), "Asian" = "ambitious" (unscrupulous) and so on. If an individual's identity consists primarily of marginalized (negative) elements, his or her self-esteem will suffer accordingly. When exploring her identity as a woman or an Asian, then, the Asian female is severely hampered by such deep-seated biases from conceiving of those identity components in a positive light.

Several scholars have observed a connection between postmodernist theory and multiculturalism.[8] Although the latter does not necessarily derive directly from the former, there is no mistaking the usefulness of certain postmodern categories to multiculturalist arguments. Specifically, both stress that the metanarratives of modernity,[9] and the power relationships effected by them, no longer hold validity for an increasingly diversified world. Modernist universal principles, regardless of their possibly humanist impulses, are now understood to be the outgrowth of Eurocentric values and, as such, limiting. Steven Rockefeller and others may still argue that, "from the democratic point of view,"

> our universal identity as human beings is our primary identity and is more fundamental than any particular identity, whether it be a matter of citizenship, gender, race, or ethnic origin.[10]

However, the very existence of a "universal identity" is questionable when one reflects, as Taylor does, that "the democratic point of view" and other well-intentioned "'blind' liberalisms" are themselves "a particularism masquerading as the universal."[11] Like postmodernism, multiculturalism abandons the metanarratives of "humanity" and "democratic principles" for more localized narratives. In the place of nationality, for instance, regional phenomena, religious particularities, or ethnic matters are placed center stage. Increased understanding of minority groups is thought to be the means toward securing a stable identity for all individuals, since all of its constituent elements can be pursued with confidence by the individual and be affirmed in the societal context. Again, the dialogical relationship between individual and society is of crucial importance. Each person needs the informed recognition of all aspects of his or her identity in order for that composite identity to be a source of confidence; in turn, the person thus accepted and educated is in a position to recognize and affirm a multitude of others' identity components as they occur in manifold combinations.

Franz Werfel: Identity and Community. The Great Human Community and Its Collapse

Identity questions arise out of turbulent events or during times of disorienting change. Most individuals are unlikely to second-guess their own self-concept without having received impetus from an outside source. Europe of the early twentieth century presented some individuals and groups with cause for redefining themselves. The unprecedented event of a world war and the ensuing situation of political change, economic depression, and chauvinistic attitudes literally forced the issue. Some found themselves given a nationality that had never before existed, others had to come to terms with the fact that their country's borders had been redrawn to enclose a (comparably) miniscule territory, still others experienced an abrupt change in social standing. All of these changes brought with them some form of the question, "Who can I be now?" The conditions giving rise to multiculturalism and those which made nationalism possible in the earlier part of the century do differ greatly, yet they have in common that most fundamental question of an identity in need of redefinition. If we consider any text as the answer to a question being posed, we can find that same identity question at the center of Franz Werfel's *oeuvre*. Many of his works address this question, offering a variety of attempts at an answer as the historical circumstances changed. At times the answer, or attempted answer, achieved nothing more than a reformulation of the question. By 1933, however, he was able to give his most complete answer with *The Forty Days of Musa Dagh*.

Werfel is situated entirely within the context of modern metanarratives. His works consistently exhibit the assumption and affirmation of universal liberal principles: fundamental human equality and dignity, democratic rights, humanistic values. Creativity and individualism are highly regarded, but Werfel understands that individual identity is possible only in a relationship

1: THE THEME OF IDENTITY IN THE WORKS OF FRANZ WERFEL

with a broader community. The dimensions of "community" change radically for Werfel as his experiences demonstrate the pitfalls and even impossibilities of different community types. He ranges from finding community in vast humanity, to seeking it in the *Volk,* and ultimately realizes that in some historical situations, the communal ties requisite to identity exist only on a much smaller scale, such as the nuclear family.

In his earliest poetry, Werfel proclaimed the great human community. Punctuated with countless exclamation marks, his verses confidently assure the reader of an intimate bond of humanity linking all individuals. His first volumes of poetry are characterized by an ecstatic tone celebrating interpersonal encounters. Twice he expresses in the first stanza of "For I have done a good and kindly deed"[12] that playing a part in others' lives gives meaning to his individual existence, which otherwise would be "lonely." "Sweetest gratification" is imparted to him as a result of a good deed he has performed for a stranger, and the bonds of their common humanity allow for the brief episode to hold meaning for both persons involved.

> Oh heart rejoice!
> I have done a good and kindly deed.
> Now I'm no longer lonely.
> Someone lives,
> There lives a man
> Whose eyes grow moist
> When he thinks of me.
> Heart, rejoice!
> There lives a man!
> No more, no, no more am I alone,
> For I have done a good and kindly deed.

It is more than just gratifying to participate in a larger human community, it is indispensable for a happy existence: his loneliness is dispelled because of his unselfish deed. Werfel assumes there to be a basic commonality which makes possible the insight into the lot of all humans' lives, and in "To the reader" would have the readers accept him (and, by implication, each other) as a brother: "My only wish is to be related to you, oh human!"

> Denn ich habe alle Schicksale durchgemacht: Ich weiß
> Das Gefühl von einsamen Harfenistinnen in Kurkapellen,
> Das Gefühl von schüchternen Gouvernanten im fremden Familienkreis,
> Das Gefühl von Debütanten, die sich zitternd vor den Souffleurkasten stellen.
>
> [...]
>
> So gehöre ich Dir und Allen.
> Wolle mir, bitte, nicht widerstehn!
> Oh könnte es einmal geschehn,
> Daß wir uns, Bruder, in die Arme fallen![13]

[For I have experienced all fates: I know / The feeling of lonely harpists in resort orchestras, / The feeling of shy governesses in a strange family circle, / The feeling of novice actors who take trembling refuge in front of the prompt-box. / [...] So I belong to you and all. / Please do not resist me! / Oh if only once / We, Brother, might embrace one another!]

The positive, affirming tone of *The Philanthropist* and *We Are* disappeared with the advent of the First World War. *One Another* (1915) is a testimony of the disgust and incomprehension Franz Werfel felt in response to such large-scale human destruction. Unlike many of his contemporaries, Werfel did not view the war as a potentially cathartic event for Europe. He condemned the separatist factions stemming from nationalist trends among the peoples of Europe. In addition to witnessing the failure of his vision of a human community without dividing lines, Werfel suddenly found himself unwillingly alienated from his Bohemian compatriots. While the Czechs and Slovaks of his Austrian homeland pursued their nationalist aspirations and the rest of Europe was embroiled in a war which precluded any hope for the unity of humanity, Werfel was at a loss to know where a person in his situation might look for a community to replace the failed one.

Werfel's disorientation is evident in many of his works from this point forward. In prose and poetry alike, themes of confusion and insecurity abound. His 1915 poem "Inscription" indicates the level of despair resulting from the lack of a community to call one's own. Every line is heavy with emotion: the longing, the search for a framework in which to develop a secure identity, the regret and homesickness for the situation prior to the loss of community. Werfel finds nothing which could adequately define him—in his circumstances, the possibility of finding it is nonexistent (the "framework which is absent").

Aufschrift

> Niemals im Andern, nie im Ich zu Hause!
> Bestand und Zeit zugleich wie Nichts und Pause!
> Nimmer ein Jetzt und stets Erinnerung.
> Und nur der Wille: Ewig sich zu teilen,
> In jeder Form vertausendfacht zu weilen,
> Und wieder Heimweh auf der Wanderung,
> Sich aus Verlorensein zurückzuretten,
> Und Sehnsucht, die sich elbst zerfrißt,
> Dem Namen, den man trägt sich anzuketten,
> Und dem Gestelle, das nicht ist.

[Never in the Other, never in myself at home! / Continuance and time the same as nothing and lapse! / Never a Now and constantly remembrance. / And only the wish: ever to divide oneself, / To tarry in every form thousandfold, / And again homesickness on the journey, / To retrieve oneself from being lost, / And a self-consuming yearning, / To link oneself to the name one bears, / And to the framework which is absent.]

He is denied positive recognition from his subjective community. Worse still, he is given a demeaning self-image. Taylor writes, "Nonrecognition or misrecognition can inflict harm, can be a form of oppression, imprisoning someone in a false, distorted, and reduced mode of being."[14] As has been discussed, the attempt to satisfy the need for identity simply in terms of the individual is in vain. Here, the dialogical negotiation process of establishing identity is marked by animosity on one side. The identity desired by the individual is denied by the community with which he would like to identify, causing low symmetry between subjective and objective identity. The negotiation process is stalled until one side (the weaker of the two; here, the individual) makes concessions. As "Inscription" indicates, reconceiving one's identity is both difficult and painful.

The *Volk* as a Basis of Identity, and Werfel's Czechoslovakian *Heimat*

In late-eighteenth-century Germany, it had become increasingly difficult to orient oneself within society according to the familiar feudal system. The modernization of contemporary life, the alienating phenomena of the industrial metropolis, and the changed conceptions of societal order brought about by the French Revolution eclipsed many traditional sources of identity. Seeking a new point of reference for the individual, many romantic authors looked to old German folklore for a foundation for historical identity. In particular, the *Volksmärchen* and *Volkspoesie* seemed to contain a uniquely Germanic quality which was capable of reinvigorating an essential German spirit with which one could identify. Especially the Heidelberg romantics promoted a conscious kinship among Germans as a *Volk,* positing a German *Volkscharakter* that had grown out of a common connection to the German landscape and shaped the collective values and eternal character of that people throughout the generations. With growing hostility toward the French presence in Germany, and with the popularization of racial theories in the following century, the term *Volk* took on more reactionary, exclusionist connotations. No longer merely a historical grounding for individual identity, it became a source of unreflected pride and a rationalization for bigotry, the roots of the *Völkisch* ideology to emerge decades later.

Once confronted with a failed human community after World War I, Werfel seeks fellowship in smaller communal groupings. His works from 1915 on often portray the *Volk* as an essential source of sustenance for the individual. National heritage replaces the human community as the overarching, identity-granting principle. Ironically, in absorbing the popular rhetoric of the *Volk,* he latches onto the very impulses that had splintered the human community into warring factions. Although he does not ascribe to chauvinistic conceptions of superiority, pitting one *Volk* against another in competition, his ideas must be regarded as utterly naive. The war had graphically illustrated the kind of bigotry and aggression that can result from taking excessive pride in one's nation or *Volk*. Werfel has unwittingly replaced the unifying principle with one of exclusivity. Still, he sees the *Volk* only as a community rich with unifying customs, a shared history, and an intimate bond with the land upon which it has lived. "Permanence" (*Sleep and Awakening*, 1935) is Werfel's strongest lyrical representation of the value of traditions and community based on the *Volk*.

Permanence[15]

As long as the Tatra winds blow
On Slovakian blossoms aglow,
So long girls will work the gay flowers
And embroider them through bright hours.

As long as the axe at dawn-gray
Through Bavarian Wood greets the day,
So long lonely man in his hut
Will God and the holy saints cut.

As long as the sea scans the ships
Of its men on Ligurian trips,
So long wives will watch from its strand
As they make bobbin laces by hand.

You folk of the earth, in my breast
Stirs the permanence you manifest.
I, myself, without folk, without land,
Now bury my face in my hand.

In each of the first three stanzas, the link between natural surroundings and local customs is stressed: the plants and geographical features indigenous to a region are incorporated into the *Volk*'s heritage in the form of crafts or artistry. Thus, the Slovakian flowers gracing the slopes of the Tatra Mountains are reproduced in the girls' embroidery—a custom that will be passed down as long as the flowers keep blooming. In similar fashion, the Bavarian forest and the Ligurian Sea are represented in traditional handiwork as a reminder of the enduring bond between people and land. It is this enduring relationship, the community traditions, the "permanence" which touches

Werfel precisely because of its constancy from generation to generation. He recognizes the value of ethnic heritage as something one can turn to for identification. The traditions of ethnic groups provide a firmly located point of orientation for the individual. It is also such a heritage of traditions, however, which eludes the Jewish, German-speaking native of Prague, particularly (though not exclusively, as will be discussed) after the collapse of the Austrian-Hungarian Empire and the establishment of an independent Czechoslovakian state. Werfel opted for Czechoslovakian citizenship after World War I, but he was painfully aware that this isolated him even more than ever. With the exception of gender, every component of his identity had minority status: "I, myself, without folk, without land, / Now bury my face in my hand."

Volk, land, and the age-old traditions binding the two together are primary components of *Heimat*—a term of community far richer in emotional content than the English "homeland." "Permanence" is a tender illustration of the qualities of *Heimat* in general, not restricted to the Bohemian atmosphere most familiar to him. K. Hyršlová, in an article addressing the question of *Heimat* in Werfel's works, asserts that Werfel "can ... only consider Bohemia as his true homeland."[16] Bohemia was his place of birth, the land of his ancestors, and the setting of both his childhood and early adulthood; as such, it was, indeed, the only place he could *consider* as a *Heimat*. His essay, "I Am a Czechoslovakian," witnesses the tenacity with which he attempted to lay claim to this region as his own. That a Bohemian *Heimat* for Werfel was, nevertheless, ultimately an impossibility will be shown in the following discussion. However, Hyršlová is correct in positing that Werfel had a special relationship with Bohemia that could not be duplicated elsewhere. Accordant with this relationship with the region is his active interest in its people: the Czechs and, to a much lesser degree, the Slovaks. Werfel admired what he believed to be the national traits of these people: simplicity, strength, and loyalty. While Slovaks and especially Czechs comprised the overwhelming majority in the population of Prague and the smaller surrounding towns and villages,[17] their status in Austrian Bohemia was subordinate to that of German Austrians—an incongruity not lost even on the young Franz Werfel. As a result, his works featuring Czech or Slovak characters exhibit two main themes: admiration for the *Volk* and its simple but hardy people, mixed with a certain amount of poignant longing to share in their community; and sympathy for their underprivileged status.

Werfel's humanism is his most defining characteristic. He constantly strove to achieve humane treatment of minority groups, be they disadvantaged in the numerical sense, as a social class, or culturally. Hugh Puckett recognizes a "preoccupation with the underprivileged" in Werfel's work and stresses that the repeating theme is no affectation.

> [T]his interest has nothing at all to do with "armer Leute Poesie" or any of the other economic or sociological motifs affected by one or another literary school. There is no pretense or dilettantism in it, rather it is a deep-seated principle and in general the mainspring of his action.[18]

His "devotion to the lowly"[19] manifests itself in his character portraits, such as that of the Czech servant girl in "The Mishap" who drops a serving bowl at a dinner party hosted, presumably, by a leading German family. (Heinz Politzer goes so far as to assume that "Of course, the hostess and the master of the house stand for Werfel's own parents."[20]) The girl is so stunned at her mistake that the other servants must attend to clearing away the spillage, while she retreats to the kitchen.

> Sie aber ging ganz wunderschön von Kindheit und Heimweh hinaus.
> In der Küche setzte sie sich auf die Kohlenkiste, legte die Hände in den Schoß,
> Und weinte vielfach, in allen Lagen, nach aller Kunst, voll Genuß, laut und grenzenlos.
>
> [But she withdrew, lovely in her childhood and homesickness. / In he kitchen she sat down on the coalbox, laid her hands in her lap, / And wept diversely, in every manner, artfully, with full enjoyment, loud and unrestrained.]

Here, her genuine and simple nature is apparent. In crying without shame, she expresses a basic emotion, nor does she feel self-conscious about it. She is "lovely" in her childlike lack of inhibition and in the visible "homesickness," which distinctly identifies her as an outsider. The guests, who pity her as "a victim of circumstances," express their sympathy at the end of the evening in giving her especially generous tips. Politzer correctly identifies her "circumstance" as "the national and social difference that separated [Werfel's] life from that of the Czech people," but does not do justice to Werfel's fundamental principles when he attributes his concern for the girl to feelings of "guilt."[21] Anna Jacobson, in a 1927 article, also finds "deepest sympathy for the privations of the poor, the helplessness of the small and the old" to be prominent in Werfel's poems and plays. Unlike some Werfel detractors, however, she does not question the motivation for Werfel's genuinely humanistic impulses. His sensitivity to the plight of the underprivileged is not restricted to isolated moments of compunction but rather is one of his most consistent themes. Jacobson continues: "It is not an impressionistic portrayal of the poor maid, . . . the old suburban prostitute; their misfortune moves him and compels him to sympathetic, humanistic protestation. . . ."[22]

In her study, "The Czechs in the Work of Franz Werfel," Lore Foltin identifies "a social awareness and political commitment" in Werfel's essays, but does not find that tendency duplicated in his other works. Her concluding paragraph asserts that this same social awareness, so central to his essayistic work, "is absent in his plays, novels, and stories, and nearly absent in his poems."[23] With this assertion, however, Foltin seems to contradict her own findings stated earlier in the same article:

> Whether the oppressor and oppressed appear as Turk and Armenian, Fascist regime and Italian citizen, German and Czech, whether Werfel expresses himself in poem, drama, novel, story, or essay, he is always sympathetic to the problems facing minorities, always defending the right to individual existence.[24]

Werfel's sympathy for minority groups is, indeed, a thread of continuity visibly winding through every phase of his work. Foltin is accurate in observing that Werfel's portrayal of Czechs is almost entirely restricted to the simple folk of the lower social strata. The Czech intellectual, the revolutionary leaders " . . . are not to be found in the pages of his books."[25] Hyršlová, too, comments that Werfel's sympathy and admiration for Czechs is ". . . accompanied by a lack of understanding and misunderstanding, especially in view of the further development of the Czech nation."[26] However, this fact should not necessarily be the target of criticism. Werfel's one-dimensional portrayal of Czech characters can be attributed to two facts: first, that his knowledge of Czechs stemmed mainly from his contact with maids (such as the girl in "The Mishap"), nannies, and laborers; second, that he is much more in a position to stress the Czechs' minority status when portraying the vulnerable, impoverished Czech. Still, such characters are not a literary invention; day laborers and servants comprised fully 57 percent of the Czech population in Prague and its suburbs in 1910 (workers: 47.95 percent, servants: 9.68 percent).[27] In no way does Werfel's concentration on working-class Czechs and Slovaks diminish the validity of his commitment to minorities. It should again be emphasized, however, that his uplifting of the *Volk* principle is unreflected. The celebration of particularism flows quite readily into the oppression of the different. In this case, Werfel's sympathy goes out to the victims of German-Austrian prejudice, but he does not recognize the correlation between *Volk*-romanticism and bigotry.

The 1923 poem "The Slovak" (*Conjurations*) is another representative example of Werfel's overromanticized image of Czechs and Slovaks in a German-dominated society. In this instance, it is the Slovakian Janoušek whose daily routine is depicted. The old man, wandering from farm to farm and repairing metal goods in return for the most basic sustenance, is very consciously shown to be an anachronism ("A strange creature, and not as though from these times"). Werfel, however, endows his outdatedness with a kind of beauty similar to that which he admired in his young serving girl. "An ancient song coos from the aged throat," signifying his belonging to a community rich with tradition. Again, the geographical bond is indicated in the sky's blue, reflecting the color of the regional gentian blossoms, mentioned in the poem's opening lines: "September winds have blown into the land. / But above still rests the gentian blue." Janoušek is a simplistic portrait of Werfel's naive notions about national character:

> Höflich nimmt er ganz ohne Gier
> Seinen Lohn, diesen Trug von Papier,
> Schlägt ein Kreuz, um weiter zu ziehn,
> Schwankend auf seinen umwickelten Füßen,
> Und vergißt auch keine Seele frohmütig zu grüßen.

[Politely, with no greed, he accepts / His wage, this paper deception, / Makes the sign of the cross in order to move on, / Staggering on his swathed feet, / Nor forgets to greet every soul cheerfully.]

Werfel's Slovak is respectful and devout, poor but friendly. He is treated badly by everyone, including the farmers who stand only slightly above him on the social ladder, and Werfel predicts even further victimization in store for him at the close of the poem:

> Enzianblau. Die Winde haben
> Gefährlichen Anschlag im Sinn.
> Tief unten schon schaukelt der Alte dahin.
> Doch ihn umfetzt ein Geschlecht von Raben.
> Oktobervögel, frostkündende Meute.

[Gentian blue. The winds carry / Dangerous tidings. / Far below the old man sways ahead. / But ripping about him is a family of ravens. / October birds, frost-portending pack.]

The small nationalities are shown to be in a position of vulnerability when the political winds become threatening. Werfel fails to understand the folly of deriving one's identity primarily from one's *Volk,* but once the inevitable competition between the *Völker* has led to hostilities, he does recognize that minority groups, hopelessly outnumbered by large *Völker,* such as the Germans or the French, are in grave danger of being thoroughly overpowered—even erased—in an era of national chauvinism. He appeals to the Czechoslovakian public's sensibilities in presenting his literary works from exactly that perspective. Press releases of the *Prager Presse* for his novel *The Forty Days of Musa Dagh* (1933), for example, relay the message that the small community is threatened. Werfel was closely connected with the *Presse;* even while living in Vienna, he made regular contributions to the newspaper.[28] It is, therefore, likely that any press releases concerning his works were supplied by him, if not verbatim then at least in content and emphasis. An article announcing a reading from Werfel's novel still in the preparatory stages, informs the public that it will be hearing "the exciting epos of the decline of an ostracized national minority."[29] A later article bearing the headline "The Mission of the Small Nations" reports to the Prague German readership that Werfel had been interviewed by the Czech *Pestrýtýden* on the occasion of the Czech *Musa Dagh* translation. He used the opportunity to comment publicly "on small nations in general and on the Czech Volk in particular." In a declaration of solidarity with and understanding for the Czechs, Werfel states:

> I believe that I understand with all my soul the great virtues and burning humanity of the Czech Volk, in whose territory I was a child and experienced my youth and the years of so much mysterious preparation. I believe that the Czech Volk will not become estranged from its mission and its genius.[30]

THE PURE IN HEART: THE EFFECTS OF INVOLUNTARY AND VOLUNTARY ISOLATION UPON IDENTITY

Running parallel to the affirmative characterization of the community in Werfel's work is a sustained contrasting theme: isolation. As was evident in both "Inscription" and "Permanence," there can hardly be a more fundamentally demoralizing dilemma for Werfel than being excluded from a vital community. It is in *The Pure in Heart* (1929) that this dilemma comes most prominently to the fore in the protagonist, Ferdinand K.[31] His strongest emotional attachment is to his Czech nanny, Barbara, who has cared for him on a daily basis since his birth. When Ferdinand becomes orphaned as a young boy, he is allowed a short trip with her to her home in the Czech countryside. Already at this age, his future isolation is apparent. With the exception of an uncaring aunt, he lacks the most primal communal bond: the family. Barbara, now more than ever, is his "foster mother." (84) Although she considers Ferdinand to be "her child" (83), their different national origins clearly separate the two—a fact that does not dawn on the boy until much later. On their excursion to her home, he feels only the bond with her.

> Ferdinand had his share of Barbara's home. . . . It mattered nothing that the child should only half understand the langage that was spoken all round him (Papa had instructed Barbara to talk only German to his son)—the Austrian officer's child did not yet know that what every peasant boasts, a home and a family, were denied him, or realize himself as uprooted and alone in the world. (84–85)

The novel continues as the story of Ferdinand's search for community. The rest of his childhood and early adulthood is a nebulous sequence of adjustments to impersonal situations: first as a cadet in a military school; then, upon becoming a ward of the state, in a Vienna seminary. Indifferent to both the military and the priesthood, Ferdinand strives only for physical survival. His emotional detachment is finally interrupted by the outbreak of World War I, which awakens patriotic feelings for his Austrian *Heimat*. "The Austrian officer's son within him had awakened.[32] That sacred flame of valour which darted up in the best of his generation lit him too, filling him with a horror of staying behind, the despised of his contemporaries, with no uniform." (152) But Ferdinand's newfound patriotism does not outlast the war. In addition to being horrified by the destruction and atrocities, he is also the victim of an antagonistic superior who, in an attempt to have him killed, sends him to the most dangerous trenches possible. It becomes clear to him that the common national cause does not create a reliable, brotherly community.

While waiting out the war's end in Vienna, "Ferdinand, the solitary," as Werfel calls him (343), is driven by the desire to find a surrogate community. He seeks out human contact in a murky cafe he calls the "realm of shadows," where he was first persuaded not to return to his regiment. "So day after day Ferdinand went forth in quest of a friend in unutterable hunger for companionship, inner contact, perception. . . ." (376) After having his patriotic feelings disillusioned by his war experiences, he is inclined to find community in even the most contradictory theories. It is not surprising that he is receptive to doctrines of Catholicism and communism vaguely promising collectivity:

> Catholicism here, Communism there, both impersonal, collective doctrines of salvation, both armed against a common enemy: liberalism, democracy, the hateful bourgeoisie! Both turned towards the thousand-year empire and absolute opponents to war and money![33]

However, he soon recognizes this attraction, too, to have been only self-deception. He derives no fulfillment from his visits to the "realm of shadows." Instead, he departs every night "with a feeling of life uselessly squandered...." (376)

Werfel puts the finishing touches on his portrait of an absolutely isolated individual when he sends Ferdinand back to his childhood home—now Czechoslovakia—several years after the war's conclusion. It is now clear that he is a complete outsider in his former *Heimat*.

> Ever since yesterday when he had crossed the Austrian frontier, he had lived in a state of constricted self-consciousness. ... He belonged to the overthrown, defeated, ruling class (but how little he really belonged to it!), spoke German, and was even ticketed by his appearance as a member of the ranks of those who counted as fallen enemies. (565)

Heimat is an impossibility for Ferdinand. He lacks an emotional attachment to the geography of truncated postwar Austria-Hungary; living within the familiar countryside of Bohemia is equally alienating, since he would be linguistically and physiognomically distinct from his compatriots. As Israel Stamm shows, Ferdinand "accepts his isolation as an irrevocable fact of life. He surrenders all hope of finding spiritual satisfaction in his relations with other men and with the world."[34] Ferdinand chooses a career symbolically appropriate to his isolation: as a ship's doctor, his permanent home is transitoriness on the sea.[35] From this point forward, his contact with other humans is of the most superficial nature. The "self-consciousness" he had felt in his homeland persists in all of his inter-personal relations. Instead of further pursuing a human community, he cultivates a personal relationship with God. Stamm sees in his "devotion only to God" a "shift of emphasis in Werfel's religious attitude from a social, humanitarian idealism to a greater concern for his own private contacts with God."[36] However true it is that Werfel strongly promoted having an intimate bond with God, it is imperative to stress that Ferdinand does not represent an ideal character for him. One admires his serenity and religiosity in the end, but there is, nonetheless, an unmistakable insufficiency surrounding him. Keeping in mind the positive terms in which Werfel wrote about community and *Heimat,* it is easy to identify the source of Ferdinand's insufficiency.

Ferdinand, then, is a tragic figure insofar as he is incomplete, having lost any connection to family and to *Heimat* and *Volk* through the circumstances of the war. Equally tragic in the novel is the character of Alfred Engländer. Coming from a wealthy, assimilated Jewish family, he represents the folly of willfully disengaging oneself from one's community: in this case, the cultural-religious community of Jews. The process had, of course, already started with his family's assimilation. Engländer compounds the problem, however, by rejecting any communal underpinnings that Vienna's assimilated Jewish community, such as it was, could offer. In becoming obsessed with the Catholic church, he alienates his family members. He renounces as misdirected Jewish traditions in both the religious and the cultural sense. In an act of total rejection of his community's cultural heritage, he develops a theory that Jews and Catholics should unite in accepting Jesus Christ as the true Messiah. Thoroughly convinced of its indisputability, he endeavors to argue his case to prominent representatives of Judaism and Catholicism: the eastern Jewish "Dunajow Rabbi" and the Archbishop of Vienna.

For the occasion of presenting his findings to the Dunajow rabbi, Engländer is accompanied by a fellow Jew, Simon Kurz, whom he has won over to his cause and who is to act as an interpreter, and the Christian Ferdinand. Kurz, who with his Polish language ability stands much closer to traditional Jewry than Engländer, makes little headway with his prepared speech. With so many Jewish eyes fixed on him, his voice becomes "halting, shameful and terrified." (405) Prior to this attempt at presenting Engländer's ideas, Kurz had shown another sign of his closer proximity to the Jewish community: while Engländer sat motionless during a song sung by the rabbi, Kurz "began to hum and sway." (403) He has allowed aspects of his historical identity, hitherto denied, to resurface in the presence of the community he had shunned. His guilt, which ultimately moves him to discontinue his blasphemous words, indicates the realization that he had betrayed himself by severing his ties to his community. Engländer, so far removed from his origins and so obsessed with his own plan to form an all-inclusive community, has no chance of reconciliation with his Jewish identity.

By far the most curious experience in this episode is reserved for the Christian Ferdinand who sought no purpose in visiting the rabbi save to lend moral support for his friend. Seated at the rabbi's feet, he finds himself forced to participate in a strange ritual: the rabbi cuts a small, greasy herring in two, takes the half with the head for himself, and offers Ferdinand the tail. Following the rabbi's example, Ferdinand quickly swallows his half, bones and all. Kurz later attempts to interpret the procedure for him:

> The smaller, less precious tail, which Ferdinand had received from the Rabbi, had been meant to symbolize Christianity. The Christian was perfectly welcome to his share, the furthest removed from the truth as symbolized by the head, for since almost twenty centuries the unity of Israel's teaching had been broken.(408–9)

The rabbi stresses in this way that there is no singular religious metanarrative, that Christianity and Judaism are two separate entities. Kurz comes to realize, however reluctantly, his membership in one, and it is demonstrated graphically that Ferdinand belongs to the other. Only Engländer, who would have the two communities combine into one, is a complete outsider to both. His refusal to acknowledge and accept his origins renders him unable to function effectively; predictably, his condition culminates in his institutionalization. Where Ferdinand represents the tragic loss of community through uncontrollable forces, Engländer and Kurz stand for Werfel's belief that denying one's community is an act which always returns to haunt the individual finally confronted with his or her origins: in the form of guilt and self-doubt, as with Kurz, or in prolonged and damaging existential confusion, as with Engländer. Two things result from an individual's attempt to be part of a community other than that to which he or she naturally belongs: an identity thus "selected" can only be affected, inauthentic; and the individual becomes alienated from his or her community's wealth of identity-granting resources (history, traditions, language, religion, etc.).

POGROM: A MISSED CHANCE FOR COMMUNITY

Werfel's 1926 novella fragment *Pogrom* addresses similar problems.[37] The narrator-protagonist of the story, thirty-three-year-old Baron von Sonnenfels, fancies himself an "imperial and royal civil servant" despite the fact that he is writing in the year 1920, and the term is an anachronism. (60) Sonnenfels saves the revelation that he is Jewish for later in his narration, but the terms of his self-description reveal to the reader early on that this character is approaching an identity crisis. His enthusiastic characterization of his profession demonstrates his innermost desire to be nondescript. All the benefits of civil service as he understands it have one thing in common: the complete lack of distinguishing traits. Sonnenfels enjoys the drab "impersonality" of the office; the weather outside his window always seems to be the leaden opacity of late Autumn ("Yes, November, that is the eternal and comfortable season of the civil servant."); the tasks he performs are marked by their "distance from reality"; in all, he is content not to have anything disturb his "nebulous peace." Particularly pleasing is the "colorlessness" of his colleagues who, through the "work of generations," have been transformed from representatives of Austria's many peoples to a "human destillation of all these races." The passing of generations has had a leveling effect; all that remains is a breed of Austrian bureaucrats, a breed to which Sonnenfels thinks he belongs. "For these civil servants were, after all, for the most part celibates of their repressed national character. And among these celibates I felt comfortable" (61–62).

There are hints that Sonnenfels, in fact, is not as indistinguishable from the other civil servants as he would have the reader believe. On occasion he has noticed that his superior's relationship with him is "as delicate as the breadth of a single hair," unlike his behavior toward the other colleagues. "Whereas the governor associated with all his employees in a manner which could be considered perfectly becoming to our lifestyle, with me he was bothered by a vague awkwardness of which he was hardly aware, and which in turn affected me." (64) As a soldier as well, he is kept at a certain distance by the others in his regiment. (96) Serving the State in the late years of World War I in a small provincial town, he notes an unsettling difference to working in Vienna. "I was accustomed to working in Vienna, the big city with no attitudes: but here in the province there was a narrow and angry attitude in people's eyes, an aggressive narrowness which I can hardly bear." (63) Sonnenfels has so thoroughly convinced himself of his "colorlessness" that he does not register anti-Semitism: he neither suspects why he causes irritation to his superior and fellow soldiers, nor does he recognize the antagonism in the eyes of the provincial populace for what it is.

Sonnenfels's illusions are finally shattered when he is sent to Eastern Galicia as a representative of the government to organize housing and improve living conditions for Ruthenian war refugees, among them a congregation of Jews. The house occupied by the Jews evokes a sense of familiarity, as if the scene before him were something he had dreamt long ago. Only later does he realize that the filthy house crowded with foreign-looking people, indeed, was reminiscent of a long-forgotten childhood memory of a funeral he had attended with his father and grandfather. In addition, this was the only occasion on which he has ever seen the two men together (a fact which points to the lacking continuity and connection with the past even within his own family). It is in *Pogrom* that the strange fish-dividing scene we know from *The Pure in Heart* originates, with Sonnenfels being forced to sit next to the rabbi and consume half of the fish as Ferdinand did. The earlier written *Pogrom* fragment was first published posthumously, but Werfel allowed this part of it to reach the public during his lifetime by incorporating the very vivid four-page segment almost verbatim into Ferdinand's story, as described previously. Reference to this fact has been made only by Gunter Grimm, but then without further analysis.[38] In Ferdinand's case, being the recipient of the fishtail signified his separateness from the Jewish community. Sonnenfels is also being shown where he belongs, but here the ritual constitutes a "nightmarish initiation or re-initiation to his ethnic origin," Judaism.[39] That Werfel considered such an episode relevant to the life of two so different characters indicates that he was less concerned with a specifically Jewish problem than with more general aspects of identity crisis and community. The experience puts Sonnenfels into a trancelike state—or rather, breaks him out of his old trance of "colorlessness"—and he reports that had a coworker not suddenly appeared, he may have been fully taken in by his surroundings. Much like Simon Kurz in *The Pure in Heart,* who had started to hum and rock back and forth when the rabbi sang, Sonnenfels's spirit is also not immune to "the substratum of his origin, the unadulterated, unadapted form of his ethnicity."[40] He admits: "If my secretary hadn't suddenly stood before me with a despairing expression on his face, I don't know—perhaps I would have fainted, or I might have danced along."(76)

This experience, however unsettling, is not enough to effect a lasting change in Sonnenfels. He comes to full realization of his ethnicity only when a young man from the Jewish congregation seeks him out at night, requesting a favor for his brother. Acting consistently with what he considers to be his identity, Sonnenfels answers that he, as a civil servant, cannot be of help: "I don't believe that I am the authority responsible for such requests. . . ." But this last effort to retain the distance between himself and the Jewish community is to no avail, for the Jew states bluntly: "The gentleman will help. For the gentleman is himself a Jew!" (94) This confrontation strikes at the very core of his existence. With his declaration, the Jew "dealt a fatal blow to my life's certainty." (97) Sonnenfels recognizes that he has not only taken on a false identity, but in so doing, he has also deprived himself of true membership in his own community, because none of those things that constitute a community are accessible to him anymore: language, customs, a knowledge of the history, a common geographical home.

> Strangers were the Jews of the Miracle Rabbi from Hodow, as strange as a similar assembly of Chinese or Arabs would be to me. I had nothing to do with them, not one feature of my face, not one word from my mouth, not one stirring of my soul resembled them. . . . So I was a Jew! I was an Other! . . . But unlearned, everything was unlearned! The homeland forgotten! And in other lands very little gained! A stranger here and a stranger there! A stranger beyond all imagination! Strangeness, the core feeling of my life, now I could penetrate the reason for it!!(97–98)

Now even the reader for whom Sonnenfels's revelation had come as a surprise can reflect on other aspects of his story with greater insight. It is clear, for example, why Sonnenfels would have felt embarassed at a social gathering with a windbag Jewish intellectual, Professor von Wertheimer. Wertheimer spent the afternoon monopolizing the conversation with his windy excursuses on every subject imaginable ("Thomas Aquinas, New Catholicity, Comenius and the Bohemian Idea, Goethe and Europe, Goethe and Vorarlberg, Goethe and the Pope, Goethe and Islam . . ."). (81) In the process, he irritated all the guests including Sonnenfels. Although he does not state it explicitly, Sonnenfels is obviously mortified by such an exhibition of "Jewish intellectualism," since Wertheimer lives up to every negative expectation from this popular stereotype. When Wertheimer is finally embarassed into silence by a barb from another guest, the group celebrates his humiliation with laughter that "grew into an exultation." At this moment, Sonnenfels forgets his irritation and instead feels instinctively that the hurtful laughter is directed not only toward Wertheimer but toward all Jews. He has not yet admitted to the reader, or himself, that he is also a Jew at this juncture, but his reaction to the incident indicates an awareness of the truth at a subconscious level. "I was ashamed for him, I was physically ashamed. For I too had blood rush to my face, as if I, the harmless civil servant, and he, who perhaps had a famous scholar's name, were one and the same person." (83)

Another clue to Sonnenfels's subconscious inklings about still-existing ties to his origins is his fondness for the Hofmannsthal verse: "The weariness of forgotten peoples / I cannot remove from my eyelids," the first half of which is used as a heading to the story segment containing the nighttime confrontation scene between Sonnenfels and the Jew. Hofmannsthal, Sonnenfels writes, "is the poet of *my* soul." "No other has expressed more discretely the misgivings about blood! And am I a question of anything else?" (86) In spite of his assimilation, Sonnenfels carries the negative aspects of his community's legacy with him—the weariness resulting from anti-Semitic bigotry and persecution. Because of his assimilation, however, his Jewish experience is limited to only those negative aspects. Like Alfred Engländer, he is not alone to blame for his predicament. The family's assimilation began with his great-grandfather's conversion to Catholicism. (96) A fragile link to the Jewish community is maintained over the next three generations via marriage to Jewesses, but no attempt is made to derive any spiritual sustenance from the link. Its hollowness culminates in Sonnenfels's father, a man who personifies Austrian aristocracy, is a renowned horseman and snob, and who in his elegance represents assimilatory perfection. "For me he represents the greatest physical-spiritual distancing from Judaism that I have ever observed of a Jew." (97) The father rejects all ties to the family's Jewish past: "Papa had always disregarded descent, names, families with a slightly disgruntled indifference." (90) The distance between father and grandfather has already been alluded to: Sonnenfels has seen the two men together only on the one occasion of a relative's funeral. Otherwise, he was always taken to see the grandfather by a servant. (90) And although there exists no enmity between him and his own father, there is also no intimacy. His father does not function as a teacher or mentor; he too keeps Sonnenfels "at a friendly but disappointed indifference." (88)

Werfel sees the family as the smallest possible community in which one can gain a sense of identity. Such poems as "Father and Son" stress that it is necessary for each generation to establish an identity separate from its parents'. However, this individual identity must also include ingredients from childhood, lessons from parents, and a familiarity with family history in order to have any authenticity or inherent value. For Werfel, the individual without community is the ultimate tragic figure. Ferdinand's story, for example, would be far less tragic if he had at least not been devoid of family. Considering Sonnenfels's situation, then—no ties to the Jewish community, no sense of family heritage in his upbringing—there is little question why "strangeness" is the "core feeling" of his life, nor can there be any doubt that he faces an imminent identity crisis. Egon Schwarz correctly notes that although the protagonist has not yet reconciled himself with his true identity before *Pogrom* breaks off, the construction of the story leads logically to that conclusion.[41]

FATHERS AND SONS. COMMUNITY IN FAMILY

Werfel had already explored the central importance of the parent-child relationship (in his works almost always in the form of the father-son relationship, true to his expressonist

1: THE THEME OF IDENTITY IN THE WORKS OF FRANZ WERFEL 37

background) in his first lengthy story, "Not the Murderer" (1920).[42] A slightly revised excerpt from his "Father and Son" leads in the novella's opening chapter, functioning as an introductory motto.

> Severed we stay
>
> Severed, as in a dream
> Dimly we see our gathered loves serving
> Love's immortal ends by boundless loving,
> And pity, like a gentle tide renewing
> Drowns space away.

With the son's maturation, two distinctly separate identities are established, yet the familial bond remains an essential component of each of the two. "Not the Murderer," told in the first person by the protagonist Karl, reports at the outset that such a bond is absent from Karl's life. He has always wished for a simple, loving father like those he observed in other social classes:

> How I always envied those boys whose fathers sat on a Sunday afternoon comfortably and cosily smoking their pipes in the porter's lodge or on the bench outside it! Still more the pupils who spent it in their simple civilian homes, wit the master of the house in his shirt-sleeves, a Virginia in his mouth and a half-empty beer-glass before him, sitting at the clean white table. (569)

Karl's family experience is far removed from the *comfortable, cozy* atmosphere he longs for. As a cadet at the military academy, he sees his parents at home only on Sundays and holidays. For the other cadets, Sundays mean freedom and the warmth of the family circle. On Sundays

> [t]hey escaped from their prison in the morning, trembling and flushed with joy, to go to homes which might be poor but yet which welcomed and cherished them with marks of love.... What was my Sunday like? I left the school at ten; sick at my stomach, my heart pounding horribly.... For at half-past ten precisely I had to present

> myself before my father in the pay-room of the batallion, and feel his eye measure me with a cold official stare.... (571)

Karl's father uses the occasion of his son's visits to quiz him on his progress at school. On his only day at home, the boy is consistently and mercilessly criticized, degraded, ridiculed by his father. He feels fortunate to escape these confrontations, which he terms "inquisitions," with "only" contempt: "I got no praise, but a full complement of army oaths; that was a blessed Sabbath for me when I came off merely with silent contempt." (571) Even an unprecedented outing with his father to an amusement park is soon spoiled when his father turns a carousel ride into an infantry exercise: "'Sit up! Body well back!' ... 'Stick to the saddle!' ... 'Grip with your thighs! Point your toes!'" (580) Despite such a disastrous birthday experience, Karl reflects that he desires nothing more desperately than the love of his father.

> This was my Father, here beside me! The great, the all-knowing, the all-powerful, the all-admired! Whom else had I in all the world save him? I did love him! Through long bitter nights I yearned for his love, the pain of all my humiliations was as nothing beside the torture of that recurring dream wherein I saw him, leading his battalion in a fog of smoke, suddenly clutch at the air and fall! (583)

A nurturing relationship between father and son should be the natural state of affairs; when this love is denied and the bond between parent and child is broken, serious damage is sustained to the child's ability to relate to others. Like Ferdinand, Karl lacks the most important reference points for identification. His self-esteem, and with it his ability to make friends, has been systematically destroyed by his father. Taylor asserts that "a person or group of people can suffer real damage, real distortion, if the people or society around them mirror back to them a confining or contemptible picture of themselves."[43] This is true already in the case of minorities that have been marginalized and rejected as a group by utter strangers. The effect is incalculably more damaging to the individual who is rejected by members of the family: the smallest possible community and last remaining safe haven for a secure identity. Karl is not liked, even by himself, and has no possibility to form a community for himself. Later, as a lieutenant in the province, he is incapable of socializing with the other officers, who would be his most natural community in this situation. Instead, he seeks out the murky pubs of the local population. "Even here, among hawking and spitting Polish drovers, cursing Ruthenian peasants, and Jews shrieking and tearing at their hair, I felt happier than among my comrades." (591) However, association with strangers is no substitute for a real community. His life having been made miserable by his father's abuse, Karl longs to avenge himself. The opportunity finally presents itself when he takes his father by surprise in the middle of the night. In the end, though, Karl foregoes revenge on the past, embracing instead the future (at the end of the novella he is newly married) as an opportunity to create community for himself and especially his son by endowing him with the family bonds he had been denied.

The works examined above may be considered representative of how Werfel approached the theme of identity in other works so numerous that it would be redundant to study each separate instance. These examples reveal an interest in identity questions which is both enduring and carefully reflected. In Ferdinand K. and Karl, Werfel demonstrates that the human existence denied communal bonds, such as nationality and family, is an existence with no hope for achieving a meaningful identity. Both are incapable of relating to any societal group. Engländer, on the other hand, willfully declines a community that is prepared to accept him. As with Sonnenfels, the symmetry between objective and subjective identity is low: he is unwilling to categorize himself in the same way as society does. His identity crisis can be ascribed to this asymmetry. Sonnenfels knows nothing of Jewish traditions and is at a loss to interpret the implications of his community's history. Upon realization of his irrefutable Jewish identity, he laments most bitterly having "forgotten," "unlearned" his own historical background.

Werfel's views on ethnic identity are somewhat mixed; however, on the whole, he tends toward the optionalist school. Many of his characters previously described have successfully shed their ethnicity. Those who have done so intentionally are portrayed as being regrettably misguided, for they have discarded a treasure that can never be regained. Those characters who have been deprived of ethnic identity through no fault of their own (parents' assimilation, sociohistorical events) are among his most pitiable. Regardless of the cause, Werfel shows us repeatedly that the loss is permanent and that attempts to take on a new (inauthentic) ethnic identity ultimately fail. However, there remains a faint expression of the primordial school that cannot go unnoticed. Even once true ethnicity is irretrievably lost, Werfel seems to believe that a small instinctual trace of it still remains in the individual—something akin to "feeling" an amputated limb long after the fact: it cannot be recovered, but its memory persists. For this reason, Simon Kurz is moved to hum and sway in the company of the Jewish congregation. The same holds true for Sonnenfels, who is so strongly affected by Hofmannsthal's words, "The weariness of forgotten peoples / I cannot remove from my eyelids." Werfel's belief in a biologically given "memory" of earlier generations finds expressions in the first stanza of his own poem "Where is . . .", similar in content to the Hofmannsthal verses:

> Ich trage viel in mir.
> Vergangenheit früherer Leben,
> Verschüttete Gegenden,
> Mit leichten Spuren von Sternenstrahlen.
> Oft bin ich nicht an der Oberfläche,
> Hinabgetaucht in die fremdeigenen Gegenden bin ich.

[I carry much within me. / The past of previous lives, / Submerged regions, / With faint traces of star-beams. / Often I am not on the surface, / Plunged down into the strange-familiar regions am I.]

The open-endedness of the poem's title gives pause for thought. Eduard Goldstücker speculates that it could be a reference to "Where is my *Heimat?*", the title of the Czech national anthem.[44] As he notes, this is only one of several plausible educated guesses. However, the phrase "Where is my *Heimat?*" could easily serve as a motto for Prague's Jewish German citizens. It is reasonable to surmise that Werfel's ability to portray identity problems with such insight stems from a familiarity gained from firsthand experience or observation of his immediate surroundings. Trying to find Werfel in each of his characters who grapple with identity would be an oversimplification, but it is likely that his upbringing in Prague as an assimilated,

German-speaking Jew helped to cultivate a sensitivity for such issues in him.

The Prague Connection

The position of German-Austrian citizens of Prague has attracted the attention of scholars in a variety of fields, most notably social and literary historians. In fact, a sophisticated and industrially vital urban center dominated by the cultural influences of a small minority vastly different from the remainder of the regional population, while not historically unique, does represent a phenomenon inherently replete with wide-ranging investigatory opportunities. The greater part of the attention focuses on the Jewish portion of that community. This is especially true of literary studies, due to the proportionately large contribution of Jewish artists to German cultural life in Prague. A commonly emphasized theme of such studies is the relationship between the writer and his or her social surroundings, or, in a word, identity. Perhaps best known is the study of Kafka by Pavel Eisner, himself a native of Prague. Eisner discusses Kafka in terms of being "a citizen of Prague and a German Jew."[45] He argues that in Prague, being a German Jew meant that one was "a stranger in three senses." The Prague German Jew was

> German, but around him there was no German people, no naturally constituted national community, and he rejected the provinciality of the "Sudetengau" just as much as it rejected him. At most, the Prague Jew clung outwardly to the Jewish community; he was Jew on the books, but in him the faith of his fathers had dwindled down to a few attributes and symbols.... But in the eyes of the Czechs, the German Jew was a stranger in three senses: as a Jew, either owing to creed or to unmixed blood; as a generally comfortable, prosperous and, often enough, rich citizen, in the midst of a crowd of proletarians and small bourgeois; and thirdly as a "German."[46]

Peter Horwath refers to the same phenomenon as "the problem of ethnic identity of the so-called 'Prague cultural Jew,'"[47] which is further defined by Kurt Krolop as "that lack of a nationally definable collective authority between the Self and the world."[48] In each instance, the same themes surface: the Jews' inability to identify wholly with any one particular reference group (Germans, Czechs) and the low symmetry between objective and subjective identity. For the Jews to accept the community with which society identified them, they were not sufficiently conversant with key elements of their ethnic identity: language, religious belief and practices, and knowledge of a distinct history separate from that of the other ethnic groups in Prague.

A Jewish community had called Bohemia its home for centuries, dating back at least as far as the Middle Ages.[49] The "Prague Cultural Jew" was relatively new to the scene. It was not until 1781 that Jews were granted the opportunity to pursue a university education, made possible by the Austrian Edict of Tolerance. Hillel Kieval traces Joseph II's reform measures and their effect on the Bohemian Jewish community.[50] The Edict of Tolerance brought with it not only new liberties for Jews but also new regulations. In particular, ordinances involving the use of language were both immediate and of lasting consequence. It was mandated that Hebrew and Yiddish could no longer be used in business records. Children were expected to attend Austrian state schools in which German was the language of instruction. The acknowledgment of Austria's Jewish community was effected with the expectation that fundamental aspects of that community would change. Kieval lists some of the most significant changes that "transformed the social and legal character of the community."

> The juridical autonomy of the Jewish community in civil and criminal matters was suspended in 1784. An ordinance of 1786 made the granting of marriage certificates to Jews dependent on the parties' ability to demonstrate that they had attended a *Normalschule*. . . . Legislation the following year made the adoption of German personal and family names mandatory. In 1788 Jews were required to serve in the Austrian army.[51]

Tolerance, it seems, would have its price. The Jewish community was reordered in the most basic aspects: law, education, and language. Still, this was not met with an undivided front of resistance. Many Jewish enlighteners seized upon the opportunity to reshape Jewish identity after a more Western orientation. Toward this end, mandatory attendance in Austrian schools promised to be extremely effective.

The *maskilim* (Jewish enlighteners) recognized in Joseph II's call for the establishment of the German-Jewish school an invitation not only to alter the world view of traditional Judaism, but also to create a new kind of Jewish individual, educated in Western science and languages, committed to the use of reason in determining questions of truth and value, loyal to king and to country, and loving of his fellow citizen.[52]

The Germanization efforts directed at Bohemian Jews met with great success, most evident in Prague where by 1890, 97 percent of all Jewish schoolchildren attending public institutions were enrolled in German-language schools.[53] The ubiquity of Jews in Prague's German cultural circles is further testimony to the extent to which Jewish identity was recast as German-Jewish identity.

However, at the same time that Bohemia's Jews gained wider acceptance as Austrian citizens, their German acculturation further alienated them from their Czech compatriots, for germanization of the Jews coincided with growing Czech cultural and national awareness. The Jewish enlighteners regarded acculturation as a chance to improve Jews' social status. They embraced German culture "on the assumption that the German language and culture were to be the principal vehicles of social advancement and national integration." Kieval discusses how their successful assimilation ultimately worked against them:

> Already by the turn of the nineteenth century, however, new demographic and political realities would call such assumptions into question. Advances in universal education, together with the beginnings of urbanization and industrialization, began to produce an articulate, Czech-speaking middle class engaged in a full-fledged cultural and linguistic revival of its own. Virtually at the precise moment that the Jews of Bohemia could be found assiduously adopting the German language and assimilating German cultural patterns, an increasingly vociferous and influential group within Czech society was challenging the very position of German in the balance of political and cultural forces.[54]

It was not long before Prague's Jews were in a position of double jeopardy: caught between anti-German national agitation from the Czechs and anti-Semitic German nationalism. Georg von Schönerer was busily propagating anti-Semitism among his Sudetenland followers and inciting German national students at the University of Prague to act in demonstration of their anti-Czech and anti-Semitic convictions. Concurrently, Czech writers were disseminating the notion of Czech spiritual superiority coupled with cultural rebirth. These efforts were based on what Horwath calls two "myths" which had become established in the previous generation: the first was popularized by Václav Hanka (1791–1861), who "told about the idyll of a safe, happy, and glorious Czech community of bygone ages, and the other myth, propagated by František Palacký (1798–1876 ...) dealt with the eternal battle between peaceful and democratic Slavs and aggressive feudal Germans." Prague Jews of Werfel's generation, with few exceptions, were grounded in German culture. With both anti-German and anti-Jewish violence becoming "frequent occurrences after 1859,"[55] Prague Jews had the unenviable dilemma of having to choose between two communities, both of which labeled them as outsiders.

An ever-widening gap separating Czech and German culture in Prague was perceptible already in the late 1830s. Representatives of both cultures collaborated to bridge the gap and to present the image of Prague culture as a dynamic combination of all its cultural groups. In 1837, the Czech-German periodical *Ost und West* was founded as a forum for Prague's cultural news and commentary in both Czech and German.[56] Werfel's generation also worked toward greater cultural understanding among Prague's citizens. Otto Pick and Rudolf Fuchs devoted incalculable time and effort to translating and publishing the works of Czech poets, to the extent that their own creative work was neglected. Many Czech works achieved international repute because of their circulation in German translation. For example, Max Brod's active support of Jaroslav Hašek, previously unheralded by the Czech populace, was instrumental in the success of his novel *Good Soldier Schweik*. *Schweik* was enthusiastically received first by the German readership and only later by Czechs. Brod effectively gave the Czechs "their national hero of the twentieth century" by popularizing this work.[57] Nor was this an isolated incident: Prague Germans' translations and sponsorship of Czech literature fueled a "Czech wave" in Germany.

1: THE THEME OF IDENTITY IN THE WORKS OF FRANZ WERFEL

> Rudolf Fuchs submitted the "Silesian Songs" by Petr Bezruč with a preface by Werfel to Kurt Wolff. . . . With the Insel publishing house, Paul Eisner published the "Czech Anthology," and in 1920 a "Slovakian Anthology." Rudolf Fuchs presented a selection of Czech verse from 100 years with Kurt Wolff under the title "A Harvest Wreath," F. C. Weiskopf published poems with Malik publishing house under the title "Czech Songs." In 1928 the book "The Czechs. An Anthology of Five Centuries" appeared with Piper.[58]

Werfel devotes a large portion of his lengthy preface to Bezruč's *Silesian Songs* to the Czechs' social struggles as a small national community. He implicitly condemns their treatment within Austria, interpreting Bezruč's poems as "the outstanding, impersonal, inexplicable final outcry of a line which has been destroyed." "Petr Bezruč," he continues, "that is a small line of the Czech people which is struggling for language and a meagre existence in linguistic enclaves within the Austrian-Silesian industrial centers."[59] Reffet reminds us that his endeavors were not without personal risk. Bezruč was a Czech nationalist, and Werfel's collaboration on the translation of his poetry occurred at a time when he was serving in the Austrian army (1917). Several of Bezruč's poems were censored, and the Czech editions of his *Songs* were taken out of circulation.[60] Werfel was willing to take risks in order to bring more German speakers into contact with the works of someone he considered a talented representative of Czech culture.

It is, as Foltin terms it, "a demonstration and a confession of solidarity with the Czechs." This case demonstrates more than the hope of many intellectuals that German and Czech culture could be forged into a unique cultural alliance in Prague; it also illustrates just how hopeless the prospect was.

> Behind these innocent facts there is great irony in the endeavors on the part of Fuchs and Werfel, both German Jews, to become the cultural mediators for the work of Petr Bezruč, a Czech gentile. For Bezruč is not only one of the great Czech poets, he is also the most consistently anti-Semitic and anti-German among them. In his revolutionary poetry, the Jews are invariably drawn as shady characters with German names and German interests, and as a demoralizing and destructive force.[61]

The attempts at cultural mediation were for naught, a fact which even the idealist Werfel had to acknowledge. In 1927, he describes "encounters with Rilke," a fellow Prague native who had sought a meeting with Werfel in 1913 after having read with great admiration the younger poet's verses. Werfel considers Rilke to be a prime example of what he calls "the inheritance of all non-Slavic Prague citizens: double and triple homelessness." Because the German-speaking Rilke was not fully accepted in Prague, Werfel argues, he led an itinerant life with no possibility of truly belonging in any one place: "In the final years of his life, this German poet, whose soul had awakened in Russia and who composed French poetry, was forced to ask himself again and again: 'Where do I belong?' Yet precisely for this question there is no answer."[62]

The homelessness Werfel projects onto Rilke by virtue of his Germanness is compounded in Werfel's case by his Jewishness. It was, as mentioned before, a position of double jeopardy in which Prague's German Jews were rejected by both Czechs and Germans. The difference between the situation of a Rilke and a Werfel is highlighted in some revealing correspondence between Rilke and Hofmannsthal. Werfel's great admiration for Hofmannsthal was apparent in the *Pogrom* reference to "this great poet" who "still lives among us."[63] Rilke, too, was a "master" whom Werfel hoped to emulate.[64] However, when the two met in Dresden at Rilke's request, the long-anticipated meeting of the souls did not occur. Rilke writes to Hofmannsthal:

> I was truly prepared to simply embrace this young man; but I immediately recognized that this would not be possible under any circumstances, that I might be able to give a most heartfelt handshake, but would otherwise have to go walking with him, being attentive and careful, with my hands behind my back. (October 22, 1913)[65]

Similarly, Werfel reports his own disappointed expectations: "I must admit that in these hours I was not really able to get close to Rilke. His sphere had something alienating about it for me, something lifeless and sophisticated which I found taxing and tiring." He attributes the initial awkwardness to the difference in age between the two: "I was quite young and my temperament resisted the idea of simply 'living in the word' for hours on end."⁶⁶ Rilke's letter, however, reveals that the age difference was not the agent at the root of the distance felt between the two Prague poets.

> The fact that part of my preconceived affection had to go unused does not necessarily mean that it waned because of that, even though it seems to be in the process of a certain transformation. The Jew, the Jew-boy to put it bluntly, would not have pulled anything on me, and yet the thoroughly Jewish attitude towards his production was indeed perceptible to me, this connaître les choses pour ne pas les avoir eu, the consequence of which is that the ecstasy, through a hint of revenge . . . becomes more passionate but also more gloomy.⁶⁷

The face-to-face encounter with Werfel transformed him from a gifted young German poet to almost an imposter: a cerebral Jew who, through Jewish intellectualism and trickery, writes deceptively artful German-language poetry, which in the final analysis is the product not of his soul and personal experience but rather of calculated rationality. Though he had been predisposed to like the young poet, Rilke was disturbed by some "Jewish" aspect of Werfel's physical appearance, which activated his assumptions about Jews. Three and a half months later, having gained some distance from the encounter and far removed from Werfel's unsettling physical presence, Rilke is able to find the ring of authenticity in his latest volume of poems, *We Are*. He urges Hofmannsthal to disregard his earlier reservations, recommending instead several specific poems to support his newly revised opinion of Werfel:

> I wrote you then following my encounter with Werfel, as we had arranged with one another, a few words regarding my impression of him,—now I feel moved to inform you anew on this topic: that in view of his new poems (which appear in the January edition, No. 5, of the "Weisse Blätter"), I have completely forgotten all reservations which had arisen from the personal; in fact, strictly speaking, I do not care to admit having had them. (February 4, 1914)⁶⁸

Rilke's attitude toward Jews in German culture is not unusual except, perhaps, for his inconsistent wavering between the two extremes of aversion and unconditional approval. The atmosphere in turn-of-the-century Prague, however, was too polarized to allow for many gray areas. There were, in fact, some Jews who identified with the Czech nationalist cause—Kieval has shown them to all have attended Czech-language secondary schools—but despite their outspoken "opposition to the cultural policies of the Jewish establishment" in Prague, they too were "recipients of a barrage of criticism from Czech national quarters."[69] The philosophy of the German and Czech national movements was both cultural and racial, precluding the involvement of Jews in either faction. In the atmosphere of exclusion and anti-Semitic aggression, especially prevalent at the University, Jewish students were given the impulse to rethink their loyalties and form Zionist groups.

> It was ... significant that the intensity of the national conflict resulted in an undercurrent of hostility toward Jewish participation in both national camps. Consequently, Zionism emerged as a serious cultural "option" for large segments of the educated and professional class even though the relative "westernness" of Bohemian Jewry in other respects appeared to militate against it. Zionism offered both German- and Czech-speaking Jews the solution of a credible middle road.[70]

That the Jewish community needed to unite in a single cause could hardly be denied anymore. More an issue of debate was what sort of Zionism the community should profess: purely political or cultural. The more influential group in Prague was comprised of those who felt Zionism must entail a Jewish cultural renaissance. Leo Herrmann, who at twenty years of age became the chair of Prague's Bar Kochba Zionist organization, believed that the retrieval of Jewish traditions was imperative if the Zionist community was to have any staying power. He stated his program as follows:

> What we want is to secure the present and the future of the Jewish people; to struggle against all that is un-Jewish in Judaism, against all of the disintegrating tendencies within the Jewish community; to revive the Jewish idea, which has preserved our people intact.[71]

Martin Buber and the Prague Zionists

Defining "the Jewish idea" and its relevance for the present was a monumental task, and the Prague Zionist students endeavored to inform themselves as thoroughly as possible of the wide spectrum of opinions and options concerning that task. Their efforts included inviting guest lecturers to speak to them in Prague. For one such occasion in early 1909, Herrmann extended an invitation to Martin Buber. He requested of Buber, considering the Prague audience to whom he would be speaking, that he address the question, "How are the remains of Jewish existence in the West to be transformed into something [that one can call] one's own?"[72] Buber's speech "Judaism and the Jews" marked the beginning of a close relationship between himself and the Jewish students in Prague. He was to return on two more occasions to speak for Bar Kochba. Werfel was not active in the Zionist movement, but he did meet Buber in Prague, and the two established a friendly personal relationship. Buber's philosophy had considerable impact on Werfel's thinking, as evidenced in their correspondence. Werfel writes him in a 1917 letter,

> For the present accept only my hand and my declaration ... that I feel myself, "nationally" speaking, entirely a Jew—with all the bad connotations of the term and some of the good ones. . . . So, dear Martin Buber, let me say only this to you, that of all the present-day literature on Jewish theoretical subjects, your writings alone are a joy to my soul and fill me with a sense of agreement, whereas I am quite put off by most of what Zionists write.[73]

With his three lectures "On Judaism" given in Prague between January 1909 and December 1910, Buber supplied terms with which Prague Jews could define their own Jewishness. Herrmann's call for the revival of "the Jewish idea" was just one expression of the need for Prague Zionism to develop into a community with distinct cultural content, beyond being solely a body for self-defense. The titles of Buber's lecture alone, "Judaism and the Jews," "Judaism and Mankind," and "The Renewal of Judaism," attest to the cultural thrust of the message he imparted in Prague.[74]

Buber probed the questions foremost on the minds of Prague's Jews: what meaning does Judaism hold for Western assimilated Jews who organize into "Jewish" groups? He raises the query in the opening minute of his first lecture: "What sort of community is this we bear witness to when we call ourselves Jews?"[75] The answer to the question, he asserts, lies in the individual's maturation process. An adult's spiritual development proceeds when she or he perceives and investigates "the innate desire ... for lasting substance, for immortal being."[76] Once the individual has become aware of this inborn wish and begins the process of inquiry and reflection, she or he discovers the concept of personal eternity—an eternity derived from membership in a community that exists not only in the present but also in the past and future.

> Stirred by the awesomeness of eternity, this young person experiences within himself the existence of something enduring. He experiences it still more keenly, in its manifestness and its mystery, with all the artlessness and all the wonder that surrounds the matter-of-fact, when he discerns it: at the hour when he discovers the succession of generations, when he envisions the line of fathers and of mothers that had led up to him. . . . He senses in this immortality of the generations a community of blood, which he feels to be the antecedents of his I, its perseverance in the infinite past. To that is added the discovery, promoted by this awareness, that blood is a deep-rooted nurturing force within individual man; that the deepest layers of our being are determined by blood; that our innermost thinking and our will are colored by it.[77]

The individual is a link in the chain of generations, guided by an instinctual heritage of earlier generations' struggles and victories, and contributing to the destiny of generations to follow. "Whatever all the men in this great chain have created and will create he conceives to be the work of his own unique being; whatever they have experienced and will experience he conceives to be his own destiny."[78]

It is a human's "natural subjective situation" to be anchored in the succession of generations. Buber adds, however, that "the natural subjective situation does not always correspond to a natural objective one." That is, when one lives among strangers, or the community is transplanted to a place other than the ancestral homeland, or a new language is adopted, the natural objective situation does not exist. This, he states, is the situation of the Western Jew.

> All the elements that might constitute a nation for him, that might make this nation a reality for him, as missing; all of them: land,

language, way of life. Neither the land he lives in, whose nature encomopasses him and molds his senses, nor the language he speaks, which colors his thinking, nor the way of life in which he participates and which, in turn, shapes his actions, belongs to the community of his blood; they belong instead to another community.[79]

The challenge facing the Western Jew is to bring the identity-shaping factors—both environmentally influenced *and* inherent blood-community traits—into balance. The deep-thinking and -feeling Jew must eventually confront a "deep schism" in his or her existence.[80] Buber concedes that "it would be senseless, for instance, to try to shed the culture of the world about us," since it too has become "an integral part of ourselves."[81] However, in order to close the schism and attain authenticity in one's identity, it is imperative to also recognize the impulses given by one's community of blood. The Western Jew must affirm the Jewish community's past and future, and increase its salience in present life. The "deep schism" will "seem insuperable to us so long as the insight that our blood is the creative force in our life has not yet become a living, integral part of us."[82] It is important to point out that although the word *blood* is prevalent in Buber's vocabulary, he hoped only to give Jews a sense of community with it. He did not imply that Jewish blood ranks higher or lower on some evolutionary ladder, or that persons lacking Jewish blood should be in any way discriminated against. It was simply a concept that was to provide common ground to a group of people who at that time lacked the feeling that they belonged anywhere in particular. As George Mosse comments, "for Buber these concepts were metaphors that defined nationality rather than race."[83] The dialogue of blood and race will receive more extensive treatment in the fourth chapter.

There can be little doubt that Martin Buber's philosophy on community and personal identity captured the imagination of the future author of "Permanence." Especially the concept of innate relatedness to a community of blood was received essentially with one accord among young Prague Jews, including Werfel. It was useful in explaining why they felt drawn together as a group despite their assimilation, and it instantly provided them with the community they had been lacking so sorely. Werfel, who felt himself to be "without folk, without land," was most definitely affected by Buber's ideas. In response to reading recommendations from the mentor-friend, Werfel wrote to Buber:

> I am reading with great enthusiasm and a completely receptive soul! The world owes you deepest gratitude. I for my part have found fatherland in unimagined quantities in the two works, often my secret drew near me. (April 18, 1917)[84]

His choice of words strongly suggests that his thoughts, too, were centered on community ("fatherland") and personal identity ("my secret"). At age twenty-seven, the issues were far from resolved for him. Many experiences still lay in store that would necessitate additional fine-tuning for his ideas: increasingly virulent anti-Semitic currents in Czechoslovakia and Austria, exile and emigration, and marriage to Alma Mahler. Community and identity were issues that accompanied Werfel throughout his life. As has been shown, they surfaced repeatedly in a large number of his works. In the following chapters, these themes will be examined as they appeared in Werfel's *Musa Dagh* novel.

2
Identity and the Historical Community in *The Forty Days of Musa Dagh*

REPRESENTING WHAT MAY BE CONSIDERED WERFEL'S MOST CONCENtrated meditation on identity issues is his 1933 novel *The Forty Days of Musa Dagh*.[1] The impetus for writing this work was provided by experiences of a 1929 trip to the Near East. In a Damascus carpet factory, Werfel witnessed the legacy of Turkish World War I domestic politics: weak, emaciated Armenian orphans, many of them crippled, worked in the factory to support their pitiful lives. Although the persecution of the Turkish Armenians was not altogether unfamiliar to him, it was this scene which helped him to gain a concrete sense of the occurrences' magnitude. Most of the remainder of his trip was spent gathering information and seeking out eyewitnesses of the atrocities. During this time, the *Musa Dagh* episode, in which a small community of Armenians successfully escaped almost certain annihilation, was related to him.[2] Werfel, ever-receptive to dramatic stories of human triumph and apparent divine intervention, immediately recognized the novelistic promise of such material.

Two years later, following the completion of other projects, as well as exhaustive research work on the *Musa Dagh* material, the writing of the novel commenced. Since its publication, analysts of *Musa Dagh* have discussed a number of its different aspects: its historical background,[3] the theme of nationalism and the lot of minorities,[4] and parallels between Jewish and Armenian historical fate.[5] The variety of perspectives brought to the work attest not to confusion but rather to the novel's rich and multifaceted nature. *Musa Dagh* went through five different revisions, altering and adding to its emphases considerably in the process; even Werfel's own account of the salience of the Jewish-

Armenian parallels changed with time. As Steiman[6] has noted, Werfel claimed in a 1938 questionaire that any parallels were "unconscious," yet a 1944 letter attributes his inspiration for writing the novel in part to a "premonition by which I was vexed concerning the Jews in Germany and all the minorities in Europe."[7] He also indicated in a 1933 letter to his parents that the meaning of the novel was evolving as the situation in Germany worsened: "'the book had acquired symbolic timeliness because of events: oppression, destruction of minorities by nationalism.'"[8] The theme of identity development and commitment to the community has also received some attention, most of which has been accurate in content and yet quite brief in its treatment. Where the topic has been touched upon, the analysis is limited to a few pages.[9] In the following, community and identity issues will be discussed at length and in several different manifestations as present in the novel.

The novel opens with the question "How did I get here?"(3), spoken aloud by the protagonist Gabriel Bagradian who finds himself atop the "Musa Dagh" in Turkey. From the summit he looks down onto his birthplace, Yoghonoluk, the largest of seven Armenian villages at the foot of the mountain. The answer to his question is provided in a few pages' space with a brief sketch of his life to this point. Born in Yoghonoluk, he lives there until age twelve when his grandfather dies. The patriarch's death allows his parents to move the family to Paris, where one of several family stores is located. Unlike his older brother who rejects Europe and soon returns to Turkey to represent the business there, Gabriel spends the ensuing years in Paris. Supported by a generous stipend from his family's commercial success, he fills his time with intellectual pursuits: art history, philosophy and archaeology. Gabriel and his French wife Juliette lead a comfortable life in Paris with their thirteen-year-old son, Stephan. His marriage has made him "more French than ever." (6) Having attended a French school and university, and now married to Juliette, Gabriel is considered assimilated. "Twenty-three years of Europe, Paris! Years of complete assimilation. They were as good as twice, or three times, that. They extinguished everything." (5) His question, then, insofar as it refers only to the circumstances leading to his current location, is easily an swered. Bagradian has returned to his grandfather's Armenian village because his older brother who lived there has died.

But the seemingly straightforward, uncomplicated answers to Gabriel's "How did I get here?" are no sooner presented as fact than they are disputed. While the explanation for his presence in Yoghonoluk is valid, there are many signals indicating that the question's answer lies on an entirely different plane. The question was not positioned so prominently as the first line of the novel simply as a flashback-prompter to orient the reader; it is there to indicate that the guiding question in *Musa Dagh* concerns Gabriel's "I," that it is his identity that is being called into question. At the outset, the contours of his question are as vaguely defined for him as they are for the reader—he utters the words "without knowing it" (3)—but it is significant that the query comes from his own lips. In the first few chapters, the narrator is the primary source of the signals of Gabriel's identity conflicts, which though they presently lie dormant, will develop into a theme of central importance to the novel.

Gabriel has been introduced early on as an example of "complete assimilation," but only one page later he is referred to as "the alienated one"[10]—and suddenly one encounters many hints that he is not the consummate Frenchman that one was led to believe. We learn, for example, that although he is an "Armenian still, but only in a sense—academically," he "did not forget it altogether, and at times published an article in an Armenian paper." His son is given an Armenian live-in tutor at age ten, "so that he might be taught the speech of his fathers," despite Juliette's objections. (She concedes to the tutor, Samuel Awakian, only because she finds his personality "pleasant.") One quickly gains the impression that Gabriel's interest in Armenian subjects, however tepid, is at the root of considerable marital strife. "Their tiffs had always the same origin. Yet, no matter how hard Gabriel might try to concern himself with the politics of foreigners, he was still sometimes drawn back into those of his people." (6) His involvement in Turkish politics is perhaps the strongest evidence that the twenty-three years of assimilation have not "erased" as much as he had thought. In 1907, he participates in the congress joining Young Turks and the Armenian National Party in one cause. He is attracted to their rhetoric of freedom and equality among the races in Ottoman Turkey. For this reason, he also serves in the Turkish army for over six months as an officer during the Balkan War. While separated from his family, he begins to fear that he might lose Juliette. "Something seemed imperilled in their relationship though he could not have given a reason for any such feeling." Upon his return, he considers applying for French citizenship: "That, above all, would have made Juliette happy." (7)

Despite the strain that his Armenian-ness puts on the marriage, Gabriel cannot commit to a final disassociation from it: "But always, in the end, the same vague uneasiness had prevented it." Henceforth, he refers to himself as "an abstract man, an individual." (7) His contact with other Armenians in Paris becomes greatly diminished, and the couple's circle of close friends consists only of other French. "Juliette, so to speak, insisted relentlessly on her blood-stream." She endeavors to create for herself a French family, and it seems that she is successful on all counts but one: physical appearance. The description of Gabriel's eyes, already on the first page, is the first indication that he is a man caught between two identities: he has the large eyes of Armenians but they are a shade lighter (read: more European) than normal. "They were a shade lighter, but not in the least smaller than Armenian eyes usually are." (3) The large, dark eyes of Armenians are a recurring image in *Musa Dagh,* one that is particularly disturbing to Juliette. She manages to raise Stephan to be a cultivated French child with one glaring exception: "she could not manage to change her son's eyes." (7) Juliette's desire to mold Gabriel into a Frenchman develops into an anti-Armenian bias that rejects more than just physical appearance. Armenians (with the exception of her husband) are endowed with certain negative traits, among them the proclivity for underhanded business dealings. This is her reason for accompanying Gabriel on his trip to look after the family's business affairs: "Matters of great importance would be involved. But he was so simple by nature and certainly not up to the Armenian *ruses* of all the others." (8) That he does not protest this sort of prejudicial statement indicates that he has internalized the opinion of the dominant group. In fact, since his subjective identity does not assert his Armenian-ness, he does not feel at all marginalized. It is nonetheless apparent from Juliette's remarks that Gabriel does occupy a position of marginality even within his marriage. Further prejudices are kept from surfacing only due to Gabriel's desire to be an "individual" and his accordant willingness to have Juliette be "the decisive factor" in their lifestyle. In effect, he surrenders his identity-formation to her discretion. However, this arrangement is immediately threatened when the family leaves Paris.

Once in Beirut, the combat in Europe precludes any thought of an immediate return to France. Juliette is able to make the best of the situation, finding a small community of similarly displaced French citizens: "Juliette found life in Beirut possible. There were crowds of French people." (9) One suspects that the second sentence is an unmarked quote of a comment by Juliette. Beirut is bearable because of the presence of other French. This is simply another expression of her perceived cultural superiority. It is all the more surprising when she, not Gabriel, suggests that the family take the opportunity to visit the newly inherited house in Yoghonoluk. Gabriel himself is ambivalent; he feels drawn to the scenes of his childhood, yet the suggestion that they visit his birthplace and ancestral home "scared him. . . . Nor could he repress a strange uneasiness mingled with longing." (9–10) When he finally is reunited with his childhood surroundings, he is greeted by "indescribable, terrifying, and yet delightful sensations." (5) In a passage reminiscent of Hofmannsthal's "The weariness of forgotten peoples . . . ," Gabriel's pre-French life is described as "a kind of life in the womb, the vague memories of which stir the soul to unwelcome shudderings." (5)

The Armenian surroundings release childhood images that had been repressed by this self-described "individual," sparking an unwanted confrontation between the French and Armenian components of his identity. Gabriel's ambivalence stems from an as yet undetected deeper knowledge of this unavoidable confrontation. Already on his first trek up the Musa Dagh he finds his actions guided by his Armenian roots. The impulse of the Western-educated archaeologist is to explore the ruin of a monastery on a nearby hill. Founded by the apostle Thomas and with stones dating back to the Selucidan period, the ruin contains finds of great archaeological significance. Gabriel collects some stones in the area, but is timid about actually approaching the main part of the ruin. The source of his hesitancy is the memory of a local legend constructed to keep the site untouched:

(It was guarded by great copper-coloured snakes, with crowns on their heads. Those who came sacrilegiously pilfering holy stones to build their houses found, as they carried them away, that the stones had grown into their backs, and so had to carry the load to the grave with them.) Who had told him that story? Once, in his mother's room (now Juliette's) old women had sat with curiously painted faces. Or was that only an illusion? Was it possible—had his mother in Yoghonoluk and his mother in Paris been the same? (11)

In this flashback, tradition and personal history are combined. Gabriel is acquainted with the local mythology; it was passed on to him by his mother. Or was it? The details of his own history are unclear to him. He questions the verity of the memories of his personal experiences, even as a superstitious legend imparted to him as a child holds enough validity to keep him from thoroughly pursuing what he considers to be his "chief occupation"—archaeology—for the time being. Although his subjective situation ("I am an abstract human being") will not acknowledge it, he has many things in common with the Armenian community: language, familiarity with the surroundings, and knowledge of myths and traditions. The list will grow and become increasingly difficult for Gabriel to ignore as the novel's events unfold.

At the beginning of the novel, Gabriel lacks Buber's natural subjective situation (since he has broken with his heritage), as well as the natural objective situation (having been transplanted to a foreign country and culture). The circumstances of the war return him to the latter. His military experience puts him in a position of leadership once the forty days have commenced, and his involvement with what should be his natural objective situation, the Armenian community, increases correspondingly. His subjective situation also mutates from assimilated French intellectual to the "natural" situation: in the end, he defines himself as an Armenian. A complicating factor is that both his ethnic community and his familial community perceive him in a way that distinguishes him as a nonmember. To the Armenians, he is primarily Western; to Juliette, he is above all else Armenian. The tension between objective and subjective identity in both cases makes the very existence of something resembling Buber's natural objective situation nearly impossible. As might be expected from a man who had so vehemently denied that he need be anything more than an "individual," the progress toward his natural subjective situation is incremental and not without considerable vacillation. One aspect of the process *is* constant: the deterioration of his relationship with Juliette.

GABRIEL AND JULIETTE: IDENTITY WITHIN THE MIXED MARRIAGE

In a convincing article on Alma Mahler's influence on Werfel's work, Peter Stephan Jungk suggests that by the mid-1930s Werfel was often using his work as a medium for venting his dissatisfaction with her in their stormy marriage.[11] At the root of their discord were his more liberal-humanistic political viewpoints and her outspoken anti-Semitism. While researching his Werfel biography, Jungk was told by numerous Werfel contemporaries that Alma routinely denounced Jews viciously at social gatherings in the presence of her husband.

> It was Alma who . . . tried to lure him away from Judaism as often as she could, who polemicized against Judaism, made digs at it, and at every opportunity launched into her anti-Semitic tirades. (The numerous contemporaries with whom I spoke in the process of my research told me, almost without exception, first of all about Alma Mahler's anti-Semitic attacks.)[12]

The noncombative Werfel was no match for Alma in their frequent face-to-face arguments. Inevitably, their quarrels broke off when he could no longer stand the frustration of trying in vain to convince her with logical arguments.[13] Jungk shows that despite Alma's considerable influence on her husband's selection of writing themes, he reached a point at which he began to write *against* Alma.[14] His artistic retaliation manifested itself in two ways: in creating negative characters endowed with Alma's worst traits and in choosing to write stories either with Jewish protagonists or with pronounced Jewish themes. Jungk cites the 1927 novella "Estrangement" as one example in which a character, here a domineering wife bent on shaping her husband in her own image, was obviously modeled after Alma. Jungk's argument can be supported by at least one additional instance: Juliette in *Musa Dagh*.

Juliette is no villain, but aspects of her marriage with Gabriel are portrayed as negative from the start. The two forces at work are Gabriel's desire to be nondescript and Juliette's wish for him to be French. As noted previously, this wish has intensified and grown into a full-blown prejudice against Armenians. Like other prejudices, hers is replete with contradictions. She looks down on Armenians with haughty eyes as uncultivated "Orientals," but she also accuses them of being excessively proud of their centuries-old culture. Armenians are, as the occasion necessitates, a race of arrogant intellectuals, conniving merchants and guileful street peddlers, or farmers almost primitive in their simplicity. Most any complimentary reference to Armenians can evoke her "ridicule of all things Armenian and Oriental . . . , with which she frequently torments her husband.[15] Gabriel is more than willing to have a French lifestyle according to Juliette's preferences, but on one point he requested a compromise: that Juliette convert to the Gregorian church which most Armenians attend. Although she agrees to the conversion, the Gregorian church becomes another target for her ridicule.

> When she had got engaged to Gabriel, she had obliged him by ceasing to be a Roman Catholic and entering the Armenian Orthodox Church. This had been one of the many sacrifices which she never forgot to mention when they quarreled. She picked holes, as her habit was. The Armenian rite was not nearly ornate enough to please her. (189) She rejected the reproach that the church uses all of its surplus monies towards education as exaggerated pragmatism.[16]

Before word of the relocation transports interrupts the quiet village life at the foot of the Musa Dagh, Juliette enjoys the months spent in Yoghonoluk. The Villa Bagradian and its inhabitants are the center of attention, and she thrives on being the local sensation. "Juliette, here in Yoghonoluk, seemed to have found her way into the hearts of his simple-minded compatriots, though in Europe she had often jibbed at the society of the most cultivated Armenians." (51) The sudden change in attitude comes as a result of the very warm, almost reverent reception extended to her by the locals. Possibly, too, she feels less threatened by simple village folk. Still, a part of her is resistant to full tolerance. Any compliment she has for the Armenians is appended by the qualification: "for an Armenian. . . ." That her compliments are simultaneously veiled insults is most apparent in her praise of Iskuhi. When Iskuhi is brought to the Bagradian house for her convalescence, Juliette's first impression is: "She's really unusual. One seldom sees such delicate-looking faces among them. She looks like a lady, even in those ragged clothes. And she seemed to speak such good French, for an Armenian." (118) Clearly, she considers beauty to be a rarity among Armenians and does not deem them capable of fluency in her native French.

Juliette's relationship with Iskuhi is marked by oscillation. In general, Iskuhi is embraced by the Bagradian household. Juliette is captivated by her beauty and attempts to win her affection by clothing her in French gowns. Obviously, this effort also serves to transform the shy Armenian at least outwardly into a sophisticated European woman—much like her attempts to modify her husband's identity. At the same time, however, reminders of Iskuhi's Armenian-ness tend to spark another barrage of derogatory comments. In one instance, Iskuhi is asked by Stephan to sing an Armenian folksong. The last stanza ends with the words, "Mother Earth embraces her well-taught child, / While ignorant nations may perish, and go." (179) Upon hearing the translation, Juliette's biting rejoinder is: "Well, there you see—how proud you all are! The well-taught child, to whom Mother Earth behaves so obligingly, is Armenian. And the ignoramuses are all the others . . ." This is apparently a topic of great conflict between Gabriel and his wife, for the narrator reports:

> Juliette was again full of a theme which had caused her husband many bitter hours. Strangely enough, Iskuhi, in Gabriel's absence, seemed particularly to inspire her to dwell on it. It took the form of a series of depreciatory remarks on the Armenians, viewed in that brilliant light of Gallic culture, which Juliette turned on their obscurity. (177–78)

Here we may recognize a portraiture of Alma Mahler as Jungk has found in other works. Indeed, it is puzzling that he omitted this example from his study, especially when the many Alma-Juliette parallels are sometimes nearly verbatim: Juliette had caused Gabriel "many bitter hours"; Jungk cites a letter to Werfel's sister Mizi in which he confides to her "that Alma's antisemitism had caused him in the two and a half decades of their relationship 'a hundred bitter hours,'" an estimate which Jungk considers "grossly underestimated."[17]

As he spends more and more time seeing to the welfare of the Musa Dagh villages, Gabriel's contact with Juliette diminishes, and the distance between them grows. After twenty-four hours of intensive planning, he returns to check on his wife—to find that he hardly recognizes her.

> Here stood Juliette's tall and beautiful body, so near, so entirely a part of his.... This body had born Stephan, had endured for the future of the Bagradians. And now? He could scarcely recognize it. He had lost the image of its nakedness. It was like having forgotten one's own name. But bad enough as it was to find some French lady standing here, with whom one had once had a liaison—this lady had become an enemy, she was on the other side, had a seat on the exterminators' councils, although she was herself an Armenian mother. (228–29)

She, too, feels their marital intimacy rapidly dissolving. With each passing hour, her husband seems more Armenian. To compound the problem, he returns after a full day's absence bearing linguistic traces of his evolving identity: having spent so much time giving speeches and holding meetings in Armenian, he struggles with the transition back to French. "He began ... in a hard, unusual accent, which seemed to set Juliette's nerves still more on edge...." (229) Her sensitivity to Armenian-spoken French was already referred to. Given the importance of language as a marker of ethnic identity, this occurrence must be regarded as a sign of Gabriel's ever-increasing identification with Armenians. Although Juliette seems ready for a break with Gabriel, she turns down an opportunity to escape the villagers' fate because she fears that she will lose Stephan, who has expressed his desire to stay.

> I, I, I! Jealous rage had hold of Juliette. Oh, these Armenians! How they stuck together! She herself had ceased to be there. Her child belonged to her, as much as to him! She wasn't going to lose him.

Yet, if she stood up for her rights, she'd lose Stephan. She came a decisive, almost an enraged, step nearer father and son. (234)

Gabriel misinterprets her motion toward him as a decision to stay with him and keep the family together. In this manner it is decided that Juliette and Stephan will remain with the others in the mountain encampment.

The forty days spent on the Musa Dagh only add to the distance between the married couple. Gabriel, as commander of the defense, sleeps with the troops and visits Juliette by day only infrequently. Her days are spent longing to be back in Paris and to have her "old" Gabriel returned to her: "But not for the present Gabriel—no! For Gabriel the *Parisien*, that sensitive, gentle, and considerate Gabriel, whose tact had always made her forget the things which are not to be bridged over." (322) She tries to imagine things as they were, but Armenian images intrude upon her daydreaming: "Coloured disks with, in the centre of each, a piercing eye—eyes that reproached and suffered, forcing themselves in on her from all sides; Gabriel's and Stephan's Armenian eyes, which would not let go of her." An encounter with Gabriel is an even more rude awakening. "When she looked up, the eyes were really bending over her, in the wildly bearded face of a strange man. She stared in alarm at Gabriel. He seemed remote, his nights all spent out of doors, the reek of damp earth clinging to him." (322) Later, she registers him as "the unknown, bearded, brown Armenian who, now and then, came in to sit with her. . . ." (417) In a short period of time, his outward appearance has been altered in ways, all of which remind her unpleasantly of the Armenian "traits" she rejects. His eyes appear enlarged as he gets thinner. He no longer shaves as she believes a cultivated person should. The constant exposure to the high-altitude sun has darkened his skin color, emphasizing his different racial descent. Finally, he even carries the scent of the land of his ancestors. Every perceptible characteristic is Armenian. When, near the end of the novel, Stephan is killed by Turks, Juliette's last link with Gabriel is broken. Her husband of fourteen years has ceased to exist as she knew him; with their son's death, she loses her last natural connection to the Armenian cause. "With Stephan's spilt blood, with the death of this only son, whom she had given the Armenian people, the whole world had indeed become French for her." (636)

Recapturing of Ethnic Identity: Stephan

With the figure of Stephan, Werfel anticipated a generational principle of ethnic identity, which gained such acceptance among historians and sociologists after its introduction (1938), that it was widely referred to as a law. "Hansen's Law," so dubbed in recognition of Marcus Lee Hansen's paper, "The Third Generation in America," asserts that "'what the son wishes to forget, the grandson wishes to remember.'"[18] In essence, it posits a pattern by which the generation assimilating to a new culture rejects all aspects of its cultural heritage as a barrier to full assimilation. The following generation, however, feels secure in its (assimilated) identity and exhibits a keen interest in the family's preassimilatory culture. "Hansen's Law" is now more often disputed than supported,[19] but Stephan may still be considered representative of this theoretical phenomenon.

Gabriel has endeavored to live in France without calling attention to his ethnicity. The only aspects of ethnicity that are passed down to his son are the Gregorian religion and the Armenian language, the latter of which seems to have been more an afterthought than a plan with clear intent: Stephan is not given the Armenian tutor until age ten. Once the thirteen-year-old Stephan reaches his father's homeland, however, he can hardly contain his eagerness to learn more about it. On the morning of Gabriel's first hike up the Musa Dagh, Juliette grants Stephan permission to catch up with his father. When Gabriel directs a question to him, he is startled to hear Stephan answer in Armenian. "Bagradian raised his head. Stephan had said it in Armenian. But had he asked his question in Armenian? Usually they spoke French to one another." (15) This is just the first of many attempts Stephan makes to meld with the Armenian environment. Unfortunately for him, he lacks all but the most rudimentary knowledge of Armenian customs. On this rare occasion of one-on-one contact with his father, he hopes to learn more. "Stephan's expectant soul awaited another remark. This was Dad's country. He longed to be told stories of Dad's childhood, that secret time, of which they had so seldom told him anything." (16) The fact that such information has been withheld has only heightened his curiosity about his father's heritage.

The new surroundings have triggered more than curiosity. Werfel depicts the experience as an awakening. Stephan has an innate connection to the land; though it lay dormant until now, he needed little more than to walk upon its soil to feel an intimate bond with it. Still expecting to be called for service in the Turkish military, Gabriel proposes that Stephan and Juliette go to Switzerland to wait out the war in safety. Stephan's response is adamant: "Stephan clenched his fists across his heart. 'No—not to Switzerland. Do let's stay, Dad!'" (17) His ethnic identity is purely of the primordial variety, while his father represents the optionalist school.

> Gabriel looked at the pleading eyes of his son in some astonishment. Mysterious! That this boy, who never had known his father's home, should feel, none the less, so deeply bound to it. This emotion had lived in him, this affinity with the mountain of the Bagradians; Stephan, born in Paris, had inherited it with his very blood. (17–18)

Increasingly, Stephan will insist upon living in Yoghonoluk as an Armenian boy, a demand that disturbs Juliette to no end. As a compromise, he is allowed to wear traditional Armenian garments when attending school with the other children, but at home he is required to wear Western clothing. Juliette's protestations will have little effect on Stephan's development henceforth. Being placed in his father's homeland—his natural objective situation, in Werfel's eyes—is all the stimulus necessary to direct the boy to his true self. Werfel suggests that without the events leading to the visit in Yoghonoluk, Stephan would have led an inauthentic life under an assumed identity.

> It was still astonishing that this child, had he not ended up in Syria by means of some mysterious fate, probably never would have experienced in a direct way his blood membership and therefore also nothing of his innermost self.[20]

Once awakened, this innermost self dominates the boy's awareness. Stephan is "no longer a child whose life one arranges, but an adult impelled by his will and blood, as destiny fully shaped, no longer susceptible to moulding." (234) Here again, Buber's influence on Werfel's thought is apparent. He explains that the basic structure of personality, though not unaffected by environmental factors, is nonetheless determined at the deepest level by the heritage of one's natural community:

> The forces that carve man's life are his inwardness and his environment: his disposition to assimilate impressions, and the matter creating these impressions. But the innermost stratum of man's disposition, which yields his type, the basic structure of his personality, is that which I have called blood: that something which is implanted within us by the chain of fathers and mothers, by their nature and by their fate, by their deeds and by their sufferings; it is time's great heritage that we bring with us into the world.[21]

When Gabriel and Stephan first get a glimpse of Iskuhi's party, battered by their Turkish tormentors and exhausted from their foot trip to safety in Yoghonoluk, father and son both feel the Armenian legacy of persecution, although neither one of them has ever been subjected to maltreatment. Along with the villagers who have gathered to witness the spectacle, they instinctively experience the fate of earlier Armenians, passed down through the chain of generations.

> Here, in the church square of Yoghonoluk, three hundred Armenians were shaken by a grief, the story of which they had not yet heard. Even Gabriel, the stranger, the Parisian, the cosmopolitan, who had long since overcome his origins—even he had to force down something which throttled him. He glanced surreptitiously at Stephan. The last tinge of colour had faded out of [his son's] face. Juliette would have been startled, not only at her son's pallor, but at the wild look of uncomprehending horror in his eyes. She would have been scared to see her child look so Armenian. (80)

Even two generations removed from the community, racial instincts take effect at critical moments.

Stephan's ethnic identity, spurred on by exposure to the Armenian community, was described as primordial. Once set in motion, it proceeds in a singular direction (from French to Armenian) and without hesitation. By the time he is killed, he is fully Armenian. As he is dying, his hallucinations feature most prominently his father, who is his link to the Armenian past, and who connects him in a blessinglike gesture to the eternal Armenian community.

> [W]hen he saw his small son waiting, Gabriel opened his arms, in a movement of unfathomable gentleness. And since Stephan was really such a little boy, Dad could lift him close to his radiant face, and then high above his head—higher and higher. (610)

Gabriel's identity, by contrast, follows a noticeably less linear route. Werfel took special pains in order to show that his progression from "individual" to Armenian, while necessary and even inevitable, constitutes a tremendous struggle between competing forces within him. He must move from rejecting Armenian identity to acknowledging and finally embracing it.

Gabriel's Return to Authentic Identity

Werfel underscored the "East vs. West" conflict in Gabriel repeatedly. The most obvious image of this conflict is his pocket watch, which he keeps set to European time. His deteriorating relationship with Juliette and simultaneous growing attachment to Iskuhi is another manifestation of that problem. Revisions made to an earlier manuscript of *Musa Dagh*[22] indicate that Werfel wanted Gabriel's identity conflict to be a complex issue whose resolution posed a serious challenge. The first version endows him with weaker ties to the Bagradian ancestral home and Armenian culture, starting with his birth: Gabriel was *not* born in Yoghonoluk. (Werfel reconsidered the point, writing on the facing page, "*Perhaps Gabriel born in Yogh. after all,*" and finally striking the "not" from his original sentence.) His fondness for the Musa Dagh is equally great in both versions, however of a somewhat different nature. Gabriel of the first version thinks of the Musa Dagh as the site of many magical childhood summers, but this sort of nostalgic attachment cannot compare with the identity-shaping ramifications of having been born there. Werfel gave the assimilated Parisian roots which were unquestionably Armenian. His transformation had to be well-motivated if it was to avoid the appearance of being superficial.

This is also the reason for references to Juliette's anti-Armenian taunts: though he does not argue with her, the taunts are hurtful to him and provide a basis for his quandary.

To balance his French education and married life, Gabriel is shown to have also a good command of Armenian culture. Apparently, he has even talked to Juliette about prominent literary figures often enough to incite her to ridicule Armenians on the level of literary accomplishments as well.

> "You may be an ancient people," she kept insisting, *"c'est bien.* A civilized people. No doubt. But in what precisely do you prove it? Oh, of course, I've been told all the names—again and again. Abovian, Raffi, Siamanto. But who's ever heard of them? No one in the world except Armenians." (178)

Revealingly, in the Vienna manuscript Gabriel does not understand a reference to Raffi's famous novel *Kaidsar.* In *Kaidsar,* a mother delivers her son to his first school day, remarking to the teacher, "The flesh is yours, the bones are mine," an Armenian saying which means so much as: Do with him whatever is necessary, just don't break any of his bones.[23] When Gabriel takes Stephan to the Yoghonoluk school for the first time, he witnesses this same ritual without comprehending it.

> An old woman approached the teacher and shoved a little boy up to him: "There he is, teacher! Do not hit him!" And she mumbled according to ancient ritual an incantation, the meaning of which Bagradian did not understand: "The flesh is yours, the bones are mine!"[24]

Werfel's margin notes suggest that the teacher was going to explain the scene to Gabriel. The finished version of *Musa Dagh,* however, omits the cryptic expression entirely, since an explanation for Gabriel's sake would detract from his knowledge of Armenian rituals and literature, while an explanation for the reader's sake would be stylistically cumbersome.

Gabriel's cultural knowledge extends to the area of adult etiquette, even though he has spent his adult life in France. He is cognizant of what "custom ordained" and follows precisely the "ritual of reception" when seeking out an old family friend, the Agha Rifaat Bereket. Needing advice after his passport has been confiscated, Gabriel pays him an unannounced visit. He violates one custom in arriving at a time of rest and can assuage his uneasiness about such a blatant disregard for tradition only by convincing himself that time is of the essence.

> His heart was still beating fast as the Agha Rifaat Bereket's servant conducted him into the selamlik, the reception-room. . . . His watch, which, idiotically, he still kept set to European time, pointed to the second hour of the afternoon. It was, therefore, the sacred domestic hour, the hour of kef, the never-to-be-encroached-on midday peace, in which every visit was a very serious piece of tactlessness. He had got here far too early. (33)

The Agha makes him wait. Despite his anxiety, Gabriel makes no further attempt to press the issue. First, he follows a greeting procedure according to custom: "Gabriel, who knew his manners, found the right formula for reply." (34) Then, in another gesture of respect for convention, he allows the Agha to steer the conversation as he sees fit: "Custom ordained that this young visitor must wait for the old man to give him an opening to direct the conversation as he desired." (35) It is significant that he is not only aware of etiquette, but also adheres to it unquestioningly. Like his knowledge of cultural figures, it demonstrates a strong Armenian component in his identity of which he is not yet aware.

More apparent to the reader is his Armenian identity on the subconscious level. The loss of the family's passports engenders more worry in him than Juliette can understand. She appeals to Gabriel's sense of logic: "What's changed? This business with the passports? We shall be given new ones. Why, you yourself said that in Antioch you heard nothing terrible." (63) Gabriel has no direct personal experience of Armenians' past ordeals in Turkey; still, he instinctively feels that danger is lying in wait for the Armenians. His instincts draw on the chain of generations, again reminiscent of Buber's philosophy. Gabriel replies, "Perhaps, really, very little may have changed. But it always comes suddenly, like a desert storm. It's in my bones. The fathers in me, who suffered incredible things, can feel it. My whole body feels it." (63) Like Stephan, he feels the suffering of previous generations: his community's history is a part of his identity. The similarity in vocabulary between the previous passage and one from Buber is striking: "[O]ur being and our character have been formed not solely by the nature of our fathers but also by their fate, and by their pain, their misery and their humiliation."[25] Gabriel's connection to past generations remains vague, subconscious through a large portion of the novel. Clearly, he must still contend with his strong French component, the component he prefers. When he makes a conscious effort to recall the image of his Armenian grandfather, something within him rebels: perhaps the grandfather was nothing but a storybook tale.

> Had he really ever known his grandfather, or only read of him and seen his pictures in a story book? A little man with a white goatee, in a long black-and-yellow-striped silk gown. His gold eyeglass dangling from a chain upon his chest. In red shoes he had walked over the grass of the garden. Everyone bowed deeply. Tapered old man's fingers stroked on the boy's cheeks. Had it all happened, or was it no more than empty dreaming? (5)

The image of his grandfather is too exotic, too specifically Armenian for the Parisian "individual" to accept as a true memory; thus, the memory is enshrouded in doubt. However, in moments of vulnerability, Gabriel's Armenian subconscious emerges with greater clarity. While taking a nap on the Musa Dagh, for example, he is revisited by childhood fantasies of saving his people from the evil Turks. In his dreams, he relives his old fears:

> The mad dreams of every Armenian boy. (Could they be otherwise?) ... Abdul Hamid, the blood-stained Sultan, had issued a ferman against Christians. The hounds of he Prophet, Turks, Kurds, Circassians, rally to the green banners, to burn and plunder, to massacre Armenian folk. But they had reckoned without Gabriel Bagradian. He assembles his own. He leads them into the mountains. With indescribable valour he fights off this overwhelming power and beats it back. (13–14)

This vision of heroics is easily recognized as a foreshadowing of the novel's events, a "daydream that anticipates everything," as Werfel noted in the preparatory stages.[26]

It is a lengthy process before Gabriel comes to regard the Musa Dagh Armenians as "his own." Having been thrust by circumstance into a situation in which the majority Turkish population sees him unequivocally as an Armenian, he is forced to ponder this identification. As much as he may identify with the finer offerings of Armenian culture, he finds it nearly impossible to accept the nonintellectual manifestations of his *Volk*. At the street bazaar in Antioch, he is confronted with an entirely different image of Armenians than the one with which he is willing to identify:

> So these were his brothers, then? These battered faces, these glistening eyes, alert for custom? No, many thanks, he refused such brotherhood, everything in him rebelled against it! ... Jesus Christ! Couldn't one be an individual, free from all this seething, stinking hostility, as one had been that morning on Musa Dagh? (29)

However, the predominantly Turkish society has gone to great lengths to ensure the marginalization of Armenians: religiously and otherwise, they have been identified as fundamentally different from the rest of society. It is impossible for a member of a minority group to be an individual at a time when that minority group is being persecuted. Gabriel recognizes this quite quickly. To a certain extent, he even accepts it: he is willing to engage himself in an attempt to combat the persecution. His involvement, however, does not amount to more than "an act of will and necessity."[27] In him there remains a very basic conflict between Western and Eastern mentality. As long as he is planning the Musa Dagh defense independently, he can envision it much as he did in his boyhood dreams. However, when the plans leave the intellectual plane, the differences between him and his "brothers" again become painfully evident. In a meeting with village leaders, his concern is met with a calm that borders on resignation. Gabriel wants to take action, but in essence he is told that what will be, will be. Just one of many confrontations with "Eastern slackness,"[28] the incident tests his patience sorely: "It was too much. Gabriel rudely sprang to his feet. All the European in him was up in arms against these sleepers, these gossips, who would sink down into death without a protest, as they rotted their lives away in filth." (121) When the time arrives to present his defense initiative to the Musa Dagh communities, the reality of the villagers again strikes a blow to the concept he had formed for himself.

> As Gabriel scanned this people, his own people, a sudden horror began to invade him. His scared heart missed a beat. Once again reality looked quite different from any concept which he had formed of it. (202)

What finally lays the foundation for a more intimate bond between Gabriel and the Musa Dagh community is the beating, witnessed by several villagers, suffered at the hands of Turkish soldiers. Gabriel has donned his old Turkish officer's uniform, hoping to catch the soldiers off guard and thus prevent the execution of deportation orders. The ploy's effectiveness is short-lived: when the confrontation takes a turn for the worse, he is stripped naked and beaten in punishment for his presumption. The abuse and humiliation, so much a part of Turkish Armenians' past, draw Gabriel closer to the community. "The physical brutality he had suffered—the first, in all his sheltered, remote existence—had drawn him even closer to all the rest." (277) His identity transformation is given impetus by this initiation, but the "individual" still rebels on occasion. The most noteworthy occurrence prompting Gabriel to reject Armenian identification coincides with his first major victory in battle against the Turks. His strategy and preparations have paid off dramatically. The unsuspecting Turks, who expected to have the rebellious villagers rounded up in a single afternoon, are pushed back down the mountain in a stunning defeat. In the confusion, the Armenians are even able to supplement their weapons supply substantially. Gabriel has given them reason to hope that they, indeed, may, be able to defend themselves. When he visits the main camp area after the battle, he is received as a hero. Even those who had previously been skeptical celebrate the military leader, crowding around him for a chance to kiss his hand—a gesture of respect and devotion reserved for the father of an Armenian household. Such a display of acceptance repels him: "This hand-kissing filled him with dismay." (335) As he tries to extract himself from the crowd, he has a single desire: "To shave, wash, rub himself down for minutes at a time from head to toe and then feel a light silk pajama on his body!"[29] Slightly later in

2: IDENTITY AND THE HISTORICAL COMMUNITY 73

the novel, it is remarked that Stephan is no longer recognizable as anything but an Armenian boy, that the fourteen years spent in Europe seemed "as though they were washed away."[30] With a mature, multifaceted personality like Gabriel's, the transformation cannot be instantaneous. The European in Gabriel tries to "wash away" the effects of the Armenian community following his victory, but he has plunged himself irrevocably into a position of service to the Armenian cause. There can be no return to the "old Gabriel": "[T]he more attention he gave to this, the more impatiently he strove to get this day scrubbed well out of him, the farther away he seemed from himself. Into this marvellous cleanness in which he revelled the 'abstract man' refused to return—the 'individual,' the man he had brought with him from Paris." (335) From this point forward, his responsibility to the community supersedes all else; since Juliette is not of his community, his relationship to her loses its primacy. This is evident in the loss of intimacy between the two. After bathing, Gabriel settles down for a private evening with his wife, but all attempts at conversation are interrupted by his concerns about the military situation.

> Who could say that the Turks weren't planning a nighttime attack! Gabriel no longer belonged to Juliette nor even to himself. He tried to hang on to his escaping self. Sweat ran from his pores. When he got close to Juliette he was unable to prove his love, for the first time in their marriage.

His impotence signals the final alienation from his wife and all things French.

Johannes Lepsius is a character based on the real German minister who made the plight of the Armenians his personal holy cause. Werfel has him utter the words, "Every human being, whether he lives it or not, belongs to a national community, and remains a part of it." (555) This very succinctly summarizes Gabriel's experience. He shares this realization with Iskuhi:

> All my life I'd only sought for what was foreign to me. I loved the exotic. It enticed me, but it never made me happy. And I attracted it, too, but I couldn't make it happy either. One lives with a woman, Iskuhi, and then meets you, the only sister one can ever have in the world, and it's too late. (615)

Buber wrote that the individual who lacks the natural subjective community can (re)gain consciousness of his or her membership through participation, and that by participating, the individual comes to understand his or her distinct role in the continuing life of that community:

> [T]he individual is not situated within a community from the very outset; he must instead find his own niche. His sense of belonging will only gradually lead him to a genuine belonging, to participation, in the life and labor of the community. This process will become intensified as he penetrates more deeply into his personal individuality, into the secret of his uniqueness; simultaneously, he will discover what he and no one else is called upon to contribute to his people.[31]

The same Gabriel Bagradian who denied the existence of any connecting forces between himself and other Armenians now feels a familial bond with them, personified in the figure of his "sister" Iskuhi. "Always it was the same sensation, that what he felt for her was the most intimate thing he had ever known. Her warmth, as of a clear fire, seemed to reach far back, beyond any frontiers of conscious memory." (487) The connection to his community extends beyond his personal experience; it is a historical force transmitted through the chain of generations. It was noted that Gabriel could not—or would not—remember his grandfather as a real person in his past. Another indication that the chain of generations lay dormant and unacknowledged within him is provided by Werfel's manuscript notes. After telling Juliette that "the fathers in me" sense impending danger, Gabriel lay his head on her lap in an effort to ward off the "fathers'" influence. Werfel's notes on the facing page read, "*Sleep, everything within him wants to sleep! The fathers within him want to sleep.*"[32] He is still seeking refuge from his identity in "the foreign."

However, the protagonist at the end of the story is *not* the same Gabriel Bagradian as the one who arrived in Yoghonoluk. He is explicitly referred to as "the new Gabriel." Indeed, nearly every basic aspect of his identity has become Armenian. The Armenian language is now the most natural for him. His marital ties with Juliette have effectively been severed. The land of his ancestors has even taken hold of his spirit: the Musa Dagh provides him with a sort of mystical power.

> The huge mass of Musa Dagh . . . seemed to renew Gabriel's strength and give him courage for the torturing hither and tither of thoughts which had robbed him of sleep ever since the arrival of Pastor Tomasian. But the instant he left the shadow of Musa Dagh the courage to think such thoughts ebbed out of him. (158)

Similarly, Iskuhi's company has the effect of "a mystic spring" upon him. (450)

Gabriel has accepted and served his natural community. He has discovered "what he and no one else is called upon to contribute to his people." When, after forty days' struggle for survival, a French battleship rescues the starving Armenians, it is no surprise that Gabriel opts to forego the rescue. His identity is complete: there is no service he can perform for his *Volk* to supplement it, and a return to his previous life is impossible.

> In those first minutes of general safety he had sensed at once that for him such return to life would be impossible, merely because the real Bagradian, the Bagradian come to life in the forty days, would have to be saved. (813)

Although he has no chance for survival, the chain of generations has been restored. The "fathers" no longer sleep, they are fully part of him. This consciousness exists not merely on the level of instinct, but rather as unquestionable knowledge: "Now he knew his father as powerfully as he had known him only in his childhood."[33] Rounding out the chain, Gabriel's last moments are spent at Stephan's grave on the Musa Dagh. Here he is discovered by the Turks, who symbolically connect him in eternity with the youngest generation. The novel closes: "Gabriel Bagradian was lucky. The second Turkish bullet shattered his temple. He clung to the wood, tore it down along with him. His son's cross lay upon his heart." (817)

3
Franz Werfel, the Historical Novel, and *The Forty Days of Musa Dagh*

THE HISTORICAL NOVEL: THEORETICAL ASSUMPTIONS

DESPITE ITS POPULARITY AMONG THE READING PUBLIC, OR PROBABLY in part because of it, the historical novel traditionally has not been regarded as a prestigious subgenre of the novel. From its inception, literary critics have generally cast a skeptical eye on it as a dilettantish and opportunistic misuse of material best left in the hands of professional historians. The historian could be counted on to present facts without embellishment and in an objective manner, while the novelist would likely take artistic liberties in order to sway the reader to his or her particular interpretation of the historical event. "Hardly invented, it became universal, and while praised, became universally suspect. Its utility as history, as historically accurate information, tends to contravene its ability to delight as fiction, and vice versa."[1]

It is generally acknowledged that the diametrical opposition of historiography and novel, fact and fiction, scientific analysis and inventive manipulation of "facts" has since been rendered anachronistic in light of work undertaken in diverse fields, including both history and literature. The dividing line between history and fiction, earlier assumed to be impenetrable, has become porous at several junctures. We have come to reject the notion that historiography can be a scientific undertaking on the same level of objectivity as, for example, "pure" mathematics. Hayden White's studies have shown how literary narrative modes, such as tragedy and satire, are employed for historiographic narration. With this observation, he attempts to narrow the differentiating gap between history and fiction. History is "fictionalized" by association with poetic modes of narration.[2]

There have been objections to his rather extreme conclusion that historiography is, therefore, fictional in nature.³ However, White's contribution to the study of historiography remains significant in having drawn increased attention to the role and nature of narration within that field. In general, both the historical novel and conventional history are now looked upon as "discursive representation(s) of the collective past";⁴ that is, they have in common the dereified historical source with its questionable status as fact, and they both employ the same tool—language—in which to document it.

This does not mean that historiography and the historical novel have merged into one vague, amorphous entity. Rather, new categories of distinction have been sought and proposed. While the factuality and objectivity of the text have been deemphasized, much attention has been directed toward the reader. In this context, a primary consideration is the expectations with which the reader approaches the literary or conventional historical text. Rigney suggests that we "distinguish between historiographical discourse and novelistic discourse in terms of the implied contract which they establish with their public." The insights that call historical fact and historians' ability to be fully objective into question notwithstanding, the historian is still held to a higher level of accountability on a professional level than the novelist. Sources must be duly cited and faithfully reproduced in their original form; speculation, if at all present, must be identified as such; and the omission of pertinent information is unacceptable.⁵ Novelists, by contrast, may manipulate historical details and use them selectively, refer to historical events without documentation, and create characters or situations freely, indeed, while the general historical framework must not divert from what is commonly known to have happened, a certain amount of invention is not only tolerated but expected.⁶ The novelist "generates historical expectations" but "operates within a different set of generic conventions" than the historian.⁷

Helmut Koopmann provides another possible perspective on the historical novel. In his study on historical novels written in exile, he completely removes the stipulation of factual accountability, stressing instead the interpretive nature of these works. He would have us consider them as philosophical statements rather than artistic reproductions of historical occurrences, pointing to their therapeutic content for the present as their primary offering.

> Everything about it indicates that the historical novel of the exile period is not fact-oriented, but rather is fundamentally an anti-realistic novel. . . . In the end existential questions are cloaked under historical garb; it is not a matter of the portrayal but rather the interpretation of history, and with the interpretation of history also an orientation in the present and the intellectual mastery thereof.[8]

Whether a given novel's historical content induces reflection more on its relationship to the present or simply on the nature of the past itself, it is clear that the historical novel has more to offer than merely an engaging fiction set in an earlier time. As P. M. Wetherill comments, "ideally," [historical novelists']

> products offer a perfectly serious and flexible way of thinking about the past. In this, the historical novel is merely an extension of the novel in general: a unique instrument for thinking about the complexity of human experience in all its diverse and simultaneous forms.

Though not mentioned in Lukács' seminal study of the genre,[9] it is generally agreed that one function of the invented protagonist is to give the historical episode a concrete beginning and end. Rather than trying to find two natural breaks in the historical sequence of events, the novelist can set the parameters in a plausible fashion.[10] Koopmann shows that this is a particularly important feature of the historical novel written in exile. Historical episodes are chosen in which the crises parallel current ones but are known to have had a positive outcome.

> As a rule, the historical novel portrayed not a randomly selected segment, but rather a self-contained and tightly defined episode; that is, not the story of an eternal exile but rather that of a situation of escape, usually a successful one.[11]

He goes on to describe the historical novel as "one of the most self-contained forms of the novel . . . that the twentieth century has produced."[12] Aust also identifies the "curve device" as an oft-occuring feature of historical novels. The first and final sentences commonly refer expressly to one another, creating a heightened consciousness of how the end was already contained in the beginning. "Both passages have the same horizon, under which opening, awakening, greeting and introduction occur as well as closure, 'putting to sleep', taking leave and dismissal."[13] Within this closed system, the novelist has a great deal of latitude the historian lacks. It is not necessary to narrate in a strictly linear fashion; ellipses[14] and flashbacks are common, and their use can greatly improve the quality of the novel. One is often transported to the prehistory of the past in which the novel is set. That is, the narrated past can be invoked to explain the narrated present. The "*order* in which material is communicated to the reader" affects the reader's ability to draw conclusions, form opinions, and make critical assessments.[15]

Koopmann focuses on the ways in which the historical novel's parallels to contemporary crises were able to convey an optimistic message to the contemporary reader. The exile situation necessitated that hope for the future be found in encouraging past episodes. However, the conscious allusion to historical precedents of contemporary occurrences is not unique to the historical novel of the exile period. This connection between historical episode and contemporary issues is a common feature in the historical novel, on which—as Lützeler points out—Lukács fails to highlight in his study.

> What Lukács overlooks is the fact that the historical novel not only participates in the "realistic" novel tradition of the late eighteenth century, that it not only seeks to portray historical phases of the past, but that it also tries to shed light on contemporary problems.[16]

Historical novels are intended not only as a presentation of historical events; rather, they are written with an eye on contemporary and future problems. In addition, the relationship between historical novels and contemporary issues extends beyond mere consolation or encouragement, a fact that further seems to be lost on Lukács. One of their goals is to understand who we are, and will be, by having a notion of who we were. In a word, they attempt to clarify identity. As Lützeler has formulated: "To structure identity means, first of all, to identify with stories."[17]

The provision of identity through the memory of history is a strong impetus behind Werfel's *The Forty Days of Musa Dagh*.

Werfel and the Historical Novel: Introduction

Werfel's first novel, *Verdi* (1924), falls into the category of historical biography. Though not his first artistic rendering of historical material, *Verdi* includes a "Vorbericht" that represents his earliest discussion about the use of history in literature. Werfel reports having had inhibitions about approaching the project: "It would be necessary to move at once upon two separate planes, the poetic and the historical—to walk simultaneously in the world of fable and the world of fact. And there were many dangers to be encountered by the way."[18] It is significant that the brief preface progresses from a concern with *fact* to one with *truth*. Herein lies a clue to his understanding of history and its role in the novel. Reality, meaning exact reproduction of researchable facts, is ultimately secondary to truth. In this, he echoes the spirit of Lukács's concept of historical faithfulness. Lukács is much more concerned that the novel be an accurate depiction of the trends and psychology of the populace than he is with positivistic historicism down to the last detail. Thus, his appreciation for Scott's historical novels:

> In portraying how historical necessity asserts itself ... through the passionate actions of individuals ... in showing how this necessity has its roots in the real social and economic basis of popular life Scott manifests his *historical faithfulness*. Measured against this authentic reproduction of the real components of historical necessity, it matters little whether individual details, individual facts are historically correct or not.[19]

When included, detail is used not to persuade the reader of the historical factuality of the text, but to further corroborate the authenticity of the general characterization of a time. As Foley sums up, "Telling the truth has become a matter of accurate generalization."[20]

Verdi relates a period of artistic crisis in the musician's life, a phase that is purely the invention of the author yet one Werfel feels can illustrate a deeper truth about his historical subject. In the medium of the novel, the disparate facts from the past can be combined to form a "purer" truth:

> [T]he truth of a life is not to be found in the strictest analysis of its biographical material, nor in the sum of all its doings and sayings. From these we must win, yea, we must create this truth for ourselves—the mythical legend of that man, that which is purely and peculiarly his.[21]

Aust writes, much in the same vein, that any discussion of the historical novel raises questions concerning truth, realism, and artistic autonomy:

> It is a matter of truth in so far as poetry, as the world of the possible, the essential and the philosophical, on the one hand defers to the narrow constraints of the real and the actual, yet on the other hand insists on "freedom of speech" and from within this tension attempts to obtain higher truths.[22]

A second clue to Werfel's perception of history is delivered in his best historical novel, *The Forty Days of Musa Dagh*. Not forty pages into the nine hundred-page saga, the wise sage of the novel, Agha Rifaat Bereket, states that history is interpretive; the events described are chosen selectively and presented subjectively. To the question, "What has occurred?", he answers, "'But what are occurrences? They are only what interpretation makes of them.'" (37) With his view that history is largely the product of the historian and his high regard for the truth-producing potential of fiction, it comes as no surprise that Werfel feels that invention within the historical novel is fully legitimate. The novel is not restricted to facts as presented by historians, nor does it sacrifice its truthfulness by inventing characters and events. It is, indeed, following P. M. Wetherill, a form of thinking about the past that is both "perfectly serious and flexible."[23] Werfel, who quotes Verdi as having said, "The truth we copy may be good, but the truth we discover is better, infinitely better . . ."[24] might even have claimed it to be superior to historiography.

Motivations for the Historical Novel
The Forty Days of Musa Dagh

Koopmann has identified some eighty-five historical novels written between 1934 and 1939, and suggests that the genre was popular among emigrants as a means of affirming their existence. The novels produced in exile "are first and foremost to be seen as emigrants' attempts at 'existence-safeguarding', and as such belong to the realm of identification-attempts, as were so characteristic of the first years of exile."[25] Stripped of their community and compatriots, writers in exile turned to historical figures with whom they could identify. In parallel historical periods they sought, and often found, answers to the existential questions raised by their predicament.[26]

Werfel's motivations for writing his *Musa Dagh* must be seen in a slightly different light, since work on the novel was undertaken already in 1932, and the finished product was published and sold in Germany in 1933. Clearly, this is not exile literature; Werfel was not in exile at this point, at least not officially, and *Musa Dagh* should not be read as the story of his own identity in crisis. However, it is worthwhile to keep in mind that his entire childhood, adolescence, and adulthood in Prague had sensitized him to the precariousness of individual identity in its constant negotiations with society. That anti-Semitic agitation of the late 1920s and early 1930s would necessarily affect the self-concept of assimilated German- or Austrian-Jews, certainly was not lost on him. To forecast, in an atmosphere of anti-Semitism, what ramifications were in store for Jews and other minorities if the current of popular opinion were allowed to accelerate undiverted, was not difficult. *Mein Kampf*, which by 1933 had sold nearly 300,000 copies,[27] and numerous other anti-Semitic publications spell out quite clearly how expendable "Hebrew" lives were considered compared to the lives of "decent, valuable Germans."[28]

Franz Werfel was a sensitive observer of his time and of human relationships. In this sense, *Musa Dagh* can be understood not as a work of exile literature, but as one written in a situation that might be described as *anticipated* exile—anticipated not for the author alone, but for many. As such, it is not so much the product of a real identity crisis suffered by Werfel as it is a more general inquiry into identity-struggles likely to be suffered by minorities in a time of popular chauvinism. It is this quality of the work that makes it a valuable and relevant novel for any generation.

Aust comments that in its "creative intent," the historical novel can be organized into two variants: "reconstructive" and "parabolic."[29] *Musa Dagh,* however, serves two main purposes as a historical novel, combining both foresight and retrospective. First, it sheds light on the contemporary situation and the anticipated consequences it holds in store for individual identity (parabolic). Second, it aims to "rescue" the tragic events of the past from the selective, forgetful field of history (reconstructive). Werfel explains in his "note" that this episode could easily fall into a black hole of history. With his novel, he hopes to ensure that the Armenians' story be permanently recorded.

> The miserable sight of some maimed and famished-looking refugee children, working in a carpet factory, gave me the final impulse to snatch from the Hades of all that was, this incomprehensible destiny of the Armenian nation. (iii)

The "note" concludes with the remark that, on a 1933 lecture tour through Germany, Werfel had repeatedly read from a particular chapter which, it is stressed, is based on "historical records." This final sentence reveals again the most important components of his program with the historical novel. Its use of historical sources is emphasized, thus reiterating its claim to historical veracity. It is also clear that he considered the historical events portrayed in his novel to hold relevance for the present. The chapter he read from was chosen because of the pertinence of its content, not for its literary merit (though well-written, many other excerpts from the same novel would have met this requirement). It deals with the central contemporary issue of the position of minorities in society. Literature is seen as a viable tool for interpreting the present; it is not divorced from history, but rather can play an active role in opinion formation about both the present and the past.

Minorities

As a field that strives for a broad, inclusive understanding of culture, cultural studies often concerns itself with manifestations of culture appearing at society's margins or expressed by minority parties and individuals. Generalizing interpretations of cultural identity as something homogeneous are rejected in favor of multifaceted cultural inquiry. Homi Bhabha writes:

> We may begin by questioning that progressive metaphor of modern social cohesion—*the many as one*—shared by organic theories of the holism of culture and community, and by theorists who treat gender, class or race as social totalities that are expressive of unitary collective experiences.[30]

Such inquiry entails the recontextualization of "forgotten community narratives" and the disclaiming of "negative figurations"[31] of minorities. As Edward Said has noted, narration is a powerful tool in the hands of minorities "to assert their own identity and the existence of their own history."[32] In *Musa Dagh,* we witness this sort of strategy of identity assertion for two minority groups. Werfel shows that the Turks were in a struggle to define and affirm their identity in competition with Western imperialist countries. He also made a conscious effort to broaden the image of Armenians, to dispel negative and totalizing figurations of that minority.

Before the turn of the century, there were few who identified themselves as "Turks." Rather, the Turkish population of the Ottoman Empire found its main source of identity in the Islamic faith. The word *Turk* in fact was a pejorative term connoting something like "redneck simpleton." In 1897, however, the young poet Mehmed Emin published a volume of poetry in which he took the word as a proud designation of his identity. With this new usage of the word, "a new concept of identity had found its way into the collective self-awareness of Turkish-speaking Ottoman Muslims."[33] Marginalized by the European colonizers to a second-rate status, the Turkish leadership sought to endow the appellation with specific characteristics and a history to complement that identity. *Turk* took on the meaning of a proud race of warriors with a glorious military past. This new Turkish pride is evident at several junctures of *Musa Dagh,* most revealingly in the discussion between Enver and Lepsius. Lepsius has criticized the Turkish government for eradicating the intelligentsia of the nation, the Armenians. Enver's response clearly indicates that the Turks are prepared to go to any lengths to assert Turkism. The new identity is one that is expressly hostile to other identities:

> Are you really so much in favour of that kind of intelligence, Herr Lepsius? I'm not. We Turks may not be very intelligent in that way, but on the other hand we're a great and heroic people, called to establish and govern a world empire. Therefore we intend to surmount all obstacles. (138–39)

In a direct challenge to European hegemony, therefore, the marginalized Turks have successfully turned the tables. The Turk is now the dominant representative of Ottoman culture; the remaining ethnic and religious groups in the empire have been reduced to minority status.

In at least two significant episodes of the novel, Bagradian attempts to challenge, in turn, this exclusive, excluding Turkish identity. The first instance is in the steam bath scene where, overhearing Turks speak disparagingly of the "traitorous" Armenian population, he contends that not only are the Armenians loyal, but that the Turkish "war god" Enver Pasha owes his very existence to Armenian soldiers:

> His Excellency Enver Pasha and his whole staff had their lives saved in the Caucasus by Armenian troops. He was as good as taken prisoner by the Russians. . . . And whosoever poisons that truth by spreading rumours is weakening the conduct of the war, destroying our unity, is an enemy of the empire, a traitor. I, Gabriel Bagradian, tell you this, an officer in the Turkish army. (32–33)

Implicit in these remarks is not only that Armenians are "Turkish," too, but also that the supposedly great Turkish military leader, having led his entire batallion into certain death, is far from being endowed with the "inherent" Turkish prowess in all things military.

Bagradian is employing the strategy of counternarrative. To achieve inclusion in the nation, the minority must destroy the totalizing (and therefore marginalizing) concepts of that nation. The Turkish citizen who excludes Armenians is, according to Bagradian, himself a traitor to the military cause; the Turkish army includes Armenians in its upper echelons. This sort of challenge to the new Turkish identity is regarded as a grave threat. "Counter-narratives of the nation that continually evoke and erase its totalizing boundaries . . . disturb those ideological manoeuvres through which 'imagined communities' are given essentialist identities."[34] The Turkish reaction is to nullify the counternarrative. It is literally silenced through physical elimination, the murderous deportations of the Armenians: "The goal of these deportations is annihilation," a government memo reads. (146) Once the problem no longer exists, the Turkish identity program may continue unchallenged.

There is an even clearer challenge to Turkish warrior identity when Bagradian dons his Turkish officer's uniform to receive the Saptiehs who have come to issue deportation orders for the Armenian villages. In wearing the most prominent symbol of the new Turkish identity, he assumes their narrative for himself and implicitly denies the Turks' power to claim the warrior identity solely for themselves. He also places their version of the Turkish past in question, demonstrating that he had participated in their military history. This type of challenge by the minority is most effective.

> The minority does not simply confront the pedagogical, or powerful master-discourse with a contradictory referent. . . . Insinuating itself into the terms of reference of the dominant discourse, the supplementary antagonizes the implicit power to generalize, to produce sociological solidity.[35]

The very terms by which the Turks identify themselves are renegotiated with Bagradian's actions. With these two episodes Werfel has demonstrated a keen understanding for minority strategies for inclusion.

HISTORICAL AUTHENTICITY AND FAIRNESS IN *MUSA DAGH*

"I never do research work," [Werfel] told me. "When I wrote *The Forty Days of Musa Dagh* I described a little storekeeper and afterwards the Armenians came to me and said: 'How did you know him?' He was not a real character. He was imaginary, but the Armenians were so pleased they greeted me as one of their own. I really didn't know much about Armenians. I don't think it is a good idea to do too much research on any subject about which one writes. One's mind gets cluttered up with too much detail. You should know enough about your subject but not too much."[36]

No doubt Franz Werfel wanted to be accorded due credit for the many convincing characters he created for his novel; however, the previous statement is only half true. It is well known that he undertook extensive research before writing his *Musa Dagh*. George Schulz-Behrend[37] was able to detail many of his sources and demonstrate their incorporation into the novel. We even know that Werfel enlisted the help of his friends to ascertain such minute details as the direction of the winds and the amount of precipitation received in the Anatolia region in 1915.[38] However, his comment regarding the mind-cluttering effects of gathering large amounts of information must be regarded as true. In all probability, it bespeaks personal experience of just that frustrating nature in his work on *Musa Dagh*. As Schulz-Behrend comments, "Werfel is known to have been a voracious reader who had the ability to absorb from printed material exactly what he needed, but who was later often unable to tell where he had obtained the information."[39]

While the exact sources of all the authentic detail in *Musa Dagh* may elude scholars (Schulz-Behrend remarks that his sources were so numerous, certain details might be attributed to any one of several books Werfel read in preparation), the result of his research was a novel that became a number one bestseller in the United States. Hans Wagener correctly identifies the primary reason for *Musa Dagh*'s success to be its believability "as a realistic historical portrait." He cites several reviewers' opinions: "I know of no contemporary novel where historical incident is given such *complete reality* (Horace Gregory);" and " . . . as a detailed record of what one character calls 'the worst crime in recorded history' it carries *authority and conviction*."(Robert Cantwell)[40] The reading public echoes this sentiment, generally appreciative and approving of what a 1942 fan letter compliments as "its fire and grim reality."[41] The novel's claim to historical authenticity received its share of negative critiques as well. In a 1934 review of the English translation, Lionel Abel takes issue with Werfel's "attempt to tell a fable of purely human valor and hatred while yet rendering an exact historical account of the Armenians' struggle against the Turks"—an attempt which he judges to have failed.[42] Ritchie Robertson also notes that it was something of a "distortion" for Werfel to have implied that Gabriel Bagradian's Western background was the key to the Musa Dagh communities' rescue: "This is hardly fair to the historical Armenians, who organized a successful resistance without a Gabriel to help them." Unlike Abel, however, he recognizes the narrative function of invented characters and events in the historical novel.[43]

Though well-researched, *Musa Dagh* certainly does not represent any attempt to render "an exact historical account" of the events in Turkey. In addition to creating fictional characters and situations, Werfel also manipulated documented facts to serve his own narrative purposes. Thus, for example, the length of the Musa Dagh struggle is changed from thirty-six or fifty-three days (the sources differ) to forty, taking advantage of the rich biblical associations with that number. Even concretely recorded dates of events are changed in order to heighten the novel's drama.[44] In all this, however, it complies fully with the recommendation of Lukács and others that the historical novel be well-informed and credible but also inventive within the bounds of "historical faithfulness." Despite the obvious departures from the facts, Werfel's novel gives a convincing portrait of popular life in the small Armenian villages. This is accomplished with the inclusion of cultural details: references to dress and dietary habits, regional architecture, practices of familial and social relationships, and local occupations and trade. These, along with titles and expressions given in Turkish or Armenian, are dispersed generously yet unobtrusively throughout the novel. The reader does not have to be actively convinced of the novel's historical authenticity; rather, the authenticity is constantly buttressed by means of such discrete reminders.

Werfel's goal was to keep his story authentic and identifiable as more than merely fiction. As was mentioned, he hoped that *Musa Dagh* would contribute to the lasting memory of the Armenian tragedy. He further aimed to evoke concern for contemporary minority issues. The novel's figures were composed with great care, and their intrinsic value as character studies should not be overlooked. Certainly, the insight into a foreign culture is in and of itself valuable. However, Werfel wanted his readers to be moved by more than atmosphere, the fates of invented characters, and single-personality issues. It is for this reason that he painstakingly researched and wrote an authoritative portrait: a historical novel with the goal of affecting change must be convincingly historical.

Consistent with this aim is the degree of authorial presence in *Musa Dagh*. In most of his works, Werfel is given to a certain amount of philosophical musing and, at times, somewhat banal generalization. In *Musa Dagh* as well, he was unable to resist the urge to express grand insights into human nature. Typical of this tendency is the following excerpt,

> It is an ineradicable human trait to relentlessly feed one's own eternally frustrated need for admiration at the costs of the lower- and more poorly-born, the deformed, yes even the foreign-born, however and whenever one can. This desire to humiliate others and the vindictive retaliation it provokes are highly significant levers of world history which can be only very inadequately shrouded by the ragged cloak of political ideals.[45]

which, in its pathos, is almost a tribute to his expressionistic roots. Such passages are among the artistically weakest in the novel. They also count to the few instances in which authorial presence is perceptible. Other authorial intrusions come in the form of questions anticipating readers' doubts ("What? Among these thousands, who now bellowed and raved in this unchained torrent of desperation, had there not been one to conceive this very simple thought in the long days of suspence allowed them? . . . Had it needed a 'gentleman from Europe,' a 'strong man,' to come and speak it?") (209), or of direct mention of historical references ("In after-years those Armenian chroniclers who described the battle on the Damlayik wrote only of 'the heroic action of a young sharpshooter' without naming him.") (390). Nonetheless, such instances are kept to a minimum; indeed, comparison with the earlier manuscript indicates that Werfel took pains to drastically reduce reminders of the novel's inherent fiction. The few interspersed explicit references to historical sources serve only as reminders of the extratextual reality, and they are toned down considerably from their original form. As evidenced in the latter excerpt, he did not want the reader to lose sight of the real historical events. This final version, however, incorporates the documentation much more subtly into the flow of narration than does an earlier version:

> What is now to be reported was compared quite appropriately to Coopers Lederstrumpf-story by Doctor Johannes Lepsius, who included the Musa Dagh story in his research files. There can be no doubt that "the deed of a youthful marksman" mentioned there is the subject of his comparison. But this here is a documented event and not a cowboys and indians story from the creative pen of Cooper or Karl May.... Let us then present only the bare facts as they occurred, without any thrilling embellishments.[46]

Here he nearly begs the reader to accept his story as truth. The passage not only identifies the source of the information ("look it up yourself!"), but also calls attention to the difference between documented fact and narrative invention. Clearly, the passage was much too distracting to leave as it stood, and Werfel, who rightly considered himself best when writing on inspiration, was in this case able to improve on his first draft. For the same reason, he also removes overt speculation about developments beyond the scope of the storyline, such as "Digran, Howsannah and Iskuhi are among the few who escaped the systematic extermination of their people. Perhaps they are still living today—and hopefully in happiness and without any permanent injuries—somewhere in Egypt or, more likely, in America."[47] Again, this only detracts from the narrative flow and the element of suspense, which is very consciously cultivated.

Though not overtly present, the author is also not the neutral entity that Lukács would have. Lukács values in Sir Walter Scott's novels what he considers to be "the great historical objectivity of the true epic writer."[48] That the story is told almost entirely from the perspective of the victimized Armenian community is evidence enough that it is a pro-Armenian interpretation. Still, there is ample evidence that Werfel strives to be fair-minded. In the process of writing, he made several notes to himself to present both sides of the issue. The margins of the manuscript are replete with such reminders: "*Don't polemicize against the Turks.*" "*Caution. The Turks cannot appear to be all too dumb and militarily godforsaken. All their actions must be well-founded.*" "*Also the Armenians' hatred of the Turks. Somewhere Enver must be in the right.*" The final text reflects his intentions to be more objective. Stephan is given aid by a Turk who risks his own life by smuggling him past the Turkish military. On several occasions, it is also stressed that the average simple Turk would not approve of Enver's Armenian politics and that they weep when their Armenian neighbors are forced to depart. Werfel is particularly effective when illustrating the psychology of the Turkish soldier who must carry out orders from above:

> These saptiehs were not all brutes. It is even probable that most of them were good, plain, middling sort of people. But what can a saptieh do? He is under stringent orders to reach such and such a point with his whole convoy by such and such a scheduled hour. His heart may be in perfect sympathy with the screaming mother who tries to snatch her child out of a ditch, flings herself down on the road, and claws the earth. No use to talk to her. She's wasted minutes already, and it's still six miles to the next halt. (154–55)

The saptiehs' brutality is shown to develop in small increments as a result of their frustration. Nor are the Armenians portrayed in a singularly positive light. Sarkis Kilikian, the insubordinate deserter who must finally be killed for his betrayal of the Armenian community, is only the most obvious example. In fact, his actions are almost comprehensible in light of his past, marked by terror and brutality, but other Armenian characters are also shown to be far from perfect. The rich villagers, for example, selfishly want to resist the communalization of property. Hrand Oskanian is plagued by paranoia and considers no member of the community beyond suspicion. Hapeth Schatakhian is a portrait of extreme vanity and self-involvement, and even the good pastor Aram Tomasian becomes a ridiculous figure in his clinging to the idea of feeding the community with fish. Even in the situation of shared danger and uncertain fate, life on the Musa Dagh has no shortage of petty arguments and gossip. Thus, despite an undeniable bias toward the Armenian side of the conflict, *Musa Dagh* does not paint the issues strictly in black and white. The author is not an overt source of opinion, and although his stance may be pro-Armenian, the novel itself is presented more objectively than one might expect.

Echoes of Colonialism

> We grow and increase, but not in a huge land abounding in everything needed for a living,—fruits of the fields, mines and raw materials—for we are confined between narrow and by no means favorable frontiers. Every year we have to import more food to appease our hunger and more material to keep our factories busy.... The markets of the world! We need them today for our existence as positively as we need our own land, and the day is approaching with irrevocable certainty when we shall need them even more.[49]

Paul Rohrbach, who only a few years later would engage in an energetic public campaign in Germany, taking an unpopular critical stance toward ally Turkey's Armenian policies, was in 1912 obviously caught up in the heady, nationalistic competition between European powers for colonial primacy. His *German World Policies* is an interesting specimen among the many pro-expansionist commentaries of the time because of the direct link he indicates between economic and cultural influence. He expresses great confidence in the value of what he regards as the "new" (in the sense of being reinvigorated through political unity) German intellectual and moral life, and hopes to see its influence spread by means of a strong colonial presence in the world. "In speaking of the German idea in the world we mean the ideal force of Germanism as a formative power in relation to the present and future happenings of the world."[50] "Our existence," therefore, is not simply a matter of physical survival. Rather, an expanding German population and economy will make possible greater global representation of the "German idea." For the good of all involved, Germany should become a "co-mistress of the culture of the world."[51] Cultural influence is clearly seen as the goal of economic colonialism, not as a resulting necessity.

Turkey is one of the primary targets for Rohrbach's cultural expansion. He praises the "great national process of development through which that oriental nation happens to be passing which has a future and which will continue to hold political sway over the lands from the Persian gulf to the Mediterranean."[52] Whereas it was necessary for Europeans to bring "productive labor" into "those countries in which for untold millennia barbarians and primitive people have eked out an existence"[53] through settler colonies, Rohrbach argues that the Turk is "the only Gentleman of the East"[54] and, therefore, should be treated more in the manner of poor brothers. Already the Turks are well on their way to political predominance in the Near East, and within their own borders are making great strides toward more sophisticated government. Germany's role should not be one of settler colonists but rather of a positive cultural influence.

> Here then is an opportunity to advance the German idea without any regard to political rule or material colonization—provided we comprehend the task in time![55]

Naturally, Germany was not the only country to recognize Turkey's probable prominence and strategic significance in the near future. England and Russia were competing for influence in eastern Asia, to which end the completion of the Siberian Railroad would give Russia the distinct advantage. The Baghdad Railroad project took on monumental importance as a result. In order to prevent Russia from gaining control of this critical passageway, England was willing to offer Germany a "junior partnership" toward gaining transit privileges.[56] The project of cultural colonialism, even if this were truly the sole German ambition, necessarily involved political-economic colonialism as well. France, too, was very much involved in the European struggle for dominance in Turkey and was one of Germany's major rivals. The *Encyclopaedia Britannica* identifies the Baghdad Railroad project as the symbol of "German ambitions to push eastward, challenging French financial dominance in the Ottoman Empire."[57] Rohrbach laments at length the extent to which France has successfully gained a foothold of cultural influence there, citing the French language schools available to all walks of life in Turkey, the foreign exchange programs, and the fact that all the Western-educated Young Turks had received their education in France.

> French is the tongue in which the Turk and every educated Oriental converses with a westerner. The newspapers in which he learns of the happenings of the world, are French. The two French journals *Stamboul* and *La Turquie* are the most widely read non-Turkish newspapers of Constantinople.[58]

Continuing his effort to portray the historical events in a fair-minded fashion, Werfel includes many references to the role that Europe's aggressive colonial pursuit of Turkey played in that country's domestic politics. The French cultural influence is hinted at when he has Talaat Bey, the Minister of the Interior, speak French in the most private government chambers: "In the autumn I shall be able to say with perfect candour to all these people: *La question arménienne n'existe pas.*" (146) The influence of early-1900s colonialism on Turkey's evolution is even more apparent in Werfel's portrayal of Turco-German wartime relations. Although he would not shift the responsibility for the Armenian massacres to another party, he does refer to colonialism as an evil which gave impetus to the tragic historical developments.

Turkey at the outbreak of World War I has been described as having a "semi-colonial and dependent economy."[59] The defeat in the Balkan War had depleted her resources and left the country with considerable foreign influence upon it in the form of the Capitulations agreement. In addition to the terms of the Capitulations, Turkey was dependent upon foreign loans to restimulate its own economy and prevent domestic chaos. On several occasions, the Turks petitioned to have some of the more damaging terms of the treaty—especially the limitations on custom duties they were allowed to impose and the inability to levy income taxes on foreigners residing in Turkey—removed or relaxed. Resentment of the Capitulations increased with each denial of their relaxation.

The outbreak of the First World War further depressed the struggling Turkish economy. The ports were closed and export goods rotted away in storage. The war presented itself as an opportunity to assert Turkish national sovereignty. Every political move by Unionist leaders was designed to exploit the war situation to this end, beginning with Turkey's alliance with Germany. As one historian remarks from the Turkish perspective,

> The alliance with Germany . . . can be understood only in light of the Unionist desire to obtain total independence for the state and society they were in the process of making. While the European powers continued to enjoy extra-territorial privileges under archaic

and anachronistic treaties known collectively as the Capitulations, Turkish sovereignty would be only a fiction.[60]

The Turco-German alliance offered Turkey the prospect of considerable war gains. It was an opportunity to abrogate the terms of the Capitulations and, in the event of a German victory, annul their indebtedness to France and England. The Turks further hoped to regain territories lost in the Balkan War and to rid their country of foreign economic control. Support for an alliance with Germany was not unanimous, however. Neutralist and pro-Entente stances were also well represented in the government, but as Ahmad points out, all of these factions had in common the single goal of asserting national sovereignty.

> In terms of their goals and aspirations for Turkey there was ... no significant difference between the neutralists and the interventionists, just as there were no differences between the "pro-French," the "pro-English," and the "pro-German" Unionists, as all were in the final analysis "pro-Turkish."[61]

Once the war was underway, the Entente powers were reluctant to challenge Turkish disputation of the Capitulations. Of primary concern was to keep Turkey neutral. A growing pan-Islamic movement, instigated by Abdülhamid as an Eastern parallel of nationalist movements in direct response to the increasing European colonial presence in Muslim countries, was rallying around Turkey as its leader and threatened an anti-European chain reaction.

> Even after the deposition of Abdülhamid, the Young Turks continued to enjoy the support of the Muslim world in their struggles against their Balkan enemies, and pan-Islamic solidarity was a matter of grave—indeed exaggerated—concern to the Allies in the First World War.[62]

Although the Pan-Islamic threat was overrated by the concerned Entente powers, it was strong enough to greatly enhance Turkey's strategic position.

Werfel shows that Turkey was both a pawn in and a beneficiary of the Europeans' competing colonial interests and that the Armenians were the ultimate victims of the maneuvering of all parties involved. At the root of the problem was the strategic importance of Turkish Armenia. "The Armenians," the German Geheimrat remarks to Lepsius, "are going under because of their geographical position." (535) Rohrbach describes in detail how pivotal the possession of this territory was for the survival of Turkey, and exactly why it should be the object of colonialists' desires:

> Whoever is in possession of Armenia controls eastern Asia Minor as well as upper Mesopotamia. Two natural routes lead from East to West through Armenia. The northern one comes out of Persia, crosses the Iranian-Armenian border mountains, leads through Bajasid and Karakilissa to Erzurum, the key to Asia Minor, and then continues through the valley of the western Euphrates to Erzincan. From there the approach to the northern part of the Anatolian highland opens up. The second route starts at the basin of the lake at Van which connects with the Iranian highland through various crossings, and proceeds through the valley of the eastern Euphrates, by Mus and Palu, to Charput and Malatya. These last places similarly control access to middle and southern Anatolia, as Erzurum and Erzincan do the access towards the North. Possibly even more dominating is the position of Armenia in relation to the South towards Mesopotamia.... [63]

As noted previously, British Oriental interests were threatened by the territory gained by the Russians with the Treaty of San Stefano. Britain, therefore, endeavored to ensure the good treatment of Armenians by the Turkish government so that they would not be inclined to turn to Russia for assistance.[64] Reforms demanded of the Turkish government were bitterly resented as further foreign influence in Turkish domestic affairs, and the resentment transferred to the beneficiaries of these reforms: the Armenians.

For the same reasons as Britain, Germany also wanted to prevent a Russian-Armenian alliance. During the war, Germany, too, protested the treatment of the Armenians at the hands of their Turkish allies. As one Turkish government official reports, however, the Turks saw through Germany's motives for their alliance with Turkey readily.

> What we said to ourselves was this: ... "The Germans want to exploit us economically, and will stop at nothing to prevent their interests

being menaced. The only purpose of their intervention ... is to prevent Russian influence extending beyond the Baghdad railway. Otherwise it would never occur to the Germans to aid us if danger threatened."[65]

Similarly, German protests of the abuse of Armenians were seen as a purely economic issue. When Lepsius makes a Christian appeal to end the massacres, the Turkish response is bluntly accusatory: "You only send out the cross before you so that the Baghdad railway and the oil trusts may pay better dividends." (556)

Well aware of their strategic position, the Turks took on an attitude of arrogance. Again, this is apparent in Werfel's novel. Talaat Bey's response to German protests is filled with haughty self-importance: "These Germans ... may have to come begging to us for more important things than Armenians." (146) German officials could only protest weakly, resigned to the situation. When Lepsius admonishes the privy councillor to threaten with the withdrawal of all German aid to the Turkish war effort, he responds that such a move would be tantamount to threatening with Germany's own suicide.

> [A]ren't you even aware that the Turks by no means feel indebted to us—on the contrary, they consider themselves our creditors. I don't see why you shouldn't be told that a very powerful group on the Committee would be perfectly ready at any minute to change horses, and negotiate with the Allies. You might easily live to see France and England, who today raise such a howl over Armenian atrocities, shut both eyes to the same atrocities tomorrow. You speak of truth, Herr Lepsius. The truth is that the Turks hold trumps in this particular game, that we have to mind our p's and q's and keep well within the limits of the possible. (534)

Simsir argues that the Armenians' downfall was their conversion to "Western inspired nationalism and ethnic exclusiveness." The colonial powers cleverly seduced them to enmity with the Turks with the sole purpose of gaining that critical territory for their own colonial interests. "The Armenian leaders, unwillingly perhaps, joined the perfidious game of the Big Powers and ended by bringing unrest and suffering to their own people as well as to their Muslim neighbours with whom they lived in peace for centuries."⁶⁶ This interpretation is also offered in *Musa Dagh,* nor can Lepsius effectively deny the accusation that

> [t]he nationalism which dominates us today is a foreign poison, which comes from Europe. Only a few decades ago our whole people lived faithfully under the banners of the prophet—Turks, Arabs, Kurds, Lasas, and many more. . . . But today even the Arabs, who really had nothing to complain abut, have become nationalists, and our enemies. (554)

In his consistent effort to avoid painting the historical incidents in black and white, Werfel went to great lengths to understand what forces were at work in and upon Turkey at that time. He correctly identifies colonialism as a major player in the events. In his eyes, the extenuating circumstances still do not exculpate the Turks for their crimes against the Armenians, but Werfel is successful in communicating that "*Somehow Enver must be in the right.*" The reader gains a firm sense of colonialism's contribution to the demise of Turkey's Armenians.

Structure and General Content of *Musa Dagh*

As was indicated earlier, a function of the historical novel's main character is to clearly delineate the narrative time frame, providing the work with a distinct beginning and end. Gabriel Bagradian supplies *Musa Dagh*'s boundaries, starting with his arrival in Yoghonoluk and ending with his death on the mountain. In this way, *Musa Dagh* achieves the closed form typical of many historical novels. It also contains the element of optimism in its resolution, much like the historical novel of exile, for Gabriel's death is one of victory, and his Armenian compatriots are rescued. The resolution is especially important here since the novel is unusually contemporary in its subject matter as a historical novel—there is very little temporal distance between the author and the novel's events. The proximity to the real events is indicated in the prefatory "note," which tells of the Armenian orphans Werfel saw in a Damascus factory, and it might have been difficult to avoid giving the story an open end. Centering the story on Bagradian is the device that allows for this closure. The Musa Dagh fighters literally disappear into the sunset without further speculation on their fate beyond the refugee camps, and Bagradian's story concludes in the most concrete sense.

It would be wrong, however, to describe *Musa Dagh*'s structure as one shaped solely by the protagonist. Several lengthy chapters or subchapters exclude him entirely, notably the section on Zeitun, the Lepsius scenes in Constantinople, and the journey undertaken by Stephan and Haik to Aleppo. These chapters are among the most pivotal in the novel. Nor do the chapters in which Gabriel figures as a character revolve solely around his development. The various settings contribute substantially to the novel's structure as well. There are at least seven different arenas of action, each of which familiarizes the reader with a different segment of Turkish society. By shifting the scene now and then, Werfel achieves a broader picture of World War I Turkey without attempting to be exhaustive. The reader gains a fairly accurate general picture even though the story of the novel relates an isolated incident.

Gabriel's spontaneous trip to Antioch may serve here as an example. The chapter "Konak-Hamam-Selamlik" has multiple functions, only one of which is to explore the extent of Gabriel's identification with Armenians. Within the short chapter, the place of action changes three times. Gabriel's visit to the central office of the Konak provides a picture of the new, westernized breed of Turkish bureaucrats. Then the scene shifts to the marketplace bazaar, where one encounters the many different peoples, with their different cultures and religions, who populate Turkey. In the steam bath scene, historical facts are transmitted to the reader through novelistic devices: in addition to containing the first reference to Zeitun, the overheard conversation there communicates Enver Pascha's military record from both an Armenian and a Turkish perspective. Finally, Gabriel's visit at the home of the Agha Rifaat Bereket introduces the reader to yet another subsection of Turkey: the devout, old-school Turkish Moslem.

If the novel is, following Wolfgang Iser, "a system of perspectives,"[67] it is easy to see that the historical novel in general, and Werfel's historical novel in particular, offers a considerably more varied range of perspectives on historical events than historiography generally does. The Zeitun chapter is exemplary in this function. It was necessary to include this disastrous episode in order to identify the successful Musa Dagh defense as an exception in two regards: most Armenians acquiesced to the "relocation" without a fight and died or suffered miserably en route; those communities that did opt to defend themselves were defeated by the superior Turkish forces. Thus, Zeitun remains in the reader's mind as the ever-present threat of complete annihilation.

Werfel also had to communicate this story without resorting to dry, historiographical presentation. He achieves this by means of talented portraiture of minor characters. Most important among them is Nazareth Tschausch, the elderly mayor of Zeitun. His story covers a negligible number of pages, but his character is so deftly conceived and realized that the tragedy of Zeitun is personalized in him. Tschausch has always accommodated the Turkish authorities unquestioningly; even when their threats and accusations become dangerously ludicrous and provocative, he wisely cooperates in every way. Finally, he is sent away on the pretext of making a mission of peace. Recognizing the ploy for a trap, he leaves Zeitun sorrowfully but with great dignity. "'Oglum, bir, daha gelmem.' My son, I shall not come back." (88) are his parting words. With uncharacteristic economy, Werfel has penned one of the novel's most poignant scenes while simultaneously underscoring the historical significance of the fate of Zeitun's Armenian population.

The Zeitun chapter is instructive on additional aspects of the Armenian persecution in all parts of Turkey. We see how relocation affected different groups within the Armenian community. Instead of accompanying the transports, able-bodied men were often separated from their families and used as forced labor. The experience of the foot transport was also widely varied. For women, the transports meant being exposed to sexual harassment by Turkish soldiers and the possibility of being given into marriage with a Muslim—effectively, the loss of their religious faith. The children, it is shown, commenced the ordeal unknowingly: at first they had a sense of adventure, then increasing exhaustion and discomfort, and finally the experience of incomprehensible physical pain. The Zeitun characters who manage to escape to Yoghonoluk serve as constant reminders of the brutality that has transpired and what might lie in store for the Musa Dagh community. Hence, the recurring mention of the wild-eyed orphan Sato; the dancer Kework who is half-witted as the result of a beating as a young boy at the hands of Turks; and most prominently, Iskuhi's lame arm which was injured in a lustful attack by a Turkish soldier.

"The people" and their everyday life comprise a large portion of *Musa Dagh*'s content. Before disaster sets in upon the villages, Werfel paints a detailed picture of normal life at the base of the mountain. Making good use of his sources, he acquaints the reader with the local industries, familial relationships and practices, religious customs, and so on. The Bagradians' social gatherings reveal many details on the quality of life and gender roles in the villages. Local flavor is added with the people on the street exchanging the customary evening greeting, "Bari irikun!" The harisa meal, described minutely in its preparation and all the festive significance it holds for Armenians, is reproduced artfully.[68] Even architectural descriptions reveal more than a certain aesthetic leaning: the lack of ornamentation in the church is explained by the fact that Armenians put all available monies toward their schools. This high valuation of education is stressed repeatedly throughout the novel. Children's free time activities also receive detailed attention. Details such as these allow the reader to become familiarized with everyday life so that the tragic events to follow can be better understood as a tragedy of "the people."

Portrayal of Historical Figures

The "great historical personality" on par with Richard Lionheart or Mary Stuart, such as is featured in Scott's novels, is absent from *Musa Dagh*. Real historical leaders, for example, Enver Pasha and Djemal Pasha, are admittedly prominent but negative figures who are more likely to go down in infamy. As such, they could hardly qualify in Lukács's sense as an optimistic reflection of "the people." The great humanitarian Johannes Lepsius provides a more positive historical model; however, he lacks historical prominence outside of specifically Armenian history. He died in relative obscurity even in his native Germany. In addition, his historical mission ultimately fails; he proves to be no match for Enver Pasha. Thus, Werfel's selection of historical figures would not satisfactorily meet Lukács's expectations. Nor can his method of portrayal be described as abstract. The reader is given much more psychological insight into these characters than Lukács would deem appropriate. Many passages even grant direct access to their thoughts, making it possible to identify with them as human beings.

With few exceptions, Werfel does not alter facts concerning historical characters' actions or whereabouts. As mentioned before, the dates of some events are changed in order to build more suspense for other aspects of the story. The date of Lepsius's interview with Enver, for example, was moved up from August to July in order to make it occur before the deportation orders were delivered to Yoghonoluk.[69] This allows him to appeal specifically for that region, giving the impression that the Musa Dagh villagers' fate hangs in the balance at that historical moment. However, the conversation between Lepsius and Enver is reproduced in *Musa Dagh* almost verbatim from Lepsius's account.[70] Werfel clearly recognized that the source, highly detailed and dramatic, demanded few artistic embellishments.

Werfel presents as fact all the thoughts, worries, and jealousies of the historical figures, taking advantage of the novelist's license to extrapolate from facts. Where the historian cannot effectively defend speculatory assertions regarding figures' inner workings, Werfel the historical novelist is under no obligation to provide documentation. This allows him to work in the realm of his greatest literary asset: the ability to put himself into others' positions, to understand their feelings and concerns. In response to the question of the character with whom he most strongly identified in his work, he stated, "I identify with every character on every page of my books. I am every bit as much Bagradian or Jeremiah as I am Enver Pasha and Nebukanezar. My enjoyment of the latter is even greater than that of the hero."[71] Two instances will exemplify Werfel's ability to convincingly present speculation as fact in *Musa Dagh*.

In both of the following cases, Werfel's material was extracted from previously unknown historical sources. The first of these is Djemal Pasha's *Memories of a Turkish Statesman, 1913–1919*, available also in German in 1922.[72] It is likely that Werfel came across this source via a reference in a *Meyers Lexikon* article on Turkey.[73] Both sources are indicated in his manuscript notes ("*revise according to Meyer!!*"; "*see Dschemal Pascha*"), and a sketched map of Turkey in his *Musa Dagh* notebook (UCLA) is clearly copied from the map in the *Meyers* article. In his memoirs, Djemal Pasha records having disagreed with Enver on the allocation of troops. Specifically, he was asked to send army divisions from his desert forces to Bagdad and Constantinople, thus seriously weakening his own military forces. The memoirs indicate that it was a hardship but that he did comply with the requests:

> Ultimately I found myself in such a state that the troops in the army zone, the vilayets of Adana, Aleppo, Syria, Lebanon and Palestine, and including those in the desert, were reduced to twelve batallions, and in the whole region not a single quick-firing battery nor a single machine-gun company was left.[74]

In addition, there are hints that Djemal had been excluded from certain policy-making meetings: "A few days later . . . , I saw another car in which Enver Pasha, Talaat Bey, and Halil Bey were seated. . . . I at once suspected that my friends might be engaged in the discussion of affairs which they did not want me to know." Werfel augments this raw material, portraying Djemal as secretly resenting Enver's demands for his troops, and endowing him with the paranoid conviction that the other Turkish leaders had plans to ruining him. However well motivated it may seem, competition between Enver and Djemal is not corroborated by these sources. Werfel, however, transforms Djemal's annoyance to a state of bitter persecution mania.

> This wire, with its insolent beginning, was the last drop in Jemal's cup of hate, which was running over. Enver, for several months, had made monstrous demands on the general, who had always complied without a word. . . . At the moment the dictator of Syria commanded no more than sixteen to eighteen shabby battalions, and this in a huge war area extending from the heights of the Taurus to the Suez canal. . . . The general-in-chief, with his usual pickpocket methods, had disarmed him, drawn his teeth, at the same time depriving him of any possibility of a victory. (411)

This characterization is of the utmost narrative importance, for Djemal's patience is shown to have snapped at a critical juncture of the Musa Dagh defense. Had he sent additional troops, it is implied, the Armenians would have met their end swiftly. Once again, their fate hangs suspensefully in the balance, and it is a personality flaw that extends their survival:

> Gabriel had found an involuntary ally. This touchy potentate neither answered, nor would he send one cannon, one machine-gun, to Antakiya, to smoke out Musa Dagh. (413)

A similar example of artistic liberties taken in the portrayal of historical figures comes in the person of Enver. Here again, Werfel works freely with his sources, in this instance combining what he considers important characteristics of several historical figures into one. Talaat Bey, the Minister of the Interior, has a few brief appearances in the novel, in each case without extensive characterization. However, another probable historical source of Werfel's attributes a comment to him which, in light of the novel's general theme of minorities' positions in society, must have seemed necessary to incorporate somehow into *Musa Dagh*. The source in question is Henry Morgenthau's autobiographical *Ambassador Morgenthau's Story*.[75] Djemal Pasha's *Memories* attempt to contradict Morgenthau on numerous "allegations," referring repeatedly to his "well-known book in which he speaks of me in anything but complimentary terms . . ."[76] When considering the extent of Werfel's research on this project, it is unlikely that he would have left such a prominent source unexplored—especially since his primary source, Johannes Lepsius's publications, often refers to Morgenthau's documentation as the basis of its historical accuracy.

In his book, Morgenthau relates a conversation he had with Talaat Bey in which the Armenian question was the main topic. Talaat attempted to neutralize his pro-Armenian stance by appealing to racial concerns, asking why Morgenthau, as a Jew, should be concerned about a Christian people such as the Armenians: "'You are a Jew; these people are Christians. . . . What have you to complain of?'"[77] This incident finds an echo in *Musa Dagh* during one of Lepsius's discussions with Enver. Here Enver questions Lepsius's information and asks for his sources; in response, Lepsius asserts that he has "a most consistent account of the whole business by the American ambassador, Mr. Morgenthau." This source is waved aside as unreliable: "'Mr. Morgenthau,' said Enver brightly, 'is a Jew. And Jews are always fanatically on the side of minorities.'" (134) Thus, Werfel is able to condense what he considers to be Turkish attitudes into the characterization of a few historical figures. By putting Talaat Bey's racist remark into Enver's mouth, he avoids unnecessarily developing yet another historical character. At the same time, he gives a different figure an entirely believable trait. Telling the truth, as Foley remarked, has very much become a matter of "accurate generalization." Lützeler confirms: "The intent to provide the truth does exist in both literature and historical writing, but it is aimed in different directions."[78] As discussed previously, this sort of condensation in the service of truth is a common feature of the historical novel, one of several "narrative techniques reserved for purely fictional narration."[79] Again, historiography and historical fiction are demonstrably categorically different despite their shared characteristics. Werfel uses this difference to his advantage in his portrayal of real historical figures.

Relevance of History for Invented Character: Gabriel Bagradian

In the previous chapter, the connection between history and personal identity was discussed at some length. The most basic, and most important, observation was that individual identity exists only in the societal context. It is determined by means of a dialogical relationship between the individual and the community in which she or he lives. A sense of belonging, shared by both parties, is essential to a well-balanced self-perception. If an individual's perception of him- or herself is at odds with general opinion, some sort of compromise is required to restore the symmetry between the individual and society.

In identifying with a certain community, one also identifies with that community's past, present, and future. The past is a constant component of community identity, manifesting itself especially in the form of customs, religion, language, traditional practices and attitudes, and the awareness of a shared heritage. Such issues combine to produce a common "historical style," or ethnic identity. The development and acceptance of Gabriel's ethnic identity was treated in the first chapter, but history's significance for the individual is not restricted to the communal experience. The historical novelist illustrates the direct experience of history in individuals' lives. Accordant with this requirement of the historical novel, Werfel shows historical occurrences to have great influence on the course Gabriel's life takes.

The most obvious historical occurrence affecting his fate is the outbreak of the First World War. This strands him in his ancestral home and supplies Turkish authorities with a pretext for revoking his family's right to move freely within Turkey or to leave the country. Certainly, this is the circumstance that compels him to finally confront his identity. In addition, Werfel endows Gabriel with a pre-World War I history that is also markedly shaped by historical events. His daydreams recalling the brutal reign of Sultan Abdul Hamid evidence just how deeply his boyhood experiences of Turkish domestic politics have shaped his psyche. In the isolated village of Yoghonoluk, Gabriel was never directly affected by anything more than an abstract fear stemming from the knowledge that elsewhere in Turkey, Armenians were being persecuted. As a contrast, the reader is provided with a graphic picture of the sultan's terror in the flashback on Sarkis Kilikian's life. This enigmatic character owes his personality and current predicament almost entirely to the forces of history that have wreaked havoc upon his life: the witness of a massacre in his boyhood home, his sole obsession is his own physical survival. The outbreak of the war means conscription into the Turkish forces and the demotion to forced labor, and ultimately leads to his desertion. Kilikian, now hardened and himself capable of atrocities, is a victim of historical circumstances. Werfel highlights the difference in attitude between those who, like Kilikian, had felt the force of history upon them, and those whose knowledge is only second hand. The doctor Bedros Altouni, it is stressed, was "a survival of those Armenians who, unlike the younger generation, seemed to bear on their shoulders the whole load of a persecuted race." (47)

Even his more abstract historical awareness is a powerful determining force in Gabriel's life. Memories of his fellow Armenians being persecuted are in fact so trenchant that not even his early departure from Turkey and his Western upbringing can extirpate an enduring interest in Armenian affairs. Even such minimal exposure to historical events induce him to participate in major aspects of Turkey's radically evolving political arena: the 1907 Congress and the Balkan War. The effects of the Balkan War upon Gabriel's life are twofold: for one, his service as an officer supplies him with much of the strategic knowledge and military experience necessary later for defending the Musa Dagh against the Turks; for another, it induces him to extract himself from Armenian affairs following the war. This latter point is significant to the development of his identity. During his six-month absence from Juliette, he had feared that his involvement in the Balkan War might endanger their marriage. Safely returned to Paris, he renounces any activities that might alienate his wife from him. It is for this reason that he reduces contact with Armenians to a minimum and allows Juliette to direct their mutual social life according to her French preferences. The two years between the Balkan War and his return to Yoghonoluk are spent in an attempt to redefine himself as a Frenchman. This serves only to intensify the inevitable identity struggle upon arrival in Turkey.

Lukács argued that the historical novel teaches the relevance of the past to the present. This insight is central to Gabriel's personal development, and Werfel shows quite concretely how this realization comes as a process, in stages. The process begins with the reemergence of his boyhood fantasies: rescuing his people from Turkish enemies. Initially, Gabriel tries to dismiss them with an ironic smile, yet he does not attempt to completely ward off emotions associated with the historical enmity between Turks and Armenians:

> Gabriel could not shake off these childish fantasies. He, the Parisian, Juliette's husband, the *savant,* the officer minded to do his duty as a Turkish subject, and who knew the realities of modern warfare, was also, simultaneously, a boy who with primitive blood-hate flung himself on the arch-enemy of his race. (14)

While in the earlier version of *Musa Dagh* Gabriel denies that such memories are anything but "daydreams,"[80] the final version stresses already at this early juncture that, despite his advanced assimilation and his powers of logical thinking, the history of Turkish offenses against Armenians holds emotional relevance for him. Werfel remarks that these feelings, while natural, are short-lived: "The dreams of every Armenian boy. Just for a moment, of course!" Though only in embryonic form, Gabriel's personal connection with history is present from the start. Memory is a powerful component of his identity.

This memory surfaces as instinct. As remarked earlier, Werfel underlines the fact that Gabriel himself has never suffered at the hands of Turks. "Massacre and torture he only knew through books and stories." (7) However, the earliest indication of unusual circumstances—the confiscation of his passport—prompts him to immediate action. Nor do his instinctual misgivings prove to be unwarranted. In Antioch, he not only is treated with thinly veiled disrespect by the Turkish authorities, but he also learns of much more serious actions taken against Armenians in other parts of the country. His instinct based on general Armenian history is limited in its accuracy, however. When Gabriel remarks that he is considering moving his family to Istanbul where his name is well known, he demonstrates his deficient knowledge of recent history. His "distant perusal of the Armenian political situation"[81] has not provided him with an accurate picture of the present. The Agha Rifaat Bereket must warn him that the very fact that the Bagradian name is well known only adds to the present danger. In another conversation with Ter Haigasun, the same naiveté becomes apparent. When Ter Haigasun states that the Armenian predicament is hopeless and their fate is in the hands of the Turks, Gabriel protests that "Europe won't stand for it." Ter Haigasun refutes this belief with the mild criticism that "You see it through foreign eyes." (76)

Gabriel's historical awareness is limited to Armenia's past, and his personal development proceeds only with the realization that historical occurrences take place also in the present. For him to have insight into current realities of his historical community's present life, it is imperative that he be directly involved in that life. Real historical knowledge requires full participation and physical presence in the community, experiencing events as they occur rather than learning about them as an intellectual endeavor. His abstract, "distant perusal" of events is not adequate to the task. This conclusion is, of course, veritably forced upon him in the form of the relocation orders for the Musa Dagh villages, but once having consigned himself to his community, Gabriel's commitment is unwavering. When he makes the decision to propose that the community defend itself, he is certain that his involvement is the right decision: "He knew with his whole being: 'For this one second it's worth while to have lived.'" (206) The assimilated Westerner will rebel in his thoughts against identifying with his compatriots, but his actions consistently demonstrate an undiminished commitment to the community.

Arguably the most pitiable character Werfel created is Gonzague Maris. Of Greek and French extraction and American citizenship, he identifies with no community beyond the most casual allegiance. In this respect, he serves as a foil to Gabriel. He participates in the Musa Dagh experience only by coincidence and remains there solely to satisfy his curiosity. At the most critical juncture, he opts to escape the mountain camp under the cover of darkness. Rather than being disappointed by Juliette's failure to join him in the escape, he soon comes to prefer the freedom of having no connections to anyone. On his way down the mountain cliff, he reflects on his cherished independence: "How incomprehensible people were! All this pain and slaughter, merely because they refused to let the impartial light have power in them, preferring their stupid, untidy obscurity." (523) Maris will continue his life as a transient existence, and it is significant that Werfel's final sentence devoted to this character emphasizes both his detachment and his concern only with the future: "His eyes, under the short, slanting brows, moved alertly, scanning the way in front of him." (524) Notes in the Vienna manuscript indicate beyond doubt that Werfel considered this a pivotal scene: "*Watch out—Be careful! Gonzague's last scene! The entire figure must be summarized, its lacking of a beginning, lacking of an ending must be deliberately formed!*"[82] Without a beginning, without an end: Gonzague's existence entirely lacks history. As such, it is completely meaningless.

"*Do minorities have any right to life at all?*" This question jotted down on the penultimate page of Werfel's Musa Dagh notebook is one that guided the conception of *Musa Dagh*. Obviously, his answer was affirmative, but more interesting is his exploration of what being a member of a minority can mean. In Gabriel, he creates an unwilling minority figure who is confronted with the choice between continuing to live his life like Gonzague— in the abstract, severed from his community, unsuspecting of the historical legacy which is a part of him—and embracing that legacy in all its manifestations. This step is a crucial one toward securing a firm sense of identity. Through the course of the novel, Gabriel becomes increasingly aware of the personal relevance of his community's history, and he finally rededicates himself entirely to playing a role in it. With his leadership during the struggle, he has made a contribution to his community's history, the significance of which will be enduring in its future. So absolute is his commitment that, when the rescue is finally in progress, he cannot leave the Musa Dagh, the historical home of his ancestors, which he has reclaimed as his own, and the burial site of his son.

Musa Dagh accomplished what it set out to do: to give this historical event a permanent record. As Jungk discovered, the novel is the equivalent of the Armenian national *epos*.[83] Werfel, however, aspired to more than just historical documentation with the novel. He wrote it also as a commentary on the prevailing chauvinistic mood of the 1930s, recognizing certain parallels in the historical material. To this end, he used the medium of the historical novel to demonstrate the significance that history holds for the present. With the fictitious Gabriel Bagradian, he composed an insightful character study on the types of identity problems that accompany assimilation and discrimination. This fictional aspect of the historical novel allows for *Musa Dagh* to be general enough to hold lasting value for readers beyond Werfel's contemporaries.

4

Musa Dagh as a Participant in Dominant Discourses

Dominant Discourses; "unconscious state of consciousness" in *Musa Dagh*

"[T]HE WORK OF ART," STEPHEN GREENBLATT WRITES, "IS THE PRODuct of a negotiation between a creator or class of creators, equipped with a complex, communally shared repertoire of conventions, and the institutions and practices of society."[1] In this process of negotiation or exchange, it is interesting to examine at which instances the literary text was the giver (the influencer) and at which instances it was the recipient (the influenced). The concept of the text as a participant in social discourse effectively collapses the hierarchical contraposition of text and context so typical of nineteenth-century *Historismus*. *Musa Dagh*, it will be recalled, served (to borrow again Aust's terms) both a reconstructive and a parabolic purpose. Werfel wanted to "rescue" the events from historical obscurity; at the same time, he hoped to highlight the parallels between Turkey's chauvinism and that emerging in contemporary Germany. For that reason, he repeatedly chose the "minorities and nationalism" passage from the novel for public readings. It will be argued in the following that *Musa Dagh* was conceived as a work to participate in contemporary debates. Werfel singled out two prominent discourses, both of which were indebted to the ever-increasing prestige of science: the pseudo-Darwinist discourse of race, inherent characteristics, and racial superiority; and the discourse of secularization—the supersedence of religion by a scientifically informed attitude of "realism." Werfel engaged both of these discourses in battle, or dialogic exchange, in *Musa Dagh*. These two modern tendencies are shown to be barriers to identity formation; they must be overcome for (what Werfel considered to be) the ultimate achievement of identity. In *Musa Dagh,* we can discern Werfel's conscious effort to be an influencer in these two trends of social-political thought. At the same time, close attention paid to the role of these trends in the novel reveals just how trenchant dominant discourses are, for Werfel—despite his intentions—absorbed and reproduced in *Musa Dagh* some of those very assumptions which he tried to combat.

Without having the specifically new historicist vocabulary of "dominant discourses" at his disposal, Werfel nonetheless recognizes the phenomenon and its wide-ranging effects in the 1930s. The problem emerges as a subtopic in a speech, "Can We Live Without Faith in God?"[2], given to a Viennese audience in March of 1932, the same year during which he began work on *Musa Dagh*. In his criticism of his contemporaries' lack of religious faith, he places much of the blame on the dominant discourses of the time, citing repeatedly the menacing power of idiom to transform falsehoods into generally accepted truths. He warns, for example, "One should not underestimate the power of the slogan. It serves not as truth but as magic incantation." (100) Words, he states, have the ability to shape historical reality at the most fundamental level: "There is many a philosophy of history but none has yet shown us that historical reality, for the greater part, is caused by words and slogans." (93)

As an example of how dominant discourses influence humans' consciousness, Werfel postulates a hypothetical "average child" of early-twentieth-century Germany and relates the probable course of his philosophical development. This average child is instructed early on about the "natural, scientific character of the world and [due to his average—with which Werfel understands proletarian—social status] its purely economic purpose." (83) Already at this juncture, one can easily anticipate his two-pronged assault on *Natural Philosophists* and Marxists. First, however, the example of the "average man" continues. During a short-lived adolescent phase of voracious reading, this person comes across, among other things, Ernst Haeckel's *Riddles of the Universe*.[3] Werfel quotes from memory a passage from *Riddles* which he believes to carry weight for the readership's "philosophy": "In reality even this immaterial spirit is not conceived of as incorporeal but as invisible, gaseous. This anthropomorphism leads to the paradoxical representation of God as a so-called 'gaseous vertebrate.'" (83) One can safely assume that this passage was chosen to highlight the displacement of religious discourse by scientific or, more accurately, pseudoscientific discourse.

The result of such short-term and dilettantish occupation with popularized science, Werfel argues, is a mind muddled with concepts only partially understood yet fully accepted as truth. What remains as the legacy of this period of intense reading is nothing more than a

> tired midges' dance of jumbled concepts: all sorts of vague and distorted notions, about the origin of species, and man's unparadisiac past as an ape, about the atomic structure of matter, about thought as a function of the brain centers, and more of the like. (83)

Despite having only this minimal intentional involvement with dominant discourses, the average man is nonetheless unavoidably under their influence. Werfel refers to this as an "unconscious state of consciousness." He continues: "It is filtered into his brain by a thousand apparent and secret ways." (84) Through newspapers, movies, literature, political debates, etc., the vocabulary of dominant discourses works its way into the average citizen's consciousness and is employed at a much less specialized level—yet is questioned by no one in its validity.

Werfel takes his theoretical average child as the "embodied symbol for the presentation of that all-pervading modern state of consciousness which [he] shall call *naturalistic nihilism*." (88) In the double term, he concisely accentuates the two dominant discourses he feels pervade all of modern consciousness; at the same time, he indicates their interconnectedness. *Nihilism* is meant to stand for the loss of transcendental experience, the belief that "God is dead" and the corresponding "prevailing spirit of worldliness" (80) which comes not only in the wake of Nietzschean philosophy but also as the result of discoveries made by the natural sciences (*Naturalism*). His criticism here of the secularization of the modern world, and of the misappropriation of scientific terminology for popular discourse, is not an isolated incident. It represented such a disturbing trend to him that he came back to the subject repeatedly, in fiction and nonfiction alike. In 1939, for example, it helped him to explain the rise of the nationalistic "demons" which "never hesitated to ally themselves with the most modern philosophies of natural science and the emerging socialism."[4] Once scientific terminology was established in the minds and everyday vocabulary of the general public, it could be put to any (mis)use.

This is the danger against which he warns in his nonfictional writing of the 1930s and, as will be shown in a later section, in his *Musa Dagh* novel. Werfel argues that national-socialist racial chauvinism was given impetus by the two discourses of secularization and science. The philosophical position that God is dead was readily twisted to induce the masses to accept nationalism as a "substitution for religion" (98); meanwhile, the broadly accepted Darwinian evolutionary theories were well-suited to define nationality as a matter of race. The citizen infected by nationalistic fever looked to science to bolster his or her new "religion." The petty bourgeois, Werfel notes, "importunes anthropology in order to prove that his race excels all others." (100) It makes no difference, he continues, that the European—far from being racially pure—is a "motley mixture." (101) The currency of the discourse of racial purity gives it the status of truth. Again he points to the potency of the idiom: "[S]logans and incantations create realities that do not exist." (101) In fact, Werfel too avails himself, perhaps unwittingly but all the more revealingly, of the discourse of "race" and "blood" relations. In a plea for the return to "true" religion, he says: "It is especially as a Jew, *by virtue of a primeval affinity of blood and character,* that I feel myself justified in the following view: this world that calls itself civilized can be spiritually healed only if it finds it way back to true Christianity." (120, my italics)

The Religion of Pseudoscience

Werfel's concerns about the displacement of religion through the discourse of science were by no means an alarmist viewpoint. Julien Benda, in his 1927 *The Betrayal of the Intellectuals,*[5] laments the modern shift of perspective in very similar terms. He characterizes the early twentieth century as "the age of the *intellectual organization of political hatreds,*" aided by intellectuals' (or "clerks'") willful betrayal of their social responsibility.[6] Until recently, he claims, the clerks—philosophers, theologians, scientists, literati—had commanded respect by pursuing their fields for purely intellectual reasons and had been able to hold the political passions of ordinary persons in check. That is, without being able to prevent statesmen's actions of aggression, they "*did prevent the laymen from setting up their actions as a religion, they did prevent them from thinking themselves great men as they carried out these activities.*" Though evil was perpetrated in the world, the clerks saw to it that good was honored. Intellectuals were the watchguards of justice and morality. However, the end of the nineteenth century brought with it a "fundamental change," which resulted in an "upheaval in the moral behavior of humanity": the clerks became involved in political ideology. "The men who had acted as a check on the realism of the people began to act as its stimulators."[7] Their most grave betrayal of morality lay in claiming their political ideologies to be scientifically defensible. "We all know," Benda remarks gloomily, "what self-assurance, what rigidity, what inhumanity ... are given to these passions to-day by this claim."[8]

Recent scholarship confirms Benda's and Werfel's impressions. Nancy Leys Stepan and Sander Gilman find that by the mid-nineteenth century, science "began to replace theological and moral discourse as the appropriate discourse with which to discuss nature."[9] Increasingly, moral issues were debated in "scientific" terms of race rather than theology. Michael Biddiss notes that in the 1850s it was far from decided whether science or religion was the appropriate source of authority in moral matters, but a victory on either side promised to have wide-ranging ramifications. There was much to gain—and lose—on both sides of the debate:

> That the whole matter was so hotly contested is not surprising in view of the huge issues necessarily raised. Among them was the place of man, and of different kinds of men, within the natural order—a topic with religious implications no less delicate than scientific ones. There was the question as to whether racial determinism could be kept compatible with belief in freedom of will and moral choice.[10]

In time, however, racial discourse achieved a higher level of authority than religious discourse on such issues. Stepan and Gilman observe that "moral issues of rights and justice," which had been

> debated in political and theological terms until the 1850s and 1860s, were increasingly reduced to questions about the racial "natures" of individuals, questions that scientists now claimed had objective, neutral answers. Moral rights were thereby translated into matters of anatomy and physiology.[11]

The old Enlightenment period ideology of equality among humans was considered unscientific and idealistic, and its remaining proponents were publicly ridiculed for their lack of sophistication. In an 1866 article published in the *Anthropological Review,* for example, John William Jackson lambasts John Stuart Mill's belief in racial equality despite "proofs" to the contrary made by science: "To write of men, and to legislate for men, while rejecting the science of man, is certainly a most extraordinary and by no means commendable procedure."[12] He accuses Mill of "judicial blindness of intellect"[13] for refusing to recognize, in this case, the racial inferiority of blacks.

> The comparative anatomist agrees with the historian in placing [Negroes] on a lower level than the European. And the phrenologist agrees with the comparative anatomist. We know that Mr. Mill does not believe in phrenology, nor we presume in physiognomy. He cannot. Either the one or the other would dissipate his daydream of racial equality within an hour of its acceptance. The inferior character of the Negro is as distinctly stamped on his organisation as on his destiny, and only minds blinded by the *idola* of preconceived ideas could fail to see the one as well as the other, and to find in both unmistakeable evidence of the Negro's lower position in the scale of being.[14]

Jackson's mention of anatomy, phrenology, and physiognomy is typical of a pseudoscientific trend in the late nineteenth and early twentieth century, which attempted to combine scientific classifications with aesthetic judgments to rank the various classes of humans according to their relative value. Johann Kaspar Lavater founded the science of physiognomy with his

"Essai sur la Physiognomie" (1781). George Mosse observes that Lavater was not racist in intention,

> [y]et in the end his pseudo-science of physiognomy proved a powerful weapon against those people who were different. Lavater also held classical ideas of beauty according to which he classified and ranked the human species. But for this no scientific studies were required, only visual ability and taste.[15]

Carl Gustav Carus built on Lavater's foundations with his *Symbolik der menschlichen Gestalt* (Symbolism of the Human Form) (1853).[16] In Italy, Cesare Lombroso—also no racist—put forth the theory that humans' physical appearance in essence mirrored their inner qualities. "But as the founder of the science of criminal law, and the advocate of psychology which made physical characteristics symbolic of the state of the mind, he had a major impact upon the racial thought which he himself condemned."[17] The tenets of physiognomy quickly gained acceptance both within the field of science and among the broader public. Francis Galton, a younger cousin of Darwin, writes in 1865: "There are certain marked types of character, justly associated with marked types of feature and of temperament.... For instance, the face of the combatant is square, coarse, and heavily jawed. It differs from that of the ascetic, the voluptuary, the dreamer, and the charlatan."[18] Max Nordau's *Degeneration* (1892–1893) literally "swept Europe," as Mosse puts it, "finally establishing the concept in the vocabulary."[19]

Although many early theories of physiognomy, phrenology, and the like were intended as nothing more than innocuous scientific discovery, they popularized concepts that were "to prove fatal in encouraging racism."[20] The ideas captured the imagination not only of the masses, but also of artists who effectively perpetuated them in their work. Mosse identifies Goethe as one of Lavater's admirers, and points out that Sir Walter Scott's novels (which were immensely popular throughout Europe) "abound with physiognomist interpretations."[21] Nor was racial science's influence limited to the arts. Benda found that the most "shocking" behavior of all clerks came from historians, in particular the French Monarchists and the Pan-Germanists under Hegelian influence:

Assuredly, humanity did not await our age to see History putting itself at the service of the spirit of party or of national passion. But I think I may assert that it has never seen this done with the same methodological spirit, the same intensity of consciousness which may be observed in German historians of the past half century and in the French Monarchists of the past twenty years.[22]

Arthur de Gobineau's "Essai sur l'inégalité des races humaines" (1853) suggests that a nation's history is determined by the degree of its racial purity. The less a nation was contaminated by foreign blood, the greater its prominence in that historical moment. Like many of his contemporaries, Gobineau writes, "I was gradually penetrated by the conviction that the racial question overshadows all other problems of history, that it holds the key to them all, and that the inequality of the races from whose fusion a people is formed is enough to explain the whole course of its destiny."[23] The British surgeon Robert Knox used his medical expertise to give further credence to such theories with his 1862 book entitled: *The Races of Men. A Philosophical Enquiry into the Influence of Race over the Destinies of Nations.* Here he expounds upon a system he dubs "transcendental anatomy" which claims "that the race in human affairs is everything, is simply a fact, the most remarkable, the most comprehensive, which philosophy has ever announced. Race is everything: literature, science, art—in a word, civilization depends on it."[24]

By the second half of the nineteenth century, there were many historians and authors who understood historical developments to be a function of racial matters, "which was," as Léon Poliakov remarks, "one way of substituting a scientific for a theological interpretation of human life, or, in other words, of replacing Providence by 'physiology.'"[25] After the revolutions of 1848, there was certainly much to be explained. Race seemed a plausible answer to many mysteries. Biddiss comments that "[i]t was tempting, above all, to examine the dramatic advance of Bismarck's Germany in this light."[26] Of course, there were voices from the other side of the issue. Thomas Huxley, for example, highlighted the fact that the notion of national characteristics was spurious and at best very difficult to prove:

It is a general belief that men of different stocks differ as much physiologically as they do morphologically; but it is very hard to prove, in any particular case, how much of a supposed national characteristic is due to inherent physiological peculiarities, and how much to the influence of circumstances.[27]

The undeniable trend, however, was a racial, and finally, racist mentality. After 1850, there was a marked "tendency to enlarge the relevance of physical categories" to explain almost any human phenomenon.[28] Religion had not disappeared by any means, but many looked to science in its place to provide answers to questions about human material existence.

THE LANGUAGE OF RACIAL SCIENCE

Racial vocabulary was entrenched as a dominant discourse. In 1927, Benda sees "scarcely a mind in Europe which is not affected" by racial passion.[29] Mosse echoes: "To some degree Englishmen, Frenchmen, Poles, as well as Germans or Hungarians, used the word *race* in their daily lives without thinking."[30] The use of the word *race* was unreflected; the supposed scientific foundation, unquestioned. The term itself had evolved semantically from meaning roughly "lineage" to a human type endowed with "a package of fixed physical and mental traits."[31] Only those who suddenly found themselves discriminated against because of their racial "inferiority" would have a strong motivation to question science and reject its racial vocabulary. However, they were hardly in a position to challenge the terms and assumptions of scientific discourse, arguing as they were from a minority status. One could only expect them to deny their own inferiority, but in what terms might they convincingly make a case? Science had achieved "epistemological status";[32] the language of science, though hopelessly oversimplified and manipulated to the point of being anything but scientific, was "one of the most authoritative languages through which meaning was encoded, and as language it had political and social, as well as intellectual, consequences."[33] Any attempt by the victims of racial prejudice to assert their equality would have to come from within the discourse of science. Even this approach was thwarted by the fact that science had already been claimed by and used in the service of the powerful. In a passage very reminiscent of Greenblatt's uneasy feeling that the human subject is ultimately "remarkably unfree, the ideological product of the relations of power in a particular society," Stepan and Gilman write:

> Even as minorities at the turn of the century pinned their hopes on the possibilities inherent in the sciences for uncovering the truth about themselves, many of them saw clearly that racial science violated the standards of neutrality, and that scientists' ideas were fundamentally marked by the relations of power between the dominating and the dominated.[34]

Victims and persecutors alike internalized the terms of racial science. Both the language of race and the assumptions behind it (i.e., biological determinism) were standard fare in Europe. Given the widely accepted authority of science, it is hardly surprising that the average citizen would give credence to racial categories and their seemingly logical outgrowth: rankings. With a few exceptions, there was no extensive contact between Europeans and "lower" races on the European continent. Furthermore, the very popular travel literature of the nineteenth century related tales of primitive communities and tribal social life in Africa and South America, which only confirmed the popular belief that the white races were uniquely endowed with the intelligence and aesthetic sensibilities to develop a higher culture and civilization.[35] Racial categorization was not only considered to be scientifically validated and borne out by exploration of other continents; for many, it "appeared the key to a general science of man."[36]

Classification leads to generalization, which in turn affects the linguistic manner in which races are described. Mary Louise Pratt describes this phenomenon as follows:

> The initial ethnographic gesture is one that homogenizes the people ... into a collective *they*, which distills down even further into an iconic *he* (= the standard adult male specimen). This abstracted *he/they* is the subject of verbs in a timeless present tense. These characterize anything "he" is or does not as a particular event in

time, but as an instance of a pregiven custom or trait (as a particular plant is an instance of its genus and species).³⁷

This homogenizing *he* or *they* is typical of European and American reports on the Ottoman Empire and its various ethnic communities. Paul Rohrbach, whose 1919 *Armenien* was one of Werfel's principle sources of information on Turkish Armenians' culture, quotes liberally from writings with just this tendency. We learn from a Pfarrer Ewald Stier, for example, that "[d]er Armenier ist bildungshungrig wie wenig andre Völker, zumal des Morgenlandes."³⁸ In the same vein, a Dr. J. Greenfield asserts that the Armenian farmer is "ein fleißiger, friedfertiger, nüchterner und ernster Menschenschlag" and that the same holds true for most Armenians in general: "Das sind Eigenschaften, die im großen und ganzen für den armenischen Charakter aller Stände bezeichnend sind...."³⁹ Even an 1891 Christian *Encyclopedia of the Missions* displays an apparent acceptance of racial types and uses the same homogenizing vocabulary: "As far as moral traits are concerned, the Armenian compares favorably with the other races of the East.... The Greek is the only race in Asiatic Turkey that can compare with them in trades, professsions, business ability, and general intelligence."⁴⁰

One finds the same proclivity toward linguistic distillation of ethnic types in the writings of diplomats who had had considerable contact with the different "races" of Turkey in that country itself. Ambassador Morgenthau speaks of "the utter depravity and fiendishness of the Turkish nature,"⁴¹ the "industrious" Armenians and "the dull-witted and lazy Turks."⁴² Samuel Cox, who served as the American minister to Turkey before Morgenthau, likewise published memoirs of his time there and devotes an entire chapter to his observations of "Characteristics of Races and Classes in Turkey."⁴³ As one might expect from the title, this chapter is replete with abstracted *he* and *they* formulations and racial language. "[T]he Turk," we are instructed, "corresponds more nearly with the European than with the Asiatic type, because of his inheritance of Caucasian blood from the maternal line of Georgia or Circassia—which is the bluest of the European stock."⁴⁴ Typical here is Cox's use of the vocabulary of genetics ("inheritance," "blood," "maternal line," "stock"), as well as his desire to place the various blood types on a comparative scale ("bluest"). A sampling of quotes from this chapter reveals the same linguistic tendency in his description of all Turkey's ethnicities: "The great body of the Jews are wily, and very difficult to catch in a trade. The Greeks are always more or less timid. The Levantine is anything you please, for he has no nation."[45]; "The Bulgarian is, as a race, gifted with honesty, sincerity and economy."[46]; "The Kurd is a warrior and spilsman."[47]; and finally, the inevitable characterization of the Armenians as exceptionally intelligent, "The Armenians are the sharpest people in the world. They are the Yankees of the Orient, with much additional acuteness."[48]

Such was the trend in both thought and language concerning racial classification. Such too were Werfel's sources on Turkey for his *Musa Dagh*. It is hardly surprising, then, to find among the letters from his readership comments on the "themes" they have discovered in the novel: "not only the sufferings of minorities, but the subtler one that race is stronger than the individual. . . ."[49] There are indeed ample references to "blood," "race," and "*Volk*" in *Musa Dagh* to justify this sort of interpretation. This aspect of the novel will be examined more closely in a later section.

Werfel himself was not unaffected by the racialist trend. In 1928, he found himself, as the recipient of a Czechoslovakian national award for German-speaking artists, the focal point of a controversy. The German Nationalists were outraged that the prize would be awarded to a citizen with non-German (Jewish) blood and attempted to stage a vociferous protest in the Prague Parliament. Lacking the necessary numbers to carry out the protest, they campaigned furiously to win representatives from other parties for their cause. However, the *Prager Presse* reports, their efforts were to no avail:

> The action was fruitless, and even closed with a lecture on culture by Dr. Skülló; the president of the Hungarian Christian Socialists. Every positive religion, he wrote to the German Nationalists, has its own art, but art has no positive religion. Categorizing artists according to the religion and race they belong to is inconsistent with the thinking of Christian Socialism. It does not tolerate races and religions being made into a caste system, and insists instead on the

principles of Christianity. For that reason our party can not contribute to a process in which the question of religion or race is the deciding factor in the awarding of prizes![50]

The German Nationalists saw in this rejection merely the confirmation of their suspicions: that the national prize was nothing more than a political tool to support German Jews and humiliate "real" (biologically understood) Germans. Undaunted by their failure to lodge an official parliamentary protest, they rerouted their energies into a campaign of negative publicity. The Franz Werfel folders at the Prague Archivní Správa[51] contain numerous German-language newspaper clippings addressing this controversy. Most of the articles refer to his "race" and are bitter or sarcastic in tone; or, as in the following case, they outdo one another in both bitterness and sarcasm:

> The prize cited here is supposed to demonstrate the good will of the Czechoslovakian state towards the cultural endeavors of the Sudeten Germans. In truth it is nothing but a whitewash which is unable to conceal the repression of the völkish movement in Czechoslovakia. This is best proved in the bestowal of the literature prize upon Franz Werfel, a full-blooded Jew not only in lineage but also in conviction, which is downright amusing. But of course the Prague gentlemen found Werfel—the loving sympathizer of the murderer Gawrilo Prinzip, the enthusiastic extoller of "Good Soldier Schweik"—especially appealing. The fact that there are real, struggling artists, such as Hans Watzlik and Bruno Hans Wittek, who are in much greater need of this alleviation of life's struggle than this Jewish cosmic "writer" heaped with percentages and royalties—apparently those in Prague are not aware of this fact, or do not wish to be. One can only hope that this occasion will provide incentive for the real German poets of Czechoslovakia to draw a sharp dividing line between themselves and Herr Franz Werfel, the deserving recipient of this national prize.[52]

Werfel was certainly in a position to recognize the dangerous potential of an intellectual attitude influenced by racial thought and validated by the vocabulary of science. This is one reason for his antisecularist standpoint and for his rejection of the widely-read Ernst Haeckel.

Werfel and Haeckel: Religion vs. "Radical Realism"

Haeckel's 1868 work, *Natural History of Creation,* was described in 1924 as being "perhaps the chief source of the world's knowledge of Darwinism."[53] He rejected biblical creationism, claiming that the Genesis story was neither reliable nor convincing. In its place, he offered a version of Darwin's evolutionary theories, which placed Nature at the center of the human story. Haeckel credits the natural sciences with having explained many of the world's mysteries: "The number of world-riddles has been continually diminishing in the course of the nineteenth century through the aforesaid progress of a true knowledge of nature."[54] Nature, not God, was the force behind material evolution, and a pantheistic spiritual attitude would provide humans with a deep comprehension of its totality. "He called this understanding of Darwinist theory 'monism,' and contrasted it to all other explanations of the world which lacked such material and spiritual unity."[55]

Like Werfel, Haeckel was a child of modernity in that he believed in totalizing concepts with universal applicability. Werfel was a proponent of Catholicism in its noninstitutional sense; that is, he felt it was imperative that there be a catholic belief, shared by all humans. Haeckel, however, is far too impressed with scientific discovery to treat the belief in an active God with anything but good-humored disdain:

> Throughout the whole of astronomy, geology, physics, and chemistry there is no question today of a "moral order," or a personal God, whose "hand hath disposed all things in wisdom and understanding."[56]

However, he felt that neither philosophy nor science alone provides a satisfactory degree of "material and spiritual unity" to assume the role previously occupied by Christianity. Haeckel faults philosophy for failing to expand its domain to include the newly unearthed "treasures of experimental research." Alternatively, the natural sciences are criticized for being content to make their many discoveries for their own sake, without further metaphysical contemplation leading to "the deeper study of the universal connection of the phenomena they observe—that is, philosophy!"[57] His "monism" combines the perceived strengths of each to form a totalizing "Philosophy of Nature." As Mosse comments, this Philosophy of Nature was uniquely suited to the needs of the contemporary because it addressed such scientific issues as evolution without depriving people of a spiritual foothold. "Haeckel's *Riddles of the Universe* . . . became a best seller, for it gave the reader a feeling of being in on science while at the same time gaining the comforts of a new pantheistic religion."[58]

The concluding section of *Riddles* raises the question of the "innermost character of nature" (380)—the nature of Nature, or the deep "meaning of it all"—only to dismiss it as a problem that is currently unsolvable. Haeckel begs the question, and in doing so is himself guilty of at least one aspect of what he believes to be wrong with the natural sciences: avoiding the metaphysical. He admits that he has been unable to get at the heart of what he calls the "problem of substance": "We do not know the 'thing in itself' that lies behind these knowable phenomena." However, he argues that it is most important to appreciate (worship?) Nature and the Philosophy of Nature for the advances it *has* made. Haeckel continues:

> But why trouble about this enigmatic "thing in itself" when we have no means of investigating it, when we do not even clearly know whether it exists or not? Let us, then, leave the fruitless brooding over this ideal phantom to the "pure metaphysician," and let us instead, as "real physicists," rejoice in the immense progress which has been actually made by our monistic philosophy of nature.[59]

His is a cult of that which is understood. By contrast, Werfel's *Musa Dagh* is dedicated to "the inexplicable, in us and above us."

For Werfel, Ernst Haeckel is just one representative of a widespread "realistic conviction" he sees in his contemporaries. "Radical realism" is being practiced at the expense of "inwardness."[60] Modern science, he complains, "steadfastly clings to specialization and modestly closes its eyes to the interpretation of the universe and to pure philosophy."[61] While Haeckel would have us celebrate scientific discovery and dismiss "the interpretation of the universe" as "fruitless brooding," Werfel holds that this is precisely the attitude that is at the root of modern problems. As it exists in the early twentieth century, realism is—contrary to its claims—not "man's direct attitude toward the things of life, his most unbiased relationship to nature, unclouded by religious, political or other abstractions."[62] Rather, it has in fact "shorn the world of reality." He offers factory labor as one example:

> [W]hat does the working man's reality look like? He stands in a machine-filled workshop and performs the same speed-up manual operation six times a minute, eight hours a day. Could anything be more unreal, more unworthy of a human being, more diabolical?[63]

Haeckel's joy in the discovery of Nature is an impossibility; an attitude of "anti-metaphysics"[64] leaves one with a void that cannot be satisfactorily filled with facts: "There is no possibility of approaching a higher meaning of the universe by knowledge or sensation."[65] His "Can We Live Without Faith in God?" is answered with a resounding "No." For the believer, the confusing modern world can be infused with meaning despite its contradictions;

> The others, however, who have strayed into the blind alley of naturalistic nihilism and the realistic outlook, must first be made to realize that there can be no human life without transcendental affinity, and that even their skepticism is but a perverted faith without salvation.[66]

Werfel calls for a "revolution of life against abstract regimentation,"[67] for the end of rampant "intellect-deification"[68] and of the religion of science with its resultant cult of race. These trends obstruct human spiritual progress. To rely on such categories as race and nationhood for one's identity is to deny oneself a true identity.

Werfel's Counter-Discourse: God in Action, God in Our Hearts

Haeckel, it will be recalled, scorned the concept of a God "whose 'hand hath disposed all things in wisdom and understanding." Many shared this attitude, but Werfel's works, starting with his earliest poetry and extending to *Musa Dagh* and beyond, exhibit his unwavering belief in God as an active force in daily life. His youthful poem, "Die Instanz" (*The World Friend,* 1911), speaks of his awareness of a "guiding hand" when he opens with the stanza: "Ich fühle stets in mir ein hohes Wissen, / Das richtend über aller Handlung schwebt, / Das unbewegt sich ewig überhebt, / Und nicht Verstand ist, Seele, noch Gewissen."

In *Musa Dagh,* the presence of an active God is much more pronounced. On numerous occasions, the image of the guiding hand appears, such as during a potentially disastrous battle between the Musa Dagh defense forces and the Turkish attackers: "Here a compassionate hand had turned it all in favour of the Armenians." (696) Indicative of the generally religious tone of the novel are the three biblical quotes preceding each of the three main books,[69] all of them taken from the Book of Revelation. The first passage, "O Sovereign Lord, holy and true, how long before thou wilt judge and avenge our blood on those who dwell upon the earth?" (Revelation 6:10), is a characteristic example of the theodicy problem. Like the first sentence of the novel's main text, it poses a question. Anticipating the cruelties yet to come in the story, it is both a "request for punishment"[70] and a questioning of the very existence of evil in God's creation. However, it does not express a basic lack of faith in the wisdom of God on the author's part. As the biblical passage goes on to indicate, Divine justice unfolds at its own pace, and one must patiently and faithfully await that moment when all inequities will make sense: "Then they were each given a white robe and told to rest a little longer, until the number of their fellow servants and their brethren should be complete, who were to be killed as they themselves had been." (Revelation 6:11) Questions of justice and punishment abound in the novel, but the fundamental belief expressed explicitly by the author is that while God's justice is slow, it does ultimately prevail: "Unlike the customs of human justice, punishment here does not directly follow the deed. Divine justice is suspended in cosmic logical consistency as salt is in the sea."[71]

The biblical quote prefacing the second book, "and the wine press was trodden outside the city, and blood flowed from the wine press, as high as a horse's bridle . . ." (Revelation 14:20), tells in graphic terms of the righteous wrath of God against the wicked: bloodshed is rewarded with bloodshed.[72] Carl Steiner understands the relationship of this passage to the novel as a preparation both for the "temporary tranquility at the beginning of this novel segment" and for the "implied fermentation process about to take place, promising a stormy time ahead."[73] It is more than that. It is most importantly the answer to the question raised in the previous biblical passage. God has delivered justice with ferocious vengeance. In the third book of *Musa Dagh,* Lepsius will have a vision that anticipates the violent deaths of the Turkish leaders, although they postdate the historical boundaries of the novel, and interprets these deaths as an act of divine justice. In a half-sleep, he sees the fate of the Armenians' persecutors: "That 'attempt' on Enver's and Talaat's lives."

> Had he been granted a glimpse into the future, or only surrendered to some obscurely murderous thought in himself? The guns growled. The panes rattled. Absurd! Absurd! he tried to tell himself. But his feverish heart already knew that God had reestablished His justice, before the scales had broken under their load. (564–65)

It is interesting to note that Talaat Bey was assassinated in Berlin by an Armenian in March of 1921, and Lepsius appeared as a witness on behalf of the defense. This, in addition to the fact that the Armenian was acquitted, cannot have escaped Werfel's notice in his careful research. In all likelihood, it further confirmed his belief in God's justice.

The Revelation quote leading in the final book will hold significance for a later section of this chapter. However, Lepsius's interpretation of his own vision is consistent with another assumption of the novel: that the fate of humanity is predetermined and will unfold in accordance with God's plan. This view is expressed repeatedly in the novel, both in authorial commentary and from the mouths of its most venerable characters. Agha Rifaat Bereket, the pious Moslem who serves as a surrogate father for Gabriel, advises him to be calm and faithful: "What will happen to us has already happened in God." (40) Bagradian hears similar words from the Armenian Krikor, who quotes an old Turkish proverb to him: "Nothing happens unless predestined." (121) Initially, this attitude irritates Gabriel because he does not want to approach his future with resignation. When Ter Haigasun, asked what action he is taking in light of strong evidence that the Turks are planning an attack on the Armenians, says simply, "I pray . . .", Gabriel responds impatiently: "pray . . . But God helps those who help themselves." (76)

Increasingly, however, Gabriel senses that his own fate is predetermined. He tells Juliette, for example, that he had experienced this sensation very strongly—though only fleetingly—on his trip to Antioch. He suspects that his unplanned return to Yoghonoluk was not merely coincidence but part of an unknown plan: "Yesterday, for an instant, I felt unshakably convinced that I'd been brought here by some supernatural power, that God has something or other in store for me. My feeling really was unshakable, though it only lasted an instant. . . . And so, by His will, through Avetis, God brought me back here. . . ." (64) As he grows to accept his role in his community's fate, the fleeting feeling develops into a firm belief. The intimate spiritual bond that forms between Iskuhi and him is interpreted as another sign that his natural place is with the Armenian community. He compares his love for Juliette with that he feels for Iskuhi: "'I used to love Juliette, and perhaps I do still. At least as a memory. But this between you and me, what is it, Iskuhi? I was fated to find you now, at the end of my life, just as I was fated to come here—not by chance, but . . . well, how shall I put it?'" (615) Even his military success seems to him to have been dictated by God, for his brief training and service with the Turkish army in the Balkan War was of negligible aid to his Musa Dagh defense. What enabled him to draw up an effective strategy was information from a book he had bought years ago on a whim. He reflects:

> I bought this book without ever knowing I should use it, simply because I liked the look of the title-page, or because the unknown subject vaguely attracted me, though in those days military science didn't attract me in the least. And yet, at the instant in which I bought it, quite independently of my will, my fate was predetermining itself. Really one would almost think that my kismet is mapped out from A to Z (352)

Werfel indicates that even the Turkish enemy must finally draw the same conclusion: the successful defense of the Musa Dagh despite the overwhelming odds against the Armenians can only be a statement from God that these people are not to be annihilated. Defeated yet again after having had a stranglehold on the Armenians, the Turkish lieutenant (*Kaimakam*) questions the ultimate authority of the Turkish leadership for the first time.

> Yet now furious doubts of Enver Pasha and Talaat Bey reared up within the Kaimakam, since failure is also the stern parent of truth. Had men the right to work out skillful plans by which this or that people should be stamped out? . . . Who is to say that one people is worse or better than another? Certainly men cannot say it. And God, that day on the Damlayik, had given a most unmistakable answer. (481)

This is not an insignificant conclusion coming from a respected member of Ittihad, a man who had never before questioned the Young Turks' party line of Turkish racial supremacy and the necessity of eliminating other races (480); however, these insights can enter his consciousness only when sleep has rendered him vulnerable. The devout Gregorian priest Ter Haigasun is naturally much more inclined to recognize the grace of God for what it is: the fire that temporarily drove back the Turkish forces but also seemingly sealed the Armenians' fate by destroying their camp, was what drew the attention of the French ship *Guichen* to their plight and finally ensured their rescue. He alone recognizes God's guiding hand in this disaster turned salvation: "Ter Haigasun's eyes were sightless with ecstasy as he stammered in Armenian: 'The evil only happened . . . to enable God to show us His goodness.'" (785)

Ter Haigasun and other devout Christian and Moslem characters occupy a special place in *Musa Dagh*. They are Werfel's "children of God," and they are expressly designed to contrast the modern breed of nonbelievers. In each of the three chapters titled "Interlude of the Gods," religiosity is pitted against secularization, most explicitly in the first of these chapters, which features the conversation between Johannes Lepsius and Enver Pascha. Enver has clearly replaced Allah as an object of worship for the Young Turks, as the following description of his entering a room demonstrates: "Enver Pasha went into Talaat Bey's office. The clerks sprang up. Hero-worship shone out of their faces. That almost mystic love had still not waned which even these paper-gentry felt for their dainty war god." (144) This reference to Enver as a "war god," indicating the reverence given to him, is only one of many. Lepsius, whose mother had him baptized as "Johannes" so that she would be constantly reminded to raise him as one "who really loves his Lord and walks in His footsteps" (150) is by no means the stronger party in the confrontation with Enver. On the contrary, Enver's singleminded rejection of all logic and morality in the name of the Turkish "race" easily dismisses every argument the pastor can put forth. Finally, Lepsius recognizes with morbid fascination that he can have no effect on this man's conscience:

> What Herr Lepsius perceived was that arctic mask of the human being who "has overcome all sentimentality"—the mask of a human mind which has got beyond guilt and all its qualms, the strange, almost innocent naïveté of utter godlessness: And what force it had, that a man could not hate it!(142)

A similar confrontation occurs in the meeting between Lepsius and the German Privy counselor. Lepsius hopes to convince him that Germany, by association with Turkey as a war ally, also shares the responsibility for the treatment of the Armenians. He believes that an informed German public would be outraged by the atrocities and that the German government should threaten to dissolve the military alliance barring an end to the crimes. In his notes, Werfel sketched the Privy counselor character: "a sort of Nietzschean, completely eclipses Lepsius. He develops the absolutely logical necessity why Germany cannot provide any help. On the surface he sympathizes with the Armenians, provides evidence. . . . Inside it becomes clear that he wishes their fate upon them."[74] The final version of this scene challenges Nietzschean nihilism with religious humanism more explicitly when Lepsius points out that Enver and Talaat have usurped God's role as "historical forces." The Privy counselor counters with a paraphrase of Nietzschean philosophy: "Doesn't Nietzsche say: 'What totters, ought it not to be thrust down?'" Such arguments of "radical realism" cannot obscure the higher reality for Lepsius, however. "But Nietzsche was not the man to disconcert such a child of God as Johannes Lepsius." (535)

Although Lepsius fails to accomplish anything in his conversations with the modern "gods," he is without any doubt the moral victor. The nefarious characters of *Musa Dagh* are without exception atheists; their heinous acts are possible only because of the secularization (or, as it is often referred to in the novel, atheism) that has spread from Europe to the East. As Steiner comments, "[p]iety and religiosity are understood as essential—perhaps the most essential—parts of the human condition" in *Musa Dagh*.[75] Werfel feels that religiosity, be it of the Christian or Muslim variety, is humanity's best defender against the shallow materialism and brutal chauvinism of the twentieth century. Like the concept of predetermination, this view is given special merit in the novel by some of its most respectable characters. Early on, Agha Rifaat Bereket questions Gabriel's characterization of Turks as adherents of nationalism: "To which Turks do you refer? . . . Those traitors, those atheists, who would annihilate God's universe itself, merely in order to get money and power? Those are neither Turks nor Moslems. They are merely empty rascals and money-grubbers." (36–37) Professor Nezimi Bey echoes this opinion, asserting that the "real" Turks are "All those who haven't lost their religion." (543) The rabidly anti-Western Türbedar accuses Lepsius, as the representative European, of forcing a new lifestyle upon the East, destroying the traditional devotion to Allah in the process: "[W]e don't want your reforms, your *progress,* your business activity. We want to live in God, and to develop in ourselves those powers which belong to Allah." (553) Less aggressively but in the same vein, the venerable old Sheik tells Lepsius that nationalism has come to occupy the place in Turkish hearts that had previously been occupied by Allah. (554) The Young Turks, whom he refers to as "Europe's servants," have "robbed" Turkey of its religion. He adds, "How is it possible to hate if the heart has opened itself to God?" (556) The devout Christian Lepsius has no interest in converting these Moslems to the "true" religion. Like Werfel, he feels that it is sincere piousness—not just Christianity—that will be humanity's salvation, and he expresses his respect for the practices of these holy men of Muslim faith: "The fervour and devotion with which I saw you strive after God has filled my heart with delight. Even if I, as an ignorant foreigner, cannot understand the innermost meaning of your holy customs, at least I was able to feel your great piety." (551) Both Werfel and his Lepsius figure, it should be pointed out, have a singularly and naively positive concept of religiosity, equating religion with humaneness. Werfel is blind to the dangers of extreme religious fervor and ironically overlooks that the age-old conflict between Turks and Armenians stem from religious differences, that the racial arguments are employed in the twentieth century as a convenient means to justify the eradication of the "wrong" religion.

Reprioritization of Themes in *Musa Dagh*

As prominent as the theme of an active God may seem in the final published form of *Musa Dagh,* the Vienna manuscript shows us that Werfel had originally intended it to be even more pronounced. Historical circumstances prompted him to diminish its prominence in the novel, shifting the work's emphasis to address the more immediate (though related) threat of racial persecution instead. In this move, his conviction that literature is an active participant in contemporary debates is once again evident.

The final published version of *Musa Dagh* opens with an action performed by the protagonist: Gabriel Bagradian's "How did I get here?" spoken aloud to himself. The reader is immediately thrust into the dilemma of the main character, whose thoughts, observations, and actions continue to be the grammatical subject of most of the next pages' sentences. An earlier version, however, shows a markedly different subject matter. Bagradian himself is not introduced until the fourth page of the text.[76] In his place, the "protagonist" of the opening pages is the mountain and its rich plant life. Werfel devotes a considerable amount of space to the description of the many flowers (cyclamen, Alpine rose, Turk's cap lily, rhododendron, azalea—to name a few) and trees (olive, mulberry, pine, cypress, centuries-old holm oak, plane tree, linden) that grace the slopes of the Musa Dagh. This is not done in an effort to make use of his extensive research on the region's vegetation. The author justifies his detailed description as follows: "These green things must be mentioned in such great detail because they form the wonders of an otherwise insignificant mountain which cannot even remotely be compared with its closest neighbors."[77] What Werfel wants to establish from the outset is that the beauty of "the Armenian mountain" is a miraculous exception ("wonder") to the otherwise desertlike landscape of the region. Unlike the neighboring barren mountains and surrounding arid countryside, the Musa Dagh "always maintains its perennial life."[78]

To be fair, the narrator tells us, one could offer plenty of "natural reasons" for "the aforementioned wonders, or rather for these exceptions"; for example, the many life-giving springs that cascade into the ocean as waterfalls, or tumble down the mountainside as creeks. However, he is at a loss to explain why this water does not flow onward to the adjoining landscape where the Turks reside. "Strangely, though, the far greater number of tributaries flows toward the sea and only three streams make their way into the Antioch valley where, however, they immediately lose their life without having reached the Orontes River." The Armenians, it would seem, are the sole recipients of a rare blessing. Their Muslim neighbors, for whatever reason, are shunned by nature. Werfel offers a possible interpretation:

> One could perceive a symbol in this: The water flees the Moslem just as the steppe and the desert seek him. The water shuns his dwellings as if an ancient insult, committed in mythological times against its divinity, were still not atoned for. Other peoples and races are sought out and blessed by it. And among these seem to be the residents of Musa Dagh, the diligent and lively Armenians whose six villages are nestled at its foot.[79]

Before any mention of the protagonist, Gabriel, one encounters the Turk-Armenian issue. Natural reasons cannot suffice to explain the exceptional character of the Armenian mountain. Nature, and therewith God, has simply decided in favor of the diligent (and Christian!) Armenians.

That Werfel originally intended to stress the theme of God's grace, or God's active presence in the fate of an individual or a people, is also evident in the renaming of this first chapter. Crossed out in the manuscript are the titles "The Wonders of Musa Dagh" and "The Mountain"; the final title of the chapter is "Teskeré." This shows the gradual shift of emphasis from the miraculous nature of the mountain as the subject (God's action), to the mountain itself, and finally to the first concrete act of racial persecution: the revocation of the *teskeré,* denying the Armenians the right to travel freely within Turkey. The persecution of the minority Armenians and the ramifications it holds for Gabriel's self-understanding become the primary theme of the novel. This is also apparent in segments of the manuscript which indicate that Gabriel accepts his Armenian identity and God-given fate much earlier (barely one hundred pages into the story) and more readily than in the final version of the novel. He reflects, "At age thirty-six God has thrust me for the first time into this foreign thing which is mine."[80] "This foreign thing which is mine," which becomes the most problematic topic of *Musa Dagh* in its final form, seems here to be an issue already fully resolved.

Early in 1933, with the novel already in the late stages of production, is when Werfel apparently decided to change the focus of *Musa Dagh* from the discourse of religion to that of race. On a blank page facing the written text—a space he always reserved for notes or changes—he indicates that it has become a historical necessity to revise the book: "*Roughly from here on the terrible events in Germany robbed me of all concentration. Only with great difficulty have I fought out these sentences. They cannot suffice. Perhaps I should even completely change the plot!*"[81] Jungk remarks that Werfel, who was in Santa Margherita Ligure at the time, had been working intensively on *Musa Dagh* and to some extent was able to ignore the political developments in Germany, including Hitler's installment as Reichskanzler. "The Reichstag building in Berlin burned at the end of February, a wave of arrests swept across all of Germany, and the Reichstag elections of March 5, 1933, secured the National Socialists more than 44 percent of the vote. Now he was no longer able to close his eyes to reality."[82] In terms of the plot, this meant that the topic of racial persecution, the pseudoscientific discourse of justifiable chauvinism had to be foregrounded. *Musa Dagh* would now open with the problem of identity in the wake of racial bigotry, and Gabriel's acceptance of an unwanted identity would not ensue without a struggle.

RACE-DISCOURSE IN *MUSA DAGH*

Werfel was aware of the mechanisms by which dominant discourses become absorbed into the vocabulary and intellectual assumptions of the general populace. His own relationship to the discourse of race is curious in that light because it seems ambivalent. In *Musa Dagh*, there are many indications that his perspectives are as much colored by the late-nineteenth- and early-twentieth-century racial assumptions as any of his contemporaries', an aspect of the novel that has received some criticism. References to "blood," *"Volk,"* and "race" abound, pointing to an unreflected use of the discourse's terms. Conversely, however, there is ample evidence that *Musa Dagh* was written in part as a challenge to that discourse's authority. The protagonist explicitly questions racial determination, ultimately demonstrating that one's race or ethnicity is an aspect of identity that must be accepted and then overcome in order to reach the innermost core of identity. It is possible that Werfel intentionally included racial vocabulary and assumptions to the extent that he did, so that the reader would make the same gradual transition from acceptance to questioning of the dominant racial discourse as Gabriel. As much as he occupied himself with identity questions and although he was aware of the phenomenon of scientific discourse creeping into the general vocabulary, however, the evidence from other works—fiction and nonfiction alike—would indicate that he himself was not unaffected by the words and ideas around him. The man who cites "a primeval affinity of blood and character" as justification for an opinion is not fully immune to the phenomenon that he recognizes and at times, as in *Musa Dagh,* attempts to examine more closely.

The popular "science" of physiognomy emerges in *Musa Dagh* as an interesting example. Werfel seems to accept the notion that physical features reflect some inner quality, be it a permanent trait or a temporary emotional state. The recurring mention of Armenians' eyes may serve as an example of the former. The eyes of Armenian characters are always described as being overly large and alert. For Werfel, this is a physical manifestation of Armenian culture and history. First, their eyes mirror the supposed intellectual tradition of their culture. Second, these are the wide-open eyes of a people that has been terrorized throughout its history. The description of Ter Haigasun is typical: "His big eyes (Armenian eyes are nearly always big; big with a thousand years of terror) had a mingled look of shy isolation and resolute knowledge of the world." (72) The horror-filled history of Armenians has left its mark on their physiognomy. Samuel Awakian, Stephan's tutor, is described in the same terms: "It was the face of an Armenian intellectual. A rather sloping forehead. Watchful, deeply troubled eyes behind glasses. An expression of eternal surrender to fate, but at the same time a sharp look of being on guard, ready every second to parry an attacker's blow." (12–20) The high forehead speaks of the Armenian devotion to intellectual matters; "watchful, deeply troubled" eyes are the legacy of centuries of persecution, although Awakian himself has never been a victim. If the significance of Armenian eyes has escaped the reader to this point, Lepsius's interpretation can leave no doubt: "Such eyes as only those beings have those who must empty the chalice to its dregs. Christ on the cross may well have had just such eyes." (125)

Physical appearance is also shown to reflect negative characteristics, as for example Lepsius sees "utter godlessness" in Enver's features. Although Werfel made some effort to be fair in his characterization of Turks, their physiognomy generally reveals his true opinion of them as a less cultivated race. A parallel Turkish figure to the beautiful Armenian Iskuhi is lacking altogether; and for the most part, when a Turk's appearance is described, it is not in positive terms. Enver, for example, has uncommonly delicate features. However, the emphasis placed on his more feminine traits (fine hands, small stature, etc.) give him an overall quality that is oddly unsettling rather than attractive. (In this case, Werfel can hardly be faulted for being biased, since Lepsius's historical account of his visit with Enver contains exactly this type of description.) More blatant is the description of Iskuhi's Turkish attacker, who is given animal-like traits:

> Over her there appeared a terrible face, gigantic, with filthy stubble, snorting, rolling its eyes, stinking, inhuman. She let out another piercing scream and then struggled silently with the man, whose spittle dripped into her face, whose brown claws were tearing her dress to shreds, to fasten themselves into naked breasts. (105)

The would-be rapist has the appearance of a beast: filthy, unshaven, clawing at his victim with paws instead of human hands. By contrast, the Turkish Captain who has forsworn his violent military career and converted to a life devoted to religion has "big, gentle eyes and a sensitive fact; only his carefully trained moustache helps him to the severity of an officer. (557)

Lepsius's appearance alters drastically through the course of the novel. By the time he meets with the German Privy counselor, little of his original optimism remains that he can effect any relief for the Armenians. The many defeats have taken their toll on his physiognomy:

> Scarcely more than a month had passed since his memorable talk with Enver Pasha, yet the pastor looked alarmingly changed. His hair seemed sparser, his beard looked grayer than it had, his nose seemed to have shrunk and become more pointed. His eyes no longer beamed. The dreamy distances had gone out of him, replaced by an expectant, mocking suspiciousness. (529)

Juliette, too, undergoes an unflattering transformation. The woman who had been compared to a lovely queen when she graciously played hostess to the Armenian visitors becomes less and less attractive as she moves closer to her act of infidelity. She herself feels the transformation coming on: "She was sure she was getting uglier every day, surrounded by such general disapprobation. (360) She neglected her face, she no longer tended to her appearance because she was ashamed of her customary care and tiredness was dragging her down. Paranoia! The Armenian eyes all around her seemed to decry her and blame her alone."[83] In this case, it is the inner condition of guilt that affects outward appearance.

In a 1934 review, Lionel Abel takes issue with the racial vocabulary in *Musa Dagh*. Abel considers the "call of the blood" that Gabriel and Stephan experience in the older Bagradian's homeland to be a reactionary theme. "Who will distinguish between mechanically and mystically caused racial sentiment? The difference exists; but since race has become the catchword of fascism, any celebration of race, even though such a distinction is made to justify it, is bound to have a confusing and finally a reactionary effect."[84] The criticism is understandable, especially in light of the time period during which it was written; however, it is not fully warranted. It is doubtful whether a novel written in the 1930s could effectively address the topic of identity with-

4: *MUSA DAGH* AS A PARTICIPANT IN DOMINANT DISCOURSES 139

out at least acknowledging the complications presented by racial science. Stepan and Gilman speak of "science as an especially weighty discourse of identity"[85] in the decades around the turn of the century. "[T]he self," they write, "was understood and represented through a preexisting, racialized science."[86] In their examination of minority strategies of inclusion at that time, they ask themselves whether minorities may have served their cause better by engaging the battle from outside the scientific discourse, or in essence by ignoring the racial bias against them. Stepan and Gilman conclude that creating "alternatives" to science was simply not a viable option. The issue had to be confronted in its own terms: "[I]n the era of the successful establishment of science as an epistemologically neutral and instrumentally successful form of knowledge, standing 'outside of' or ignoring science was very difficult."[87]

Thus, racial themes and vocabulary exist in abundance in *Musa Dagh,* and in many instances, one has the distinct impression that Werfel indeed has accepted certain assumptions concerning race and inherited character to be true. For instance, the Turks are frequently referred to as a "warrior race." Werfel observes that the defeat at the hands of the numerically inferior Armenian forces on the Musa Dagh is much more distressing for this military race than it would be for other peoples: "An unfortunate war can hurl such races often centuries back, while other peoples who adopt a more reserved attitude toward combat can overcome military misfortunes far more easily and productively."[88] The language seems even to suggest that the very evolutionary process of the Turkish "race" has been dealt a severe blow by this military defeat. They can be "hurled back" to an earlier stage of their collective development.

Juliette is also shown to be essentially different from the novel's Armenian characters as a result of her race. "Being French," a passage explains, "she had a certain natural rigidity. Latins, for all their surface pliancy, are set and rigid within themselves. Their form is a perfection. They have perfected it. Northerners may still have something of the vagueness and infinite plasticity of cloud-shapes; the French as a rule hate nothing so much as to have to leave their country, get out of their skin." (359) Perhaps, Werfel continues, if Gabriel had been resolute in a long-term attempt "to guide her gently in the direction of his own people, perhaps it would all have worked out differently." Race seems to determine, if not innate and unchangeable characteristics, then at least strong tendencies that can be altered only through long-term conscious effort. Elsewhere in the novel, it is indicated that certain groups of Armenians in their diaspora have developed different traits depending on their particular surroundings. (348) Nonetheless, even if racial characteristics are not immutable, it is apparent that Werfel believes them to be biologically inherited ("natural").

The issue of race, then, is not simply dismissed as invalid. Werfel does not challenge the discourse in its entirety, but rather takes on the transcendental significance attached to it. Races may be different, he concedes, but is this our most noble source of identity? Further, is our character truly predetermined by our blood stock? Lepsius answers the first question in his conversation with the devout "Thieves of Hearts" group when he comments that "Usually the people who dwell on their race are the ones who have most need of something of that kind." (543) The amount of spiritual and cultural depravity necessary for human beings to derive their fundamental identity from race is so great, these persons are almost beyond abhorrence and ridicule. If their rhetoric were not so dangerous, they would be downright pitiable. However, it is stressed repeatedly that the outgrowth of racism is a murderous nationalism. Agha Rifaat Bereket says to Gabriel in their discussion about racial hatred: "It is the worst of doctrines, to bid us seek our own faults in our neighbors." (36) again indicating that race can only serve as an inadequate compensation for the absence of a true identity.

Juliette, who has always identified strongly with her nationality, is forced by circumstances to make herself a part of the Musa Dagh community. After spending the first several days in her tent, isolated from the Armenians, she comes to the realization that continuing to live in this self-imposed solitude is an impossibility: "I can't go on living like this," she tells Gabriel. At his suggestion that she become involved in the life of the Armenian camp, she protests, "It's not my community." She does not believe that she belongs with the Armenians in a "natural," genetically predetermined way. However, Gabriel admonishes her to fundamentally change her concept of identity. "We belong far less to what we've come from," he argues, "than to what we're

4: *MUSA DAGH* AS A PARTICIPANT IN DOMINANT DISCOURSES

doing our best to reach." (323) A racial conception of personal identity is simply too narrow to be adequate.

Naturally, Gabriel has every motivation to believe that identity transcends race. At the beginning of the novel, he is, after all, the assimilated Parisian, the reluctant Armenian. This is a man who would prefer to be "abstract," an "individual." "Bloodstream, and people!", he contemplates, "Were not these mere empty concepts? Human beings in every age have strewn the bitter bread of existence with a different spice of ideas, only to make it still more unpalatable." (29) His gradual acceptance of the minority identity in a time of racial persecution has already been discussed. Nor is his Armenian identity purely an intellectual decision: he does experience that "call of the blood" Abel identified. However, it does not become the center of his being. It emerges somewhat mysteriously at critical moments but in the end does not comprise even the main part of his identity. One misunderstands Werfel's novel in interpreting the discourse of race as an unreflected "celebration of race."

GOD IN OUR SELVES: THE ACHIEVEMENT OF TRUE IDENTITY

The most telling episode during which Gabriel's feelings and actions are controlled by his Armenian blood is the first battle on the Musa Dagh. This is the event that elevates him to unquestioned membership in the community, and more than that: to the role of an esteemed father-protector figure, as the kissing of his hand betokens. The celebration of the first victory, at the same time a ceremony of Gabriel's acceptance into the community, gives him for the first time a vague sense of what true identity must be. He realizes that his identity lies neither in the "old Bagradian," the assimilated Parisian, nor in the "new Bagradian" who has come to terms with his responsibility to the Armenian community. Though he cannot yet grasp it, he senses that there is still another step to be taken that will lead him to himself, or the "true Bagradian":

> In this moment Gabriel felt strangely relaxed. It seemed to him as if there were three Bagradians: the old, comfortably familiar Bagradian; a new Bagradian, who like a con artist was involving himself

in gruesome things which did not suit him in the least; and a third Bagradian, the actual and true one. But this one was floating without body and without a homeland between the two others.[89]

A clue to this higher identity can be found in strange sequence of events during that first battle. As the Turks' inevitable defeat becomes increasingly apparent, the Armenian soldiers are overwhelmed by a primal "call of the blood"; they fight with distinct focus but are "no longer sane." Gabriel also feels the pull of the primitive forces: "Gabriel himself had long since lost the clearheadedness of a leader, was the wild prey of some intoxication, a crazy rhythm come suddenly to life in his blood that had slumbered a thousand years." Similarly possessed by irrational behavior, Pastor Aram Tomasian runs aimlessly, waving a cross in the air and shouting, "Christ! Christ!" Unlike the other Armenians, Gabriel snaps out of his daze: "Oddly, these shouts of 'Christ' brought Gabriel back to his senses with a jerk." (332) It is highly significant that the utterance of Christ's name restores clarity for Gabriel, as it is Werfel's first indication that the culmination of his protagonist's true identity lies in God. For the first time, Gabriel transcends his "second" level of identity and approaches that final achievement of identity that will be his at the novel's close.

But that second Bagradian is indispensable to the true Bagradian; he is a necessary part of the process. It will be recalled that Gabriel feels early on that his return to Yoghonoluk is part of a higher plan, that "God has something or other in store for me." He is returned to his natural Armenian community and forced by circumstance to participate in its fate. Along the way, God occasionally provides the aid he needs to regain his Armenian identity. For example, he suddenly feels a natural ease with the Armenian language at the moment when it is most crucial that the villagers accept him as part of their community: when he proposes the defense initiative. A proposal with ramifications for the fate of an entire community cannot come from an outsider. God speaks *through* Gabriel, granting him the reconnection with his authentic ethnic identity:

> Always, when talking to these villagers, his Armenian had seemed laboured and embarrassed. But now it was not he who spoke to

them—and this knowledge brought him complete peace—it was the force which had brought him here, down the long, winding road of centuries, the short, twisted path of his own life. He listened in amazement to this power, as it found the words in him so naturally. (206)

Lepsius, who so often serves as Werfel's mouthpiece, also puts forth the necessity of ethnic identity as a fact of life. At the same time, however, he distances himself from the base nationalism that attempts to use this fact in the service of evil. Ethnicity is an important aspect of identity; however, it should not be considered a source of special pride. "[T]he peoples are slaves of their racial differences," he explains to the Privy counselor. "And their flatterers, who want to live off them, intensify such things and stimulate their vanity. As though there were any special merit in being born a dog or a cat, a turnip or a potato." (536) "Blood" may connect us so that we will preserve and, if necessary, protect our community, but it is not meant to be used as a pretext for destroying others. The fundamental commitment in one's life should be to all of humanity, in the service of God. Lepsius cites the example of Christ: "Jesus Christ . . . gives us the eternal example of the divine man, only put on human form in order to conquer it. So that on earth only the true sons of God should rule, from the very fact that they have conquered their race, their earthly conditioning." (537) Again, it is part of a process: the service one performs for the blood community out of natural impulses is akin to a trial run in preparation for service to humanity as a whole. Ritchie Robertson interprets this aspect of *Musa Dagh* in similar fashion:

> First comes the natural fact of ethnicity. If one does not acknowledge this, one leads the unsatisfying cosmopolitan life of the earlier Gabriel; one is an abstract human being . . . Hence affection for one's people, and loyalty to them under threat, are natural and good; but such feelings must be focused on places and people one knows. Otherwise they begin to approach the abstract nationalism which dominates the modern world, the chauvinism that Lepsius disclaims. . . . [90]

This message can be found repeatedly in Werfel's works. A 1939 article, published in the Paris exile newspaper *Courrier*

Autrichien and entitled "Homecoming to the Empire," also urges the public to transcend "peoplehood" and instead work for the "all-human idea." Here, Werfel argues that the Austrian Empire, nonexistent since the Anschluß, will be restored in an improved form: "The harm and damage done in the previous manifestation of Austria, the privileges and half-measures brought along from feudal times, will not be a part of the restoration." Unlike his contemporary Joseph Roth, whose nostalgia for the "multiracial state" blinded him to its inequities, Werfel seizes the historical moment as an opportunity to eliminate the weaknesses of Austria while highlighting its positive features. For him, this means first and foremost moving beyond ethnic loyalties and toward an "all-human spirit." "Sacrificium nationis," he writes,

> the sacrifice of the demonic, earthbound, blood-conditioned, ambition-driven urges of our soul in favor of a higher, worldwide unity, is that not the eternal idea of the empire, the idea of Austria? Had not that "learned Austrian" overcome within himself the peoplehood of the German, Czech, Slav etc., in order to become a new human—less colorful perhaps, but freer and more just than before?[91]

In 1931, he had already made very much the same plea. Here, too, he concedes that one's ethnicity has a bearing on one's identity; but as Lepsius in *Musa Dagh,* he hopes that these natural "racial differences" can be overcome ("conquered"). The similarity in vocabulary is unmistakable: "The individual man is the sentient representative of his physical type of constitution, of his family, of his social and national heritage, and of a hundred other relativities. Mastery over these can grow only out of a quite rare religious and ethical act, but never out of an intellectual decision."[92]

The achievement of true identity is inextricably bound to a religious act, to embracing God within oneself as a part of oneself. Werfel repeats this idea elsewhere, proclaiming that "once he has lost his empty, naturalistic *Ersatz*-faith, he will be permitted to penetrate to his innermost self, that is, to the perception of the Divine which is waiting for him to hearken unto it."[93] At the innermost core of every human being is God. To perceive God within oneself is to have arrived at one's identity. Steiner cites Werfel's poem from 1934, "Tempora mea in manibus tuis," which demonstrates that a human's relationship with God is the defining aspect of his or her identity. He comments, "After denying in it that he belonged to his family, his people, and even himself, he concludes that poem by entrusting himself fully to God: 'To whom do I belong? I am His / For being is being His, and I nestle myself, as I weep / Into his open father's hand.'"[94]

Now we may return to the biblical quote leading in the third book of *Musa Dagh*. Steiner suspects that it may in some way point to "the ultimate outcome of the novel and the possible sanctification of the victorious protagonist after death," but beyond that he considers it to be "rather cryptic."[95] The passage Werfel chose for the final segment of his novel is, like the other two, from the Revelation to John: "To him who conquers I will give some of the hidden manna, and I will give him a white stone, with a new name written on the stone which no one knows except him who receives it."(Revelation 2:17) This has been referred to in biblical scholarship as "the classical passage in the New Testament about the individual." Lynn Harold Hough offers the interpretation that each individual "is to have an eternal secret with God. There is a central citadel in each personality which only God shares." The new name on the white stone, he continues, "represents the individual personality achieved only through the grace of Christ. He is *a new man;* but he is not a new man just like every other man. He is *eternally something individual,* and different, and eternally prized by God."[96] Hough's interpretation seems a valid one for understanding Werfel's use of this passage. Looking back to earlier cited works, it will be recalled that his "learned Austrian" casts off "peoplehood" in favor of a more fundamental concept of identity, and in so doing becomes "a new human"; furthermore, when the individual discards superficialities and arrives at his or her "innermost self," she or he perceives there "the divine"—comparable to that "central citadel . . . which only God shares." This is the level of individual identity for which every human should strive.

Individuality is a sacred gift to be cherished, an essential aspect of the human condition. As Lepsius remarks, "As a Christian, I believe that our Father in heaven created these differences between us, to teach us love. Since no love is possible without diversity and tension." (555) This point is stressed when he witnesses the ecstatic dance of the dervishes. Each individual dance is admired as an expression of the individual's special bond with God: "[T]here was none of the symmetry of drill or ballet in the surge. Each obeyed his own law. Each individual in this brotherhood seemed to be alone with himself, in ecstatic invocation of his God." A comment somewhat later on the same page reveals Werfel's opinion that only a community comprised of individuals who are secure in their relationship with God can be a truly cohesive and just community: "There must be full freedom and solitude of the ego before his God, to make possible a higher community." (548)

Werfel's preparatory notes on *Musa Dagh* leave no doubt that Gabriel's final achievement of his true identity was planned to be the culmination of the novel and that his identity was to be understood as the consciousness of God's special presence within him. On one of the final pages in his notebook, Werfel planned the novel's conclusion: "*In the end.* Union with God. Against the volk, the masses, the individual, the sovereign, the prince, by the grace of God." As Robertson correctly remarks, Gabriel has "transcended community and personality"; "he has acknowledged and obeyed his loyalties and thus fulfilled his existence."[97] Gabriel himself contemplates his own development and recognizes that it was imperative for him to follow the "call of the blood," to commit himself to his natural community in order to delve deeper within himself and ultimately discover the "new" Gabriel who is defined by his relationship with God:

> The one thing possible filled him from top to toe with incredible certainty. He had shared in the destiny of his blood. He had led the struggle of his own villagers. But was not the new Gabriel more than part of a blood-stream? Was he not more than an Armenian? Once he had thought of himself as "abstract," as an "individual." He had had to pass through the pen-fold of a commune really to become so. That was it, that was why he could feel so incredibly free! (814)

Werfel and Identity: Conclusions

Werfel's lifelong preoccupation with problems of identity went through many stages. The youthful expressionist believed it possible to live in brotherhood with all humanity—it is his "only wish." When that ideal was quashed by the realities of world war and bigotry within his own homeland, the search for a convincing conception of community and individual identity began in earnest. Following the trends of his contemporaries, he probed the romantic notions of the historical community, the immutable *Volk,* even the biological family unit for an acceptable basis of identification. He was unmoved, even offended, by the Zionist movement which attracted so many young Jews in Prague, because he knew that Judaism could not provide a foundation of commonality for a group of assimilated Jews whose religious adherence was at best superficial. With the help of Martin Buber, however, he came to understand that the assimilated German Jews did comprise a community—not the least of all because of the persecution directed toward them—and that they must work toward recognition as such. This insight is similar to multiculturalists' positions, who along with Charles Taylor argue that "important consequences flow for people's identity from the absence of recognition."[98] Here, the collective identity of German-speaking Jews was at issue. Maligned by non-Jews, it was necessary for them as a group to establish a positive definition of their collectivity. Equally important was to acknowledge one's membership in that community as a component of one's own multifaceted individual identity. Werfel recognized that the "individual" leads a life that is not only empty but also a mere illusion. The latter point is particularly obvious when historical circumstances, such as the racial prejudices of the early twentieth century, confront the would-be "abstract person" with society's version of his or her identity.

In Musa Dagh, Werfel's ideas on identity issues receive their most comprehensive treatment. The problem of false assimilation was to have played a role in the novel from the start, but historical events prompted him to treat the problem as one of much greater urgency. He refuses to accept racial categories as the end-all of personhood, although he has concluded by this point in time that "Jeder Mensch gehört einer Volksgemeinschaft an, ob er will oder nicht, und bleibt mit ihr verbunden." (Lepsius) One must participate in the natural community with loyalty and devotion. He rejects the idea that racial groups are comprised of indistinguishable persons sharing the same basic traits because it is dehumanizing: human beings are defined by their differences, their individuality. Like multiculturalists, Werfel views individuality as being nonstatic: personal identity is pluralistic, comprised of many components which are emphasized or de-emphasized in accordance with the given social circumstance. An essentialist conception of identity loses sight of individuals' plurality. Jürgen Habermas, in his contribution to the multiculturalism debate, also argues against essentialist national identities, calling instead for national identity based on the liberal democratic principles of individual choice and tolerance. "National self-understanding" should be the result of a voluntary decision, not bloodlines; should be "no longer based on ethnicity but founded on citizenship."[99] A democratic, multicultural society respects a wide spectrum of collective identities in coexistence, allowing the individual to embrace, alter, or even reject his or her membership in a collectivity and thereby making individuality a matter of choice. As Lützeler observes, individual identity is in a constant state of flux and "must . . . constantly be newly negotiated and determined."[100] Habermas's democratic solution acknowledges the need for flexibility in identity and provides for a societal climate in which flexibility and plurality are tolerated. For Werfel, individuality is first asserted within the greater community through a conscious choice to act, and the highest level of individuality is located in one's relationship with God. This, however, can be reached only after having understood and played out one's predetermined role in the collective life of the community. Service to one's community is an expression of love, without which no relationship with God is possible.

That these ideas contradicted some popular opinions of the time did not elude Werfel. They were quite self-consciously "untimely observations." He felt it was especially important to confront the discourses of racism and secularization, since the popular assumptions within these discourses ruled out any possibility that his ideas could be considered seriously. The novel was particularly well suited to this task. Instead of explicitly stating his rejection of racism and secularization in a prosaic manner, the medium of the novel offered a more subtle approach: the two discourses are *demonstrated* to be invalid. On the topic of secularization, God is shown to be right in the thick of things. Believers are the wisest and most humanistic characters in the novel; nonbelievers' eyes are opened to the workings of an active God; and miracles occur for no other reason than God's will. Racial discourse is also indirectly criticized. Nationalism is repeatedly demonstrated to be the brutal outgrowth of racial pride. The main character himself must grapple with the extent to which his race determines his identity, nor is it depicted to be a trivial struggle. The reader is asked to identify with Gabriel, to understand his dilemma, and ultimately to question the validity of these two dominant discourses themselves. Gabriel's service to his community is both commendable and fulfilling, but even more gratifying is his ability to transcend the community and retain his individuality. No reader who also considers him- or herself to be an individual—and Werfel could safely assume that the majority of his readers thought this of themselves—could be unmoved by Gabriel's development. He has chosen to play the role God intended for him, and having completed his service to the Armenian community, he can now perceive in all clarity his special individuality:

> Was it imagination, or had he really spoken the words: "For some time now, I've known with the stoniest conviction that God intends to use me in some way." Now he knew the whole depths of that intention. Now it was no longer merely freedom, comfort, and joy that filled his heart. No, something new, entirely new, burst into his consciousness. The ecstasy of supernatural unity, the ghostly ray. My life is guided, and therefore safe. (815)

The supernatural connection, that comprehension of totality scientists and Philosophers of Nature like Haeckel sought in vain, is a possibility for those who go against the grain of the dominant discourses and listen for the presence of God within themselves, which is their true identity.

5
Reception and Literary Response

A READER'S RECEPTIVE DISPOSITION TOWARD A WORK MAY BE INFLUenced by a wide variety of issues concerning the author's biography, the genre and theme of the work, and the recipient's own sociohistorical situation. Acquaintance with earlier works by the same author can motivate a more skeptical or receptive initial attitude toward the new work, or even cause the reader to reject it out of hand. In the same vein, aspects of the author's biography (to the extent that they are known), such as age, political sympathies, religious convictions, or association with other contemporary literary figures, contribute to the formation of the reader's "horizon of expectations" (Hans Robert Jauß) regarding this work. Generic and stylistic expectations also play a role: does the reader hold verse (drama, historical fiction, etc.) in high esteem, is a flowery or more linguistically economical style preferred? How does this work fit into the established literary tradition? Finally, the recipient's personal history and current social situation may influence his or her final assessment of the sort of question to which the work represents an answer. To readers of different historical time periods, the same text can provide an answer to radically different questions.

In the following, these topics will be addressed in connection with the reception of Werfel's *The Forty Days of Musa Dagh*. The primary materials to be analyzed are reviews of the novel from German publications dating from 1933, the year it appeared in Germany; American and British reviews of the English translation, which became available one year later; sales promotion materials for *Musa Dagh* at the time of its publication; and more recent scholarly evaluations of the novel. Finally, Edgar Hilsenrath's novel, *The Story of the Last Thought* (1989), which also treats the topic of the Armenian genocide, will be analyzed as a literary response to Werfel's work.

Contemporary German Reception of *Musa Dagh*

By 1933, Werfel was a well-known literary figure in Germany and Austria. His early poetry had established him as one of the most promising young writers in the German language, receiving public exposure and the critical acclaim of the likes of Karl Kraus (until a childish incident made a personal enemy of the influential critic); his dramas were performed on Austrian and German stages; on speaking tours he attracted audiences of considerable size; and his first novellas and novel had also received critical as well as popular attention. In light of these facts, it seems, at a first glance, somewhat surprising that *Musa Dagh* was reviewed in only a very few German-language newspapers and journals.

One might be tempted to attribute the lack of attention to a professional bias against the genre of the historical novel. A 1933 article, although it praises some merits of the historical novel, informs us that the genre has "an era of success behind it"[1]—a quality which more often than not engenders misgivings about a genre, topic, or author. Hermann Hesse lends additional credence to the theory that historical novels were suspect in the eyes of literary experts when he reviews an Icelandic representative of the genre as a happy exception to the rule: "The historical novels that one read with enthusiasm in one's early youth later turned out to be shams; people are suspicious of this genre. All the more pleasant to find the occasional exception!"[2]

Another possible factor contributing to the unexpectedly small amount of critical attention given to *Musa Dagh* in German publications is the unwillingness to offend the Turkish ally. Anticipating a negative reaction to the portrayal of the Turkish government in the novel, the publisher himself, Paul von Zsolnay, attempted to preclude a conflict by providing not only a complimentary copy but also a conciliatory interpretation of its contents to the Turkish representative in Vienna. Although Werfel's book is unmistakably critical of the persecution of Turkish Armenians, Zsolnay writes,

> I believe nonetheless that Franz Werfel was successful in being neutral, in that he constructed figures on both sides that combine all the merits of the nations. I believe, for example, that in the characters

of the old sheik, the Agha Rifaat Bereket and Dr. Nezimi Bey, and furthermore the representative Turkish country-dwellers, he introduced the Turk into European literature in a way unlike any previous portrayal.[3]

He also takes the opportunity to remind the Turkish representative that, since the Turkish statesmen appearing in the novel had all been removed from office by the new government, "today's" Turkey was in no way the object of criticism. Such arguments proved to be ineffectual. Protests were lodged against the anti-Turkish content, and by February of 1934—*Musa Dagh* had appeared in November 1933—the novel was banned in Germany. (Later, official Turkish protests also prevented the American film company Metro-Goldwyn-Meyer from carrying out its plans to produce a grand-scale film from the wildly popular book.)

Still, it is surprising that so little was written about *Musa Dagh* before it was officially banned. For, despite the fact that Werfel was among the "burned" authors in Germany (May 1933), the novel sold extremely well while it was available: "Even though no publicity for the book was permitted within the boundaries of the Reich, German booksellers sold all the copies they had ordered."[4] The prohibition of all advertising for *Musa Dagh* provides, in all likelihood, the strongest clue for an explanation of the dearth of critical attention in Germany. Jungk notes that "official reaction" to the book was strongly disapproving because the "parallels between Young Turk nationalism and Nazi ideology" were patently obvious to "even the least sensitive reader."[5] Literary critics, more likely to belong to the category of the most sensitive readers, must have recognized the potential perils of recommending such a novel to the public.

Significantly, German reviewers either gloss over or do not mention at all aspects of the novel which could, by association, reflect unfavorably upon the German government. The World War I German-Turkish military alliance is not spoken of; there are no parallels drawn between Jewish fate and Armenian fate; the persecution of religious minorities is not among the "main themes" identified; and the fact that Werfel is a Jewish author is entirely left out of the discussions. By contrast, what does stand out in these reviews is the rootedness of the interpreters in their historical situation between the calamitous experience of the war and the growing acceptance of national-socialist rhetoric.

The earlier-mentioned 1933 article on the merits of the historical novel as a literary genre sheds some light on the effects that the war experience had on many Germans. The historical novel is praised for its ability to cross national boundaries, explain historical occurrences in an objective manner, and reunite Europeans as human beings after an ugly, divisive war of unprecedented scale. There seems to be a particular concern for the German image in the world; the laudable historical novels by German authors show the world the "real" Germany, a country much better than its tarnished postwar reputation:

> These books inspired confidence. They helped to enlighten. They demonstrated how history happened. Their knowledge was independent—their attitude was European. They initiated objectivity. That in itself had a political effect. Their authors rendered great services toward understanding. In their *Vaterland* the princes had abdicated. In their novels—the history of princes abdicated. It seemed as though they came from a better Germany. Their insight reconciled. Their stories provided lessons for life. The readers of the world had been alienated by the world history that they had experienced. By means of the history that they read, they came together again.[6]

This desire to have the German image restored is apparent in a December, 1933 review of *Musa Dagh* in the monthly journal *Der Querschnitt*.[7] After briefly describing the historical tragedy of the Armenians, the reviewer devotes the second half of his opening paragraph to extolling the virtues of the German pastor Johannes Lepsius. The fact that any Armenians had been spared during the First World War, he tells us, is "first and foremost thanks to Pastor Johannes Lepsius from Potsdam, ... who in the midst of the war never ceased to cry out to humans' conscience for these innocent victims of national policy." Werfel's main accomplishment with his novel, it would seem, is in having composed a tribute to this exemplary German: "Werfel built a monument for this crusader for holy compassion and tolerant love of humanity in his book ... An unforgettable statue of German idealism, German humanity."

Not only the redemption of the German image in the world but also the self-image of Germans as a *Volk* is palpably present as an urgent concern in these reviews of *Musa Dagh*. Clearly, the national-socialist rhetoric promoting the sacrifice of individualist concerns for the overall well-being and unity of the *Volk* has found some resonance even among the literary critics in this historical moment of continued economic woes in Germany. Instead of identifying the theme of Gabriel's personal identity in transition—which, as we have seen earlier, is in the end a highly individualistic result—the reviewers latch on to the theme of the struggle of the *Volk* to defend its existence and link it to the necessity of the individual dedicating him- or herself absolutely to the greater communal cause. So, for example, the critic for the *Vossische Zeitung* sees Gabriel's "homecoming ... from his 'individuality' to the fate of his people"—the sacrifice of his individuality for the sake of his *Volk*—as the admirable culmination of his personal development rather than as simply one stage of that development.[8] The *Querschnitt* reviewer also highlights this aspect of the book, tying Gabriel's efforts to defend his people to contemporary postwar concerns. This struggle, he writes, "has been experienced more than once by all of us who went through the war years. And we are all included in this Armenian Gabriel Bogradian [sic], ... who, in his people's hour of need, finds his way back to it and merges with it." In addition, this review reminds the reader in no uncertain terms that the *Volk* is constantly in danger from outside forces and must be protected with vigilance. He considers Werfel's novel to be "the epic story of the coming-to-be of a people, of its struggle for external and internal existence, of its victory over the constantly new danger that threatens every people, that is, that it may lose the defining aspect of its inner cohesion and become an amorphous mass."

Absolute, unquestioning dedication to the national cause is so fundamental that the *Vossische Zeitung* reviewer finds it necessary to criticize Werfel for the excessive objectivity he displays in the novel. "The non-Armenian" Werfel does a disservice to Armenians by de-emphasizing the sacred importance of the *Volk* above all else. An Armenian novelist, the review argues, would have dispensed with objectivity:

Trusting in the divine powers of his nation and the righteousness of that struggle which seems holy to him, he would have depicted the helpers as angels and the enemies as devils, which is not to be confused with black-and-white depiction, and he would have attempted in this way to link his nation's struggle with the realms of the eternal.

For similar reasons, he rejects the conclusion of the story. Gabriel's death on the Musa Dagh, in isolation from his people, seems inexplicable. Indeed, he comments, "We feel justifiably insulted in our sympathy. Why on earth does Gabri Bagradian stay behind?" Disapprovingly, he reports that Bagradian "believes only now to have become an 'individual', 'more real than all people or any nation' and also 'more than part of a bloodstream' after having passed through the 'penfold of a commune.'" Since it represents such a denial of the blood community, such a celebration of the individual, the novel's conclusion is dismissed as "nothing other than a misunderstanding and reaction." Grudgingly, however, he concedes that Werfel deserves some respect for recalling to public memory the Armenian tragedy: "The annihilation of the Armenians, this remnant of an indogermanic people with an ancient Christian heritage, should not have happened to this degree with us as mute spectators . . ."—but one suspects that the sympathy for the Armenians stems from identification with a Christian, "indogermanic" Volk.

Jewish-German reviews of Musa Dagh exhibit a markedly different horizon of expectations. The difference is apparent already in the title of the review in the Jüdische Rundschau (December 1933): "Struggle of the Weak."[9] The novel is explicitly interpreted as the story of the persecution of minorities; moreover, the position of the Armenians is directly linked to that of German Jews. Much like the Vossische Zeitung, this reviewer, Bertha Badt-Strauß, identifies the theme of the "fateful struggle of an entire nation. . . ." By contrast, however, she also praises the portrayal of Bagradian's individual identity struggle: "and yet, as befits the 'Philanthropist' Werfel who cannot shed his individualistic skin, the fate of a solitary person is portrayed." Badt-Strauß sketches the protagonist's development from involuntary but inescapable participation in the fate of his community, to his active commitment toward its rescue, and concludes that his decision to forego personal rescue and meet his death on the Musa Dagh is fully understandable: "He cannot return to the world of cities and quarreling nations. He *desires* his death; and welcome is the Turkish bullet that lays him down upon the grave of his son." This is not first and foremost the story of a community's self-preservation, as the non-Jewish reviews would have it, but rather primarily a portrayal of the effects of "racial hatred" upon the identity of the assimilated minority individual. In both recognizing and highlighting the parallels between Armenian and Jewish persecution, the reviewer is anything but ambiguous:

> there is a certain historical justice in the fact that a *Jewish* poet had to portray the Armenians' problem and therewith the problem of *minorities* overall in this invaluable book. Ktat twam asi—you are the one who suffers; you are the one who struggles—you are the one who ultimately prevails. The reader senses this in every line of this book; therein lies its final message.

Similarly indicative of German-Jews' sensitivity to their sociohistorical situation is the review of *Musa Dagh* appearing in the Berlin monthly *Der Morgen*.[10] The journal has a vested interest in Jewish topics, as evidenced in the editorial commentary directly following the *Musa Dagh* review in this issue: the editorial reports with approval on the recent consolidation of previously independent German-Jewish youth organizations into the nationally unified "Alliance of German-Jewish Youths" and notes that such unity among young Jews is necessary despite the differences existing between them. "Until now the independent alliances have justifiably accounted for their autonomy with their unique ideological stance. Now a new German-Jewish stance will have to be found."[11] Discrimination against Jews necessitated their organizing as Jews even though they may previously have felt to be anything but a homogeneous or even a separate group. This thought appears also to guide the interpretation of Werfel's novel by Herbert Friedenthal. In the forty days spent on the mountain, he sees a "symbol of a nation's coming of age, which takes place during the most difficult days of trial." Here, too, it is the fate of the assimilated individual, the reevaluation of personal identity necessitated by circumstance, which seems most compelling to the reviewer: "In this tragedy of a community the drama of Gabriel Bagradian is inserted. Assimilated in France, he is swept by circumstance into the fortunes of the nation which has become foreign to him, and experiences, like his people, a national rebirth."

Precisely this sort of interest in the inner development of an individual was regarded in national-socialist circles to be "un-German" and therefore unsavory. A 1933[12] doctoral thesis on Werfel's pre-*Musa Dagh* novels provides ample and detailed information about the horizon of expectations with which the party approached any new literary product this "celebrated poet of Germany's period of foreign infiltration" put out. Even without the thinly veiled parallels between Turkish Armenians and German Jews, *Musa Dagh* offends nearly every precept the national-socialists held dear. A survey of the titles of the thesis' subchapters within the main chapter (itself revealingly entitled: "The Basic Position of Franz Werfel's Novels as a Contrast to the Literary Will of the Present") suffices to predict with substantial confidence how the novel would be received in official party circles. The subchapter titles are all constructed to indicate an opposition: Werfel vs. German. Thus, for example, the first of these addresses the problem of individualism as discussed previously: "Egocentric Poetry—Community Poetry." Werfel is shown to be a writer obsessed with the "cult" of the individual, blind to the collective life of the *Volk,* in all his works. "Never," Rheinländer-Möhl reproves, "does the line lead beyond the purely internal individual concerns of a single, isolated person into the broader richness of collective lifestyle which lifts us contemporaries, as *the* great experience of the hour, above our self and its private feelings."[13] As Robert Weninger has shown elsewhere, professional literary critics must often operate under restrictions, be they moral or political.[14] In the case at hand, we may assume that the German reviewers of *Musa Dagh* de-emphasized the prominent theme of Gabriel's identity development either due to having political convictions similar to those of the national-socialists or in order to avoid conflict with the party in power.

A further look at Rheinländer-Möhl's categories indicates that many other aspects of *Musa Dagh* made it a natural object for denunciation along party lines; only the fact that it took several months to officially condemn the novel might be considered surprising. The slow-turning wheels of a new government are likely to blame for the delay. As a character type, Gabriel is not only too psychologically self-involved, he is also intellectual and unheroic by nature. "The present times reject intellectualism," Rheinländer-Möhl writes, buttressing her assertion with a quote from Hitler.[15] The subchapter, "The Type: the Unheroic Stranger—the Heroic Model," maintains that "[t]he present times require active, aggressive, manly-powerful literary characters...." Gabriel, who criticizes Stephan publicly for his rash but indisputably heroic capture of the howitzers, and who allows himself to be shot unceremoniously at the end of the novel, is far removed from being the heroic role model sought after in 1930s Germany. In addition, the novel is openly critical of government as a corrupt, villainous entity (subchapter: "Politics: Unconnectedness—National Awareness"), and portrays war in its ugliest manifestations ("Pacifism: Weakly Rejection of War—Power-Conscious Will for Peace"). Finally, of course, Werfel had little chance of having his novel promoted in reviews because of his Jewishness. The horizon of expectations concerning both his work and his person were manifest:

> The Prague Jew Franz Werfel was never able to think and feel in a truly German way. His endeavor was always to be an international poet who lauds a humanity which stands above all races, removed from all natural, national bonds.[16]

The German reviews of *Musa Dagh* extracted what was currently palatable and emphasized those aspects, Jewish-German reviews interpreted the novel in relation to contemporary minority problems; in all, few publications in Germany deemed it wise to give press to this "foreign" work.

"A Christmas Book for Practically Anyone but a Mohammedan" Reception of *Musa Dagh* in English Translation

Hans Wagener identifies Franz Werfel as one of the most successful, "if not the most successful German author of the twentieth century on the American book market," and credits principally the American literary critics of the 1930s with having played an immensely supportive role in popularizing his works.[17] Wagener's study traces Werfel's reception in America from its modest beginnings—sporadic and mixed reviews of early prose works (*Verdi, Class Reunion, The Man Who Conquered Death*)—to the peak of his popularity (*The Song of Bernadette*), singling out *The Forty Days of Musa Dagh* as the work that secured his reputation as one of Europe's prominent novelists.[18] This novel, which appeared in its English translation shortly before the December holidays in 1934, was an enormous hit. It was designated book-of-the-month by three different book clubs, received a great deal of press, was marketed aggressively, and was among the five best-selling books of the year 1935 in the United States (some sources list it as the number one seller). In his short treatment of American critical response to *Musa Dagh*, Wagener notes that despite its enormous popularity, the reviews, though quite positive, did not proclaim it to be a truly great work: "The novel was considered to be very good, but not a really great book, too long-winded, somewhat too schematic, above all flawed in the characterization of the protagonist."[19]

Although some reviews do indeed exhibit the sort of mixed reaction that Wagener describes, a more exhaustive examination of the English-language reviews does not bear this out to be the rule. Of the sixteen contemporary American and British reviews located for this study, nine may be described as rave reviews featuring superlatives and comparisons with other "great works" of literature almost in excess, five are of the nature described—overwhelmingly positive though reluctant to designate *Musa Dagh* as a classic, and only two are principally critical. Excluding the British reception does not affect the balance, as fully half of the American reviews are of the "rave" variety, while the two negative reviews stem from doctrinally specific (Marxist, Catholic) viewpoints.

Many *Musa Dagh* reviewers, in their profession seldom at a loss for words of criticism, find themselves embarrassed at their inability to adequately summarize what they perceive to be the novel's strengths. The reader is informed that the novel simply defies summarization. Lewis Gannett of the *New York Herald Tribune* finds it to be "too rich to spoil by summary repetition."[20] The reviewer for *The Atlantic* feels similarly unable to communicate the full range of *Musa Dagh*'s merits, recounting the plot only "in inadequate outline" and claiming that "the attempt to give any fair impression of its richness leaves one with a feeling of helplessness,"[21] a problem shared by several of his colleagues, who likewise appeal that "No description can do justice to this narrative,"[22] and that it is "not a book that can be sketched lightly."[23]

Superlatives, as noted above, abound in American and British reviews of *Musa Dagh*. The novel is touted repeatedly as an "epic" work; one reviewer surpasses his colleague's rave reviews by recommending that Werfel be awarded the next Nobel Prize for literature. However, the critical acclamation is more valuable in those instances in which the reviewers were able to formulate clearly those aspects of the novel which made it so highly recommendable. Analysis of the praise heaped on the book will provide some insight into the literary and real-world horizon of expectations specific to 1930s America and, to a lesser extent, England.

The New York Times devoted the entire first page of its book review section to "Franz Werfel's Heroic Novel. A Dramatic Narrative That Has Stirring Emotional Force," complete with a large, flattering photograph of the author himself.[24] The headline is strikingly similar to others ("Heroic Stand of Armenians Becomes Epic. Werfel Writes Magnificent Novel of Christmas,"[25] "Armenian Epic,"[26] "Armenian Heroism in Tragic Forty Days"[27]) and shares a language common to nearly all the reviews of *Musa Dagh*. What stands out is the enthusiasm for an "epic" testimonial of human heroism and courage. Professional reviewers and reading public alike seem to be searching for some evidence of human goodness. The novel was being received by an audience whose confidence in humankind had been shaken by the experience of the First World War. Unlike the German public, which had to contend with both the military defeat and the negative image of its nation's culpability for the war, Americans felt no particular need to restore confidence in their nationhood. They were, however, jaded by ugly wartime incidents and had formed lower expectations of humanity's own ability to be humane as a result. In the reception of Werfel's novel, one senses the need to have the reputation of humanity in general restored.

William Saroyan, who was just coming into his own as a literary figure in America with his *Daring Young Man on the Flying Trapeze,* outlines succinctly the pessimistic historical attitude that informs the reception of *Musa Dagh:*

> The world was mad with the lust to kill. No nation could point an accusing finger at the government for its little indulgence. Who cared about a handful of Armenians? Political crimes were the rule, not the exception. England was at war. France was at war. Germany was at war. Russia was at war. Western civilization had run amuck. Why couldn't the East enjoy its private fit of barbarism? Destruction was the major occupation of all great races. The strong were killing, the weak were being killed.[28]

The great valor and courage of Werfel's characters, the humanity of the French rescuers in the historical incident, provide the reader with a reason to cast off this pseudo-Darwinist irony (survival of the fittest) and skepticism toward Western civilization and human nature. "At a time of chaos and confusion," Saroyan continues, "Franz Werfel reveals the naked heart of man, who is weak yet strong, sinful yet virtuous, mortal yet godly, evanescent yet timeless." The *London Mercury* also refers to the spiritual content of *Musa Dagh* as a trait separating it from other contemporary novels: next to other current fiction, it claims, Werfel's novel "stands out like a mountain among molehills. It is a big book not only quantitatively . . . but also artistically and, what is rarer, spiritually."[29] The *New York Times,* which finds that the novel "falls short of greatness," notes that it nonetheless "has a kind of grandeur, and it tells a story which it is almost one's duty as an intelligent human being to read," adding that this particular duty is also a pleasure to fulfill. The historical proximity of the incident recounted in the novel increases its timeliness: "This is in every sense a true and thrilling novel; but it is concerned with a moment in history still so close to us . . . that it looms up as more than a novel; it is a social and historical document as well."

Another observation common to the majority of American and British reviews is that Werfel, a Jew, has chosen the story of a people, the fate of which is so similar to that of his own. The German reviews had made no reference to the parallel aspects of the persecution of the two minorities, and although the argument might be made that the parallels had become substantially more obvious during the year lying between the novel's appearance in Germany and its translation into English, we also cannot ignore that the Jewish-German reviews of 1933 had little trouble recognizing the connections. On several occasions, the mention of Werfel's Jewish background comes in an odd context: it is noted that the novel was the January 1934 choice of the Catholic Book Club "although it was written about members of another church by a Jew,"[30] or elsewhere, "though written about non-Catholics and by a Jew."[31] The surprise at this selection by the Catholic Book Club was apparently not unwarranted, as the unsympathetic review in *The Catholic World* would indicate.[32] Though the reviewer believes Werfel to be "a recent convert from Judaism to Catholicism," he finds his religious sensibilities offended by Gabriel's "illicit love and the adultery of his wife." He cannot understand the critical acclaim the book has received elsewhere and is led to wonder "why the Catholic Book Club should have chosen as its book of the month, this one which contains no true appreciation of Christianity (much less of Catholicism)—nor even the religious quality of the Armenians."

In general, however, discussions of Werfel's religious convictions are absent, and his Jewish background is mentioned only in connection to the timeliness of the minority theme. Typical of most reviews is Robert Cantwell's opinion that "the fate of the Jews in Germany, since Franz Werfel is Jewish, may account for the peculiar poignancy and timeliness, the urgency of 'The Forty Days of Musa Dagh.'"[33] The *Times Literary Supplement* speculates in similar fashion that "[i]t may be that the tragedy of his own race ... has inspired him to write the epic of another persecuted people, the Armenians."[34] The *New York Herald Tribune* also recognizes the greater relevance of the novel as a "saga of a minority people" which "reaches out into the world, as the saga of every minority people does"; *Time* magazine praises it as "more than a stirring tale, a passionate defense of a persecuted minority" with "implications that make it unwelcome in Germany"; and even a negative review in *The Nation* credits it with being an "epic celebration of the sufferings of a minority race."[35] Though most reviews liken the situation of Armenians to that of German Jews, few go so far as the *New York Herald Tribune* reviewer, who directly equates Turkey with Germany, and Enver Pasha with Hitler. "It would be superb irony," he feels, "if the next Nobel Prize to go to a writer in the German tongue should be awarded to a Jew born in Prague and forced out of his chosen Germany by the Turkish passions of Adolph Hitler." By contrast, the *Springfield Sunday Union and Republican* cites the discrimination against German Jews but does not consider it to be as villainous as the treatment of Turkish Armenians. In 1934, it was still possible to believe that "the provocation of the Armenians was, of course, far bolder and the manner of persecution much more cruel," for how many were able to anticipate the grisly culmination of Nazi rhetoric in the gas chambers?

Werfel was not a widely read author in America when *Musa Dagh* appeared in its English translation; therefore, the reading audience did not approach this novel with well-defined expectations about its author. There are some indications that certain expectations existed of German novels in general, however. German literature seems to have had the reputation of tending toward philosophical musing, long-windedness, and thoroughness of preparation and presentation (the American public was, significantly, well acquainted with Thomas Mann's *Magic Mountain*). *Musa Dagh* is described in a few reviews in terms of the expected "uniquely German" characteristics. The *Chicago Daily Tribune* alludes to one of these characteristics when it praises the accurate historical content of the novel: "With the usual German meticulousness of detail, he assembled every known fact about those epic days...." Robert Cantwell refers to another supposed German trait, in this case a negative one, that "Germanic, idealistic, petty-bourgeois philosophizing" Werfel had happily avoided in writing *Musa Dagh*.[36]

Although Werfel's earlier works were not familiar to the reading public, several professional reviewers were well-acquainted with the author and often compared *Musa Dagh* to his previous literary products. Several critics use the *Musa Dagh* review as an opportunity to promote earlier Werfel books that had gone unacclaimed. Harry Hansen recounts that when *Verdi* had appeared in an English translation, he had "tried, through these columns and elsewhere, to stimulate interest in this brilliant work ... But although Werfel came before the public again with other novels and plays, he never found the following awarded lesser men." With *Musa Dagh* receiving the unanimous recommendation of the judges for the Book of the Month Club, Werfel would finally have the attention he was due.[37] The *New York Post* reviewer also refers the reader back to earlier, neglected works: "if you will go back to his 'Verdi' you will find it a very fine novel, indeed, and he has written several other good ones, although none so unmistakably outstanding as his latest."[38] There is unmistakable consensus among the reviewers that *Musa Dagh* represents Werfel's finest literary achievement thus far. In fact, Robert Cantwell, who had been perplexed by the critical acclaim given to *The Pure in Heart* and *The Pascarella* by European reviewers, expresses his surprise at the quality of *Musa Dagh:* "The works of Franz Werfel were known to me through two translations, 'The Pure in Heart' and 'The Pascarella Family,' both windy and pretentious efforts, mysteriously hailed abroad as masterpieces." His expectations of Werfel were correspondingly low: "it seemed to me that if I should sit down and imagine a book in which I felt absolutely no interest, I might have thought of a novel dealing with Armenian life and written by Franz Werfel." Although he objects to Werfel's antimodern tendencies and "theories of race" (the precise nature of which remains unelucidated in his review), Cantwell judges the book to be a "great story" that will affect the life of the reader: "the story itself, the memory of Werfel's account of those days, will remain with a reader long after the author's politics and his racial theories have been forgotten."[39]

Cantwell's prediction on the effect that *Musa Dagh* will have on its readers is echoed by several other reviewers. One reviewer asserts that "the whole dark, useless tragedy, born of racial and religious differences, is indelibly impressed upon the memory";[40] while Saroyan also describes the effects of this aesthetic experience upon extraliterary life: "Its implications cling to the heart and mind of the reader." That *Musa Dagh* was a literary event not only in commercial terms but also in Jauß's sense of social implications (Jauß assesses the aesthetic value of a work in part according to the extend to which it alters the reader's literary or real-world horizon of expectations), is further evidenced in readers' letters to Werfel. An American reader relates to the *Musa Dagh* author that "this book will forever linger in my memory as a symbol of human courage and human endurance. The book has made a greater impression on me than words

5: RECEPTION AND LITERARY RESPONSE

can picture and somehow it has made the present struggle even clearer than before."[41] A Swiss reader not only tells of the novel's impact on his own life, but also recommends that it be more widely circulated for the good of his contemporaries:

> For very personal reasons the book "The Forty Days of Musa Dagh" made an especially strong impression on me, and I expressed repeatedly that every Swiss should read it, every teacher should quote to his students from it, every soldier should acquaint himself with its content, and every woman should see her own life reflected in this book. To the extent that the book was still available, I bought it and gave it to others, and many thanked me for it and had the same deep impression from it.[42]

The literary experience of *Musa Dagh* evidently had the sort of real-life implications upon American 1930s readers that Werfel had hoped for: the preservation of the Armenian tragedy in public memory, the heightened sensitivity toward discrimination against minorities, the restoration of confidence in the valor and resilience of the human spirit, and the reevaluation of popular notions regarding Armenians.

Time magazine addresses this last consideration of the standard image of Armenians, opening its review of *Musa Dagh* with the sentences: "To the ordinary U.S. reader, 'Armenian' suggests Levantine rug-dealers, massacres, Michael Arlen. But last week Author Franz Werfel gave the word a new and heroic significance." Werfel is also commended for bringing to the attention of a wide audience "a news item which few readers even noticed in the greater drama of the world war."[43] It is felt that the Armenians need a literary benefactor both to chronicle their sufferings during the First World War and to provide cultural information about the life of this little-known people. *Golden Book* praises "Herr Werfel" for "putting into a novel a race about whom little or nothing has been written." *Musa Dagh* is enthusiastically recommended as "A Christmas book for practically anyone but a Mohammedan."[44]

PREPARING THE READERSHIP: COMMERCIAL PROMOTION OF *MUSA DAGH*

[T]his book can be read as an adventure story or as a historical romance or as a study in the psychology of danger or as a tract against man's inhumanity to man. However one reads it, one cannot fail to find it remarkable.[45]

The Viking Press did not fail to recognize the potential wide-ranging appeal and historical timeliness of the most recent addition to its literary offerings. The date of its release was advantageous as well, coming shortly before the December holidays, a peak month for book sales. *Musa Dagh* was given a good deal of exposure in order to ensure that it become a well-known title and an obvious gift choice for Hanukkah and Christmas of 1934. Viking ran a full-page advertisement for the novel in the December 16 issue of the *New York Times Book Review,* taking advantage of the many early positive reviews ("unprecedented praise") it had received thus far. Little mention is made of the content of *Musa Dagh* beyond the highly condensed description, "The heroic novel of a little band of men and women fighting for their lives, heritage and faith." Instead, the advertisement reproduces short excerpts from nineteen positively gushing reviews putting Werfel's novel in the company of other "monumental" novels (*All Quiet on the Western Front, Candide, The Case of Sergeant Grischa*) and making references to its predicted lasting importance ("It will never be forgotten.") Its selection by the Book-of-the-Month Club is also mentioned to enhance the overall compelling urgency of the ad.

A 6 January 1935 newspaper ad repeats the strategy of stressing the novel's critical acclaim, however, this time organizing the reviewers' quotes into six different categories, each emphasizing a different quality of the novel. In this way, the publishing house effectively demonstrates that *Musa Dagh* offers something to a broad variety of literary preferences. Not only the literary merit, but also the excitement, historicity, timelessness of theme, emotional power, and popularity of the novel are proclaimed here—each with a boldface caption accompanied by supporting quotes from literary critics: "Work of Enduring Literature / Full-Blooded Adventure / Great Historical Import / A Timeless Epic / A Stirring Human Document / Enormous Popular Success." Offered as further evidence of its success is the note that the book has seen "five huge printings" in as many weeks.

From this point forward, the unprecedented popularity of *Musa Dagh* is consistently included in its further marketing.

"Never before have we published a book which has fired the imaginations of so many people in so short a period," Viking Press proudly declares. Great care is taken to avoid the impression that Werfel's novel is merely light fiction. "It has won recognition because it is great literature...," a 20 January advertisement assures the potential reader, while also stressing the must-read nature of the work: "[It] at once became a chief topic of conversation from coast to coast wherever intelligent people gathered."

Once the novel's success was established, Viking focused its promotional efforts on readers' fascination with its historical content. A February, 1935 advertisement sheds light on Werfel's research and the lengthy writing process by recounting in detail "The story of the writing of a sensationally successful novel." One learns about Werfel's trip to the Near East, the interviews made there, his subsequent painstaking research on Turkish Armenians, and—for the first time—many details of the story and its characters. In a conscious effort to tantalize the as yet uninitiated, a great deal of the plot and several subplots is recounted up to the fortieth day spent on the mountain. This portion of the advertisement ends, however, at this juncture with a teaser: "As for the culmination of the desperate defence—only Franz Werfel can recount the climactic happenings of that fortieth day when Enver Pasha gathered all his strength for a final not-to-be-denied attack and Gabriel, standing among the remnants of his forces, heard the sound that rose from off the sea...."

Much like the professional reviews of *Musa Dagh,* the Viking advertisement campaign for the novel prepared the American public for a literary experience that would speak to contemporary needs and expectations. Post-World War I pessimism was countered by this novel rich in its affirmation of the human spirit. In addition, *Musa Dagh* satisfied a wide spectrum of readers' requirements by offering a dramatic, suspenseful story line while simultaneously maintaining a sophisticated literary style; by demanding both emotional and intellectual participation in a fictional rendering of historical events; by presenting an accurate and at times disturbingly graphic account of events historically not far removed from the recipients' own experience, without frightening them away from the topic altogether; and by revealing the atrocities to which discrimination against any minority group can lead, thus sensitizing a substantial reading population to minority issues in general. That the timing of the English translation of *Musa Dagh* could hardly have been more appropriate is reflected in the tenor of both the professional reviews and the publisher's marketing campaign. Both contributed to the enthusiasm with which the novel was received by the public.

Recent Reception of *Musa Dagh*

With few exceptions, more recent evaluations of *Musa Dagh* come in the form of scholarly analyses published in professional journals. Furthermore, Franz Werfel's overall reputation within the field of Germanistics is a determining factor in the amount, and the tone, of the attention any single work of his receives. As Wagener notes, "Germanistics in Germany to this day has taken a distanced attitude toward Franz Werfel," an attitude he attributes to the skepticism with which intellectuals approach phenomena of mass appeal. The one hundredth anniversary of Werfel's birth in 1990 occasioned not only a new edition of his works with Fischer Verlag and a Franz Werfel postage stamp, but also renewed scholarly interest in the author. Newspaper columns gave "life-and-work" retrospectives in honor of the anniversary; a few Werfel symposia were organized to evaluate his contribution to German literature. In the former, discussions of single works were necessarily condensed to the space of a short paragraph. The abbreviated nature of these retrospectives evinces the current professional opinion on both author and work.

The enduring distanced disposition of Germanists toward Werfel is apparent. Typical of the more recent articles are Thomas Anz' comments "On the Hundredth Birthday of the Expressionist and Popular Writer Franz Werfel."[46] The skepticism toward Werfel's popular success in the 1930s is undiminished some sixty years after the fact. Werfel was and will ever remain a "popular writer," a cut below the true elite of modern literature. Ulrich Weinzierl, reporting on a Werfel symposium, similarly refers to the author as being "controversial to this day," citing the disagreement even among the attendees of the symposium as to Werfel's literary merit.[47] However, the manner in which Weinzierl opens his article provides some information on the status of *Musa Dagh* in the late twentieth century. The article begins:

> The Armenians still worship him as a national saint, they honor in him the author of the novel "The Forty Days of Musa Dagh". For the recent unveiling of a plaque on Franz Werfel's Vienna residence, a deputy Minister President of the Armenian Soviet Republic in the flesh actually appeared.

Werfel's novel is still recognized, not only by Armenians, as a momentous documentation of the otherwise little discussed Armenian genocide. The lasting significance of his humanistic service to Armenians, already extolled in 1930s reviews, is questioned by none. What separates 1980s and 1990s reviewers from their earlier colleagues is the post-Holocaust perspective they bring to the work—and on this point there is less consensus.

Elisabeth Endres stresses the humanistic character of Werfel's works, referring to him as "the Philanthropist," and contends that "much is worth reading" for today's readers. She applauds the Fischer Verlag for making these works available in the new paperback editions. *Musa Dagh* itself, seen from the historical reality of the Holocaust, "seems to us today like a premonition of an even worse genocide."[48] Artem Ohandjanian, an Armenian writing for a German scholarly journal, agrees that Werfel must have anticipated similar racial persecution of the minority Jews in Germany:

> Werfel saw indications that the genocide of the Armenians could be repeated with the Jewish people. His novel tried not only to call attention to the fate of a nation persecuted with the approval of the German military; Werfel also wanted to warn against similar tendencies in the Germans' thought processes toward their Jewish compatriots.[49]

Others are less willing to credit Werfel with such prescience. Wagener admits that although it may be "tempting to make Werfel the prophet of the fate of his own people," and despite the "uncanny" parallels between Armenian and Jewish persecution, "we must remember that Werfel finished the manuscript in March 1933,[50] well before the active persecution of Jews in Germany had begun." To support his thesis that Werfel did not take the Hitler government seriously enough to predict real trouble for Jews, he cites a letter Werfel wrote to his parents in which he expresses the hope that the current negative atmosphere would lead only to a "brief setback."[51] Lionel B. Steiman makes a similar argument against any prophetic foresight on Werfel's part, stating that, "through the thirties he was not particularly concerned with the danger to the Jews, though in 1940 he expressed the view, extreme for the time, that the Nazis intended the total, physical extermination of his people."[52] But there is other evidence that Werfel was very apprehensive about the nature of the Hitler government. Shortly before the final version of *Musa Dagh* was completed, he writes to Alma that he would like to meet her in Germany once the novel is finished but has definite reservations about the wisdom of taking such a trip. The letter conveys a palpable sense of urgency: "Do you think that we can still travel to Germany?—I will, if you agree, send a dispatch to Munich regarding the facilitation of entry.—But is it not dangerous? And even for you! Write immediately!!"[53] That he would suspect danger for the well-connected non-Jew Alma Mahler certainly indicates that he perceived Hitler to be a serious threat. It is not surprising that he would avoid alarming his parents in Prague with dire predictions.

Of the attention given to *Musa Dagh* in the last two decades, a 1980 article written by Hans Christoph Buch comes closest to resembling a review of the novel.[54] His interest in *Musa Dagh* arose from a trip taken to the Armenian Soviet Republic as a member of a West Berlin literary association, where the group was greeted with the words, "We welcome our friends from Franz Werfel's country!"[55] Like many of the American reviewers in the 1930s, Buch knew little about *Musa Dagh*. Of the author himself, Buch had little more than a quote from Kafka—not one of Kafka's more flattering descriptions of Werfel—to the effect that "Werfel was a thick-walled vessel with fermenting contents which only resounds when shaken from without."[56] His expectations of the novel were correspondingly vague.

Musa Dagh was as compelling for Buch as it had been for the American reviewers who reported that they were unable to put the book down until the last page was read. Buch also speaks of the lasting effects the novel had on him personally, the consequences on the life-world horizon of expectations as discussed previously in the case of the American reading public:

> Werfel's prose had a physical effect upon me like a heavy wine that soaks through all of one's pores and afterwards still clouds the senses. For weeks I could think of nothing else, my entire nervous system, my inner metabolism was preoccupied with the reading material, and when I finally closed the book the horrible fate of the Armenian people had become a part of my own history. At the same time, the book is very suspenseful to read—it has "bestseller qualities", we would say today—, but reading it does not simply arouse disinterested pleasure—the bloody seriousness of the topic prevents that.

As a post-Holocaust recipient of the work, Buch considers *Musa Dagh* to be uniquely qualified to re-infuse the overused word *genocide* with concrete meaning: "One must read Werfel's novel in order to regain a concept of what a genocide really is...."[57] He praises Werfel's ability to communicate the historical horror in its full scope while concentrating the story on the successful Musa Dagh defense, a positive exception to the rule. In addition, he admires the skillfulness with which Werfel moves in the realm of historical fiction, commenting that writers today would lack confidence in the genre's ability to depict a reality so abhorrent:

> An author today would probably have retreated into documentary literature with the argument that reality is after all much more monstrous than any poetic imagination. Precisely that is what Werfel does not do. He has a naive trust in the world-creating power of fiction, and in this way he is able to do what simple documentary literature can do only in the rarest cases: the invented story seems more authentic than the historical reality, because it allows the reader to identify with the victims, to experience the gruesome events through their own eyes.[58]

Although holocaust literature is anything but rare, sixty years of literary production have not added much to Werfel's legacy on the subject of the Armenian genocide. Not until 1989 did a

German author take on the Armenian theme as the main topic of a work. In the following, Edgar Hilsenrath's novel, *The Story of the Last Thought*,[59] will be examined as a literary response to Werfel's *Musa Dagh*.

A "Fairy Tale" of Genocide: Hilsenrath's Armenian Novel

Edgar Hilsenrath's literary rendering of the Armenian genocide differs from Werfel's not only in coming from a post-Holocaust perspective, but also in that Hilsenrath himself is a Holocaust survivor. The latter fact grants him some stylistic liberties, emancipating him from the documentary style felt by Buch to be the most probable choice of post-Holocaust authors. Peter Stenberg considers Hilsenrath's first two novels to be "the first and so far only examples in German-language literature of the satiric, ironic, black-comic description of the destruction of the European Jews in the Second World War," and adds that "such taboo ground can only be pioneered by a member of the victimized culture."[60] In *The Story of the Last Thought,* Hilsenrath continues to cultivate a tone of dark humor in what Frances Spalding describes as "a billowing magic-realist narrative."[61] His "fairy tale" construct allows the narrative to flit backward and forward in time, and to shift at will between story lines that bear to a greater or lesser degree upon the fate of the main character, Wartan Khatisian. Khatisian's story is told to his son Thovma by a "storyteller" who allows Thovma to observe past events and pose questions, and who, in his predilection for lengthy exposition, at times performs a function very similar to Werfel's more conventional authorial commentary. On the topic of the overuse of the word *genocide,* for example, the storyteller makes no attempt to conceal his disdain from Khatisian. The historians, he scoffs, will

> look for words to describe the great massacre and classify it pedantically. They don't know that every human being is unique, that even the village idiot in your father's village has the right to a name. They will call the great massacre "mass-murder," and the scholars among them will say it's called "genocide." Not one smart alec among them

will say it's called "armenocide," and in the end some crank will look up his dictionary and finally announce that it's called "holocaust!".[62]

Sidney Rosenfeld also commends Hilsenrath's stylistic approach to the grim topic, finding that the author is successful "against all esthetic odds" in conveying "the abysmal criminality of totalitarian oppression." Furthermore, Rosenfeld argues, "[I]n casting the novel as an Oriental 'fairy tale,' he precluded rivalry with Franz Werfel's epic on the same theme."[63]

Indeed, the *Story* contains evidence of Hilsenrath's pronounced respect for Werfel's work, for it reproduces or mimics many key elements of *Musa Dagh*. While rivalry is not intended, comparison is unavoidable. Hilsenrath is Werfel's literary successor in the theme of Armenian genocide. That his novel represents a response to *Musa Dagh* is signaled materially on the back cover of the paperback edition of the *Story,* where a literary review comparing the two novels is quoted. Whether it is to stress similarities or differences, reviews of the *Story* inevitably compare Hilsenrath's work with "Werfel's novel 'The Forty Days of Musa Dagh' (1933), that other great portrayal of the Armenian genocide."[64] For Armenians it will take some time before Werfel's novel is referred to as "that other" great portrayal of the Armenian genocide: Ohandjanian's 1990 article on *Musa Dagh* makes no reference whatsoever to Hilsenrath's *Story,* nor could any reviews of the *Story* be found in Armenian journals to date.

Werfel's motivation for writing *Musa Dagh* stemmed from the fear that the Armenian genocide might become a forgotten historical episode. Hilsenrath, who has lived to witness the serious efforts of "revisionist" historians, is equally aware of this danger. Remembering—or not forgetting—is the primary impetus behind his novel. Much of the novel's "prologue" stresses that the Armenians' story is often left out of the official history of the First World War. In a passage illustrative of Hilsenrath's ability to communicate fact through the construct of the fairy tale, Thovma relates to his "storyteller" a conversation he had with an invented "Archivist in the United Nations":

> "I'm looking for that Armenian file," I said. "It's a question of a report on the forgotten genocide."
> "The forgotten genocide?"

"Yes."
"And when is that supposed to have happened?"
"In 1915."
"That really is a long time ago. This is 1988."
"Yes," I said.
"Look here," he said.

When Thovma asks that the files nonetheless be dusted off and given to him, the archivist states dryly, "That would raise clouds of dust and make them cough." The brief scene concludes, "'What's forgotten mustn't be dusted,' said the archivist. 'It's too dangerous.' And with those words he disappeared."[65] Martin Hielscher terms the novel a "black fairy tale" and concludes that its achievement lies in its potential for resuscitating the historical memory of the Armenians who perished: "The only hope in this novel is precisely this fairy tale of the last thought: that the whispering of these thoughts which are immortal and roam the earth eternally will someday penetrate the gaps in Turkish history book."[66]

From the outset, the reader is not allowed to approach the book with expectations of a typical fairy tale. The cover and title page take care to alert the reader that this "fairy tale" is also "an historical novel from Caucasus." Like Werfel, Hilsenrath wants the historical veracity of his literature to be manifest. His fairy tale achieves credibility as a historical document through the inclusion of many elements which had served the same purpose in *Musa Dagh*. Although fictional characters and invented story lines comprise the bulk of Hilsenrath's *Story,* he incorporates the same real historical characters and situations that Werfel had worked into his fiction. The striking similarities in the presentation of the historical content of these two novels speak for the continuing relevance of Werfel's *Musa Dagh* some sixty years after its publication.

Still a source of morbid fascination, for example, is the contrast between the physical appearance and the cruel deeds of Enver Pasha. Werfel had described the Turkish "war god" as follows: "Enver Pasha looked shy, almost embarrassed; from time to time he would open his eyes like a young girl. The narrow hips and sloping shoulders gave his movements a certain delicate grace." (130) Hilsenrath's portrait of Enver also juxtaposes the appearance of feminine innocence and the reality of murderous personality:

> Enver's face is as soft as a girl's, his narrow moustache could have been stuck on. His hands, holding the reins of his horse, look gentle, and the long thin fingers might be a pianist's. An attractive man, a man with sensitive hands and a sensitive face. He is the hangman of the Armenians.[67]

Missing from Hilsenrath's cast of historical villains is Djemal Pasha, who is featured at some length in *Musa Dagh*. In both novels, however, Talaat Bey appears—in both cases only briefly, to be sure, but in precisely the same historical incident. Talaat's effrontery toward the international community in discussing his government's understanding of the "Armenian problem" represents to both authors the Turks' shameless manipulation of the wartime situation. In his brief appearance in *Musa Dagh*, it will be recalled, Talaat brags about his intentions to announce to the world that "la question arméniénne n'existe pas." In Hilsenrath's *Story*, we encounter him in this situation again, delighting in the prospect of holding a press conference during which he will assert:

> Gentlemen, I don't know what you're expecting from us. There is neither an Armenian nationality problem in the disputed Anatolian province of Turkey, nor is there any Armenian question or any sort of Armenian majority. For you see, gentlemen ... according to the best of my information, there aren't any Armenians there any more.[68]

For Werfel, Talaat Bey was the consummate representative of hard-line Turkish inhumanity. Hilsenrath also recognized his comments' symbolic potency and reproduced them to perform the same function in his novel.

As we saw in *Musa Dagh*, the Young Turks' confidence that their Armenian policies would go largely unchallenged by their allies derived from the strategic importance of Turkey during and following the war. Hilsenrath, like Werfel, seems to anticipate readers' outrage at the involvement of the German government and its reluctance to curtail the actions against Turkish Armenians. He, too, documents the vain attempts of the American ambassador Henry Morgenthau and the Reverend Johannes Lepsius to prevent or even retard the rate of the genocide in action. However, their service to the Armenian cause is documented here in more abridged form; Hilsenrath is less concerned with penning a tribute to these two men than Werfel. The storyteller recounts to Thovma a conversation between his father and the American consul:

> "Morgenthau has done everything possible to persuade Enver Pasha," said the consul. "And Morgenthau is the voice of America here."
> "I've heard of Morgenthau," said your father.
> "And a German priest called Lepsius has talked with Enver on behalf of the Armenians."
> "Lepsius?"
> "Yes," said the consul. "That man Lepsius is a German saint. The German consul in Bakir told me he was the true voice of the Germans."
> "What about the Kaiser's voice?"
> "That's the Germans' other voice."[69]

The Holocaust survivor Hilsenrath is less optimistic than Werfel about human heroism. Hilsenrath knows that the unprecedented modern genocide of the Armenians was soon followed by the century's second genocide, and that what is considered in retrospect to have been the "true voice" of the perpetrator nation is of little consequence to the murdered victims. He thus takes a less forgiving attitude toward the German involvement in the Armenian genocide. The intense colonialist competition for Turkey ("Everyone wanted to cut themselves a slice, including the Germans. . . ."[70]) and the correspondingly tricky wartime relations ("They know very well in Constantinople that the Germans won't take any drastic steps. . . ."[71]) are mentioned as they are in *Musa Dagh;* however, Hilsenrath does not finally consider them to be mitigating circumstances. Even the German officers and an Austrian journalist who appear in the novel comprehend what Hilsenrath believes is at issue: "That the extermination of the Armenians in Turkey—the execution of a whole people—depends ultimately not only on their exterminators but also on the silence of their allies."[72] One scene in particular unrelentingly implicates Germany in the crime. This scene attributes the Young Turks' rhetoric of racial difference—which was such a prominent subject of *Musa Dagh*—to European, and especially German, influence. Here a Turk is instructed by a German in racial "science" and terminology, using the corpses of three executed Armenians to demonstrate:

> "Four thousand years ago there was a dolichocephalic race living here," said the German. "But later the dolichocephalic race was driven out by a brachycephalic people." . . .
> "And what are the Armenians?"
> "Brachycephalic. Armeniod, anyway. Thought to be mixed with Dinaric."
> "I don't understand a word."
> "You can see it in those hanged men. Receding chin. Strong, rather hooked nose, light brown skin, curly, rather frizzy dark hair . . . Big, expressive, velvety eyes."[73]

The German's final remark regarding the Armenians' eyes is the height of his callousness—for their eyes had been poked out by their Turkish tormentors.

In his 1980 book, *As Others See Us,* Leo Hamalian tracks the image of Armenians as depicted in literature.[74] Armenian characters are mostly limited to bit parts in literary works; with few exceptions, there is no (non-Armenian) literature with an Armenian theme. Hamalian finds that Armenian characters consistently correspond to a few stereotypes: male characters are usually merchants, warriors, intellectuals, spies, or men-of-the-world; female Armenians are represented by the innocent virgin beauty, the woman of erotic attractions and dubious moral character, the earth-mother, or more recently the educated woman. Werfel's *Musa Dagh* is credited with being an exception both in having an Armenian theme and in featuring characters that challenge preconceptions about Armenians. As discussed earlier, one of Werfel's goals in writing *Musa Dagh* was to avoid clichés about the ruthless Armenian merchant. In portraying village life, he gently educates the reader: one learns that the majority of Armenian men are simple farmers and craftsmen, and that many of the women are educated or even respected as leaders within their communities. Hilsenrath similarly uses his novel as a forum to challenge preconceived notions about Armenians; however, his methods differ greatly.

Whereas Werfel's approach is simply to ignore stereotypes and to provide in its place a new (more accurate) image of Armenians, Hilsenrath acknowledges the old stereotypes. In a manner typical of his "dark fairy tale," he allows certain characters verbally to perpetuate the objectionable image. A conversation between Thovma's father and his Turkish interrogator may serve as an example of Hilsenrath's method of first presenting, then correcting the stereotype: "'The Armenians are a race of traders and swindlers. The trustful Turk is defenceless against them.' 'My father is a farmer, Mudir Bey. Most Armenians are simple fathers and artisans.'"[75] Like Werfel, Hilsenrath is aware of the parallels between the negative reputations of Jews and Armenians as dishonest businessmen and disloyal citizens. Ohandjanian elaborates:

> Both peoples were considered to be crafty merchants by nature, had the reputation in Europe and America of being usurers and swindlers. Journalists wrote in feature articles, authors in novellas and novels about the "unpleasant Armenian Jew," travelers in the Orient couldn't get enough of attacking the "swindling Armenian": "The Armenian is and will always be a Jew and a swindler."[76]

The comparison is repeated in Hilsenrath's *Story* during a meeting between a German major and a Turkish Müdir:

> "A few weeks ago I was in Galicia," says the major, "on the Austrian front. And do you know, Mudir Bey, what happened there?"
> "No," says the Mudir.
> "There are too many Jews there. And you know what it's like haggling over things with Jews?"
> "No," says the Mudir.
> "Just like Armenians," says the major. "Those two peoples are so alike you can almost mix them up. It's incredible."[77]

Except for Enver's comment that Morgenthau, as a Jew, would necessarily be on the side of the minority Armenians, there is no explicit reference made in *Musa Dagh* to the parallels between popular preconceptions of the two groups. In this regard, too, Hilsenrath's post-Holocaust perspective may account for the difference in tone and emphasis between the two authors.

Revising the image of a group may be accomplished by replacing the clichés with accurate information on that group's culture or history, an approach taken by both Werfel and Hilsenrath. Both novels inform the reader that the Armenians have an ancient culture and were the first nation to proclaim Christianity as its official religion.[78] One also finds references to the history of the Armenian kingdom and the traditional names attached to that history[79] in both works. The specific aspects of Armenian culture described by Hilsenrath correspond conspicuously to those described in *Musa Dagh*. Both authors demonstrate an interest in the tradition of the *Widjak* celebration.[80] The Armenians' superstitions are exemplified by the same example: the piercing of the afterbirth by seven needles from seven different households to ward off evil.[81] The reader learns in both cases about the Armenian national meal *harisa,* albeit differently. Werfel provides a long description of the meal's preparation which is almost a celebration of the dish. In Hilsenrath's novel, by contrast, *harisa* is spoken of only in disparaging terms, as he allows a Turkish official to describe the dish, which is to be served to an Armenian prisoner in order to strengthen him for a grueling interrogation: "That stuff Armenians eat on their holidays, the Armenian national dish. It's called *harisa.* Every Armenian becomes good-tempered automatically if you stick that mess of overcooked meat and pearl barley under his nose."[82]

This last example is characteristic of the manner in which *Musa Dagh* and *The Story of the Last Thought* are fundamentally different despite having so many aspects in common. Werfel's tribute to *harisa* stands in glaring contrast to the manner in which Hilsenrath made use of the Armenian national dish. While Werfel fetes the tradition, Hilsenrath has it used as part of the torture process. From the two novels, the reader gains the same information about the meal's special status and even its ingredients, but Hilsenrath's version reflects his far less idealistic view of the world.

Musa Dagh by no means trivializes the Armenians' tragedy. On the contrary, it was shown in the previous section that precisely Werfel's sober and at times graphic treatment of human brutality distinguished it as a work to be taken seriously by American readers of the 1930s. The realism with which he depicted the historical events lent the work a tone of grim sincerity to which his contemporaries were receptive. At the same time, however, Werfel selected an incident with a positive outcome—not for its representative value, since he leaves no room for doubt in his novel that the escape of the Musa Dagh villagers was a rare exception, but rather to reassert his unwavering belief in the human spirit. This idealistic aspect of *Musa Dagh* was a second contributing factor to its success in the 1930s and, as Buch testifies, still retains its power for today's reader.

With the spectre of the Holocaust now a component of Western readers' imagination, particularly for the readers of German literature, writers on the topic of genocide face challenges that simply did not exist in 1933. Rosenfeld correctly identifies in Hilsenrath's "casting the novel as an Oriental 'fairy tale'" an attempt to "surmount the impotence of art in the face of an atrocity made all the more untellable by our knowledge of the cataclysm that succeeded it." *Musa Dagh* is a "literary event" in Jauß's sense that literary successors still respond to it, that they hope to "imitate, outdo, or refute it." *The Story of the Last Thought* does not eclipse *Musa Dagh*'s relevance, but it responds to it in a manner that acknowledges the events that occurred after 1933. Hilsenrath counters Werfel's realism with folkloric fantasy, his solemnity with bawdiness and dark humor, and his message of hope with confrontational denunciation and pessimism. His *Story,* in short, does justice both to Werfel, as its literary progenitor, and to the sensibilities of post-Holocaust readers.

Notes

Chapter 1. The Theme of Identity in the Works of Franz Werfel

1. 1938 Questionaire by W. Paulsen, document in Special Collections, University of California at Los Angeles.
2. Philip Gleason, "Identifying Identity: A Semantic History," *The Journal of American History* 69, no. 4 (1983): 910.
3. Ibid., 914.
4. Quoted in Robert Coles, *Erik H. Erikson. The Growth of His Work* (Boston and Toronto: Little, Brown & Co., 1970), 376.
5. Peter Berger, "Identity as a Problem in the Sociology of Knowledge," *European Journal of Sociology* 7, no. 1 (1966): 111.
6. Alex Haley, *Roots* (Garden City, N.Y.: Doubleday, 1976).
7. Ibid., 32, 34.
8. See Gerald Early, "American Education and the Postmodernist Impulse," *American Quarterly* 45, no. 2 (1993): 220–29; also Mark Poster, "Postmodernity and the Politics of Multiculturalism: The Lyotard-Habermas Debate over Social Theory," *Modern Fiction Studies* 38, no. 3 (1992): 567–80.
9. Jean-François Lyotard, *The Postmodern Condition: A Report on Knowledge,* trans. Geoff Bennington and Brian Massumi (Minneapolis: University of Minnesota Press, 1989).
10. Steven C. Rockefeller, "Comment," in *Multiculturalism and "The Politics of Recognition,"* by Charles Taylor, ed. Amy Gutman (Princeton: Princeton University Press, 1992), 88.
11. Taylor, *Multiculturalism,* 44.
12. In Franz Werfel, *Poems,* trans. Edith Abercrombie Snow (Princeton: Princeton University Press, 1945), 13. Many Werfel poems are not published in translation. In such cases, the German will be quoted and a translation in prose provided. All such translations are mine.
13. In Franz Werfel, *Das Lyrische Werk,* ed. Adolf D. Klarmann (Frankfurt a.M: Fischer, 1967). All poems quoted in German are taken from this volume.
14. Taylor, *Multiculturalism,* 25.
15. Werfel, *Poems,* 87.
16. K. Hyršlová, "Zur Frage der Heimat im Werke Franz Werfels," *Zeitschrift für Slawistik* III, no. 5 (1958): 729. Translations are mine.
17. Gary B. Cohen, *The Politics of Ethnic Survival: Germans in Prague, 1861–1914* (Princeton: Princeton University Press, 1981). Information is taken from table, 92–93: German-speaking citizens of Prague's eight municipal zones and four suburbs comprised 15.3 percent of the population in 1880, 7.0 percent in 1910; when considering just Prague I–VIII, the numbers were 17.5 percent in 1880 and 8.2 percent in 1910.

18. Hugh Puckett, "Franz Werfel's Mission," *Germanic Review* 22 (1947): 124.

19. Ibid., 121. See also Michel Reffet, "Franz Werfel und die Tschechoslowakei," *Österreich in Geschichte und Literatur (mit Geographie)* 27, no. 2 (1983): 85.

20. Heinz Politzer, "Prague and the Origins of Rainer Maria Rilke, Franz Kafka, and Franz Werfel," *Modern Language Quarterly* 16 (1955): 55.

21. Ibid., 54–55.

22. Anna Jacobson, "Franz Werfel: Eine Würdigung," *Journal of English and Germanic Philology* XXVI, no. 3 (1927): 340. Translations are mine.

23. Lore B. Foltin, "The Czechs in the Work of Franz Werfel," in *Studies in Nineteenth and Early Twentieth Century German Literature: Essays in Honor of Paul K. Whitaker,* ed. Norman H. Binger and A. Wayne Wonderley (Lexington, Ky.: APRA Press, 1974), 20.

24. Ibid., 17.

25. Ibid., 19.

26. Hyršlová, *"Frage der Heimat,"* 731.

27. Cohen, *Politics of Ethnic Survival,* 122.

28. Reffet, *Werfel und die Tschechoslovakei,* 85.

29. "Franz Werfel liest," *Prager Presse,* 16 November 1933. Translations are mine.

30. "Sendung der kleinen Völker," *Prager Presse,* 4 November 1934. Translations are mine.

31. Franz Werfel, *The Pure in Heart,* trans. Geoffrey Dunlop (New York: Simon and Schuster, 1931). Parenthetical page numbers will refer to this edition. The translation excludes some passages from the German original, *Barbara oder Die Frömmigkeit* (1929; reprint, Frankfurt a.M: Fischer, 1988), henceforth referred to as *Barbara*. All translations from this edition are mine.

32. *Barbara,* 152.

33. Ibid., 332.

34. Israel S. Stamm, "Religious Experience in Werfel's *Barbara,*" *Publications of the Modern Language Association* 54 (1939): 340.

35. Ibid., 340–41.

36. Ibid., 344.

37. Franz Werfel, *Pogrom* (1926; reprint, Frankfurt a.M: Fischer, 1989). Parenthetical page numbers will refer to this edition. All translations are mine.

38. Gunter E. Grimm, "Ein hartnäckiger Wanderer. Zur Rolle des Judentums im Werk Franz Werfels," in *Im Zeichen Hiobs: Jüdische Schriftsteller und deutsche Literatur im 20. Jahrhundert,* ed. Grimm (Königstein: Athenäum, 1985), 262. Translations are mine.

39. Egon Schwarz, "'Ich war also Jude! Ich war ein anderer!' Franz Werfels Darstellung der sozio-psychologischen Judenproblematik," in *Franz Werfel. Neue Aspekte seines Werkes,* ed. Karlheinz Auckenthaler (Syeged: Jate, 1992), 173. Translations are mine.

40. Ibid.,

41. Ibid., 171.

42. Franz Werfel, "Not the Murderer," in *Twilight of a World,* trans. H. T. Lowe-Porter (New York: Viking Press, 1937).

43. Taylor, *Multiculturalism,* 25.

44. Eduard Goldstücker, "Franz Werfel, Prag und Böhmen," in *Bild und Gedanke: Festschrift für Gerhart Baumann zum 60. Geburtstag,* ed. Gunter Schnitzler et al. (Munich: Fink, 1980), 403.

45. Pavel Eisner, *Franz Kafka and Prague* (New York: Golden Griffin, 1950), 12.
46. Ibid., 35–36.
47. Peter Horwath, "The Erosion of *Gemeinschaft*: German Writers of Prague, 1890–1924," *German Studies Review* 4, no. 1 (1981): 9–10.
48. Kurt Krolop, "Das 'Prager Erbe' und 'das Österreichische,'" *Zeitschrift für Germanistik* (1983): 170. Translations are mine.
49. Eisner, *Kafka and Prague*, 14–15.
50. Hillel Kieval, *The Making of Czech Jewry. National Conflict and Jewish Society in Bohemia, 1870–1918* (New York: Oxford University Press, 1988).
51. Ibid., 5.
52. Ibid., 6.
53. Ibid., 45.
54. Ibid., 7.
55. Horwath, *"Erosion of Gemeinschaft,"* 13.
56. Jürgen Serke, *Böhmische Dörfer. Wanderungen durch eine verlassene literarische Landschaft* (Vienna, Hamburg: Paul Zsolnay, 1987), 9. All translations are mine.
57. Ibid., 72.
58. Ibid., 64.
59. Franz Werfel, *Zwischen Oben und Unten* (1944; München: Langen Müller, 1975), 476. All translations are mine.
60. Reffet, *"Werfel und die Tschechoslowakei,"* 85–86.
61. Foltin, "Czechs in the Works of Frans Werfel," 17.
62. Werfel, *Zwischen Oben und Unten*, 421.
63. Werfel, *Pogrom*, 86.
64. Werfel, *Zwischen Oben und Unten*, 418.
65. Rudolf Hirsch and Ingeborg Schnack, ed., *Hugo von Hofmannsthal. Rainer Maria Rilke. Briefwechsel 1899–1925* (Frankfurt: Insel, 1978), 77. All translations are mine.
66. Werfel, *Zwischen Oben und Unten*, 420.
67. Hirsch and Schnack, *Hofmannsthal-Rilke Briefwechsel*, 77.
68. Ibid., 79.
69. Kieval, *Making of Czech Jewry*, 49.
70. Ibid., 200.
71. Quoted in ibid. 127.
72. Quoted in ibid. 128.
73. Nahum N. Glatzer, Paul Mendes-Flohr, ed., *The Letters of Martin Buber* (New York: Shocken, 1991), 206.
74. Martin Buber, *On Judaism*, ed. Nahum N. Glatzer, trans. Eva Jospe (New York: Shocken, 1967).
75. Ibid., 11.
76. Ibid., 14.
77. Ibid., 15.
78. Ibid., 16.
79. Ibid., 16–17.
80. Ibid., 18.
81. Ibid., 19.
82. Ibid., 18.
83. George Mosse, *Toward the Final Solution* (New York: Fertig, 1978), 104.
84. Grete Schaeder, ed., *Martin Buber. Briefwechsel aus sieben Jahrzehn-*

ten. Band I: 1897–1918 (Heidelberg: Lambert Schneider, 1972), 491. Translation is mine.

Chapter 2. Identity and Historical Community in *The Forty Days of Musa Dagh*

1. Franz Werfel, *The Forty Days of Musa Dagh*, trans. Geoffrey Dunlop (New York: Viking, 1934). Parenthetical page numbers refer to this edition. The translation excludes some passages from the German original, *Die vierzig Tage des Musa Dagh* (1933; Frankfurt a.M. Main: Fischer, 1988), henceforth referred to as *vierzig Tage*. All translations from this edition are my own.
2. Peter Stephan Jungk, *Franz Werfel. Eine Lebensgeschichte* (Frankfurt a.M: Fischer, 1987), 189.
3. George Schulz-Behrend, "Sources and Background of Werfel's Novel *The Forty Days of Musa Dagh*," *Germanic Review* XXVI (1951); Hans Christoph Buch, "Ein Genozid, der offiziell nie stattgefunden hat. Über Franz Werfels Roman *Die vierzig Tage des Musa Dagh*," in Buch, *Waldspaziergang* (Frankfurt: Suhrkamp, 1987).
4. Lionel Abel, "A Poet's Defense of Nationalism," *The Nation* 139, no. 3623 (12 December 1934): 684.
5. Gunter E. Grimm, "Ein hartnäckiger Wanderer. Zur Rolle des Judentums im Werk Franz Werfels," in *Im Zeichen Hiobs: Jüdische Schriftsteller und deutsche Literatur im 20. Jahrhundert*, ed. Grimm (Königstein: Athenäum, 1985).
6. Lionel Steiman, "Werfel, Christianity, and Antisemitism," in *Franz Werfel im Exil*, ed. Wolfgang Nehring and Hans Wagener (Bonn: Bouvier, 1992), 66, note no. 13.
7. See 25 March 1944 letter to Mr. Kearton; 4 October 1938 *Fragebogen* by Paulsen, both located in the Franz Werfel Collection, Special Collections, University of California at Los Angeles.
8. Peter Stephen Jungk, *A Life Torn by History. Franz Werfel 1890–1945*, trans. Anselm Hollo (London: Weidenfeld and Nicolson, 1990), 141.
9. James Davidheiser, "The Quest for Cultural and National Identity in the Works of Franz Werfel," *Perspectives on Contemporary Literature* 8 (1982): 61–63; Gunter E. Grimm, "Ein hartnäckiger Wanderer. Zur Rolle des Judentums im Werk Franz Werfels," in *Im Zeichen Hiobs: Jüdische Schriftsteller und deutsche Literatur im 20. Jahrhundert*, ed. Grimm (Königstein: Athenäum, 1985), 262; Hans Wagener *Understanding Franz Werfel*, (Columbia, S.C.: University of South Carolina, 1993), 123–24; Ritchie Robertson, "Leadership and Community in Werfel's 'The Forty Days of Musa Dagh,'" in *Unser Fahrplan geht von Stern zu Stern. Zu Franz Werfels Stellung und Werk*, ed. Joseph Strelka (Bern: Peter Lang, 1992), 255, 261–63, 266–67.
10. *Vierzig Tage*, 10.
11. Peter Stephen Jungk, "Alma Maria Mahler-Werfel. Einfluß und Wirkung," in *Franz Werfel im Exil*, ed. Wolfgang Nehring and Hans Wagener (Bonn: Bouvier, 1992). All translations are mine.
12. Ibid., 29.
13. Jungk, *Lebensgeschichte*, 244–45.
14. Jungk, "Alma Maria," 27.
15. *Vierzig Tage*, 16.

16. Ibid., 197.
17. Jungk, "Alma Maria," 28.
18. Quoted in Werner Sollers, *Consent and Descent in American Culture* (New York and Oxford: Oxford University Press, 1986), 215.
19. See Sollers; also Vladimir C. Nahirny and Joshua A. Fishman, "American Immigrant Groups: Ethnic Identification and the Problem of Generations," *Sociological Review* 13 (1965): 311.
20. *Vierzig Tage*, 358.
21. Martin Buber, *On Judaism*, ed. Nahum N. Glatzer, trans. Eva Jospe (New York: Schocken Books, 1967), 17.
22. Vienna: Österreichische Nationalbibliothek, Handschriften- und Inkunabelsammlung. This handwritten manuscript of *Musa Dagh* will henceforth be referred to as "Manuscript." All translations are my own.
23. Paul Rohrbach, *Armenien. Beiträge zur armenischen Landes-und Volkskunde* (Stuttgart: Engelhorns, 1919), 82.
24. Manuscript, 168.
25. Buber, *On Judaism*, 17.
26. Page 7 in a notebook marked "Franz Werfel. Szenarien und Pläne June 1930," Franz Werfel Collection, Special Collections, University of California at Los Angeles. Translation is mine.
27. *Vierzig Tage*, 358.
28. Ibid., 353
29. Ibid., 349.
30. Ibid., 358.
31. Buber, *On Judaism*, 22.
32. Manuscript, 62.
33. *Vierzig Tage*, 868.

Chapter 3. Franz Werfel, the Historical Novel, and *The Forty Days of Musa Dagh*

1. Murray Baumgarten, "The Historical Novel: Some Postulates," *Clio* IV, no. 2 (1975): 176–77.
2. Hayden White, *Metahistory. The Historical Imagination in Nineteenth-Century Europe* (1973; reprint, Baltimore: Johns Hopkins University Press, 1990), 5.
3. Paul Michael Lützeler, "Fictionality in Historiography and the Novel," in *Neverending Stories. Toward a Critical Narratology*, ed. Ann Fehn, Ingeborg Hoesterey, and Maria Tatar (Princeton: Princeton University Press, 1992), 29–44.
4. Ann Rigney, "Adapting History to the Novel," *New Comparison* 8 (1989): 127.
5. Ibid., 132–33.
6. An exception would be what Helbig calls the parahistorical novel, which portrays alternative outcomes to historical occurrences in a sort of postmodern game-playing with the genre. Jörg Helbig, "Thema und Variation. Kingsley Amis' *The Alteration* als postmoderne Spielart des historischen Romans," *Germanisch-Romanische Monatsschrift* 42, no. 4 (1992).
7. Joseph Turner, "The Kinds of Historical Fiction: An Essay in Definition and Methodology," *Genre* XII (1979): 343.

8. Helmut Koopmann, "'Geschichte ist die Sinngebung des Sinnlosen.' Zur Ästhetik des historischen Romans im Exil," in *Schreiben im Exil. Zur Ästhetik der deutschen Exilliteratur 1933–1945*, ed. Alexander Stephan and Hans Wagener (Bonn: Bouvier, 1985), 32. All translations are mine.

9. Georg Lukács, *Der historische Roman*, 1937. Passages cited here are taken from *The Historical Novel*, trans. Hanna and Stanley Mitchell (1962; reprint, London: Merlin, 1978).

10. Eberhard Lämmert, "Der Autor und sein Held im Roman des 19. und 20. Jahrhunderts," *German Quarterly* 66, no. 4 (1993): 424.

11. Koopmann, "Ästhetik des historischen Romans," 28–29.

12. Ibid., 30.

13. Hugo Aust, *Der historische Roman* (Stuttgart: Metzler, 1994), 28. All translations are mine.

14. P. M. Wetherill, "The Novel and Historical Discourse: Notes on a Nineteenth-Century Perspective," *Journal of European Studies* XV (1985), 122.

15. Ibid., 123.

16. Paul Michael Lützeler, "Georg Lukács and the Historical Novel of the Restoration Period," in *The Modern German Historical Novel*, ed. David Roberts and Philip Thomson (New York: Berg, 1991), 37.

17. Lützeler, "Fictionality," 39.

18. Werfel, *Verdi*, trans. Helen Jessiman, (1924; reprint, London, New York, Melbourne: Jarrolds, 1945), 6.

19. Lukács, *Der historische Roman*, 59.

20. Barbara Foley, *Telling the Truth. The Theory and Practice of Documentary Fiction*, (Ithaca, NY: Cornell University Press, 1986), 145.

21. Werfel, *Verdi*, 6.

22. Aust, *Der historische Roman*, 1.

23. Wetherill, "The Novel and Historical Discourse," 119.

24. Werfel, *Verdi*, 7.

25. Koopmann, "Ästhetik des historischen Romans," 18–19.

26. Ibid., 20.

27. Karl Dietrich Bracher, *The German Dictatorship*, trans. Jean Steinberg (1969; reprint, New York: Holt, Rinehart & Winston, 1970) 129.

28. Adolf Hitler, *Mein Kampf*, trans. Rolf Manheim, 1925–28; reprint, (Boston: Houghton Mifflin, 1962), 772. Cited in Bracher, *The German Dictatorship*, 425.

29. Aust, *Der historische Roman*, 33.

30. Homi K. Bhabha, *The Location of Culture* (London; New York: Routledge, 1994), 142.

31. Angie Chabram-Dernersesian, "I Throw Punches for My Race, but I Don't Want to Be a Man: Writing Us—Chica-nos (Girl, Us)/Chicanas—into the Movement Script," in *Cultural Studies*, ed. Lawrence Grossberg, Cary Nelson, and Paula A. Treichler (New York; London: Routledge, 1992) 81.

32. Edward Said, *Culture and Imperialism* (New York: Knopf, 1993), xii–xiii.

33. Bernard Lewis, *The Emergence of Modern Turkey* (London: Oxford, New York: Oxford University Press, 1961), 343.

34. Bhabha, *The Location of Culture*, 149.

35. Ibid., 155.

36. Louella O. Parsons, "Afternoon with Franz Werfel," *Chicago Herald-American*, 26 December 1943.

37. George Schulz-Behrend, "Sources and Background of Werfel's Novel *Die vierzig Tage des Musa Dagh*," *Germanic Review* XXVI (1951): 111–23.
38. Peter Stephan Jungk, *Franz Werfel. Eine Lebensgeschichte* (Frankfurt a.m.: Fischer, 1987), 138.
39. Schulz-Behrend, "Sources and Background," 112.
40. Hans Wagener, "Franz Werfel in der amerikanischen Literaturkritik," in *Franz Werfel im Exil,* ed. Wagener and Wolfgang Nehring (Bonn: Bouvier, 1992), 8, emphasis added.
41. F. R. Stern, letter to Mr. Franz Werfel, 3 July 1942, Franz Werfel Collection, Special Collections, University of California at Los Angeles.
42. Lionel Abel, review of *The Forty Days of Musa Dagh,* by Franz Werfel, *The Nation,* 12 December 1934, vol. 139, no. 3623: 684.
43. Ritchie Robertson, "Leadership and Community in Werfel's *Die vierzig Tage des Musa Dagh,*" in *Unser Fahrplan geht von Stern zu Stern. Zu Franz Werfels Stellung und Werk,* ed. Joseph P. Strelka and Robert Weigel (Bern: Peter Lang, 1992), 253.
44. Schulz-Behrend, "Sources and Background," 123 and 118. The author details at length the historical facts with which Werfel took liberties.
45. Werfel, *Vierzig Tage,* 531.
46. Manuscript, 353–54.
47. Ibid., 104.
48. Lukács, *Der historische Roman,* 34.
49. Paul Rohrbach, *German World Policies,* trans. Dr. Edmund von Mach (New York: Macmillan, 1915), 7.
50. Ibid., 4.
51. Ibid., 5.
52. Ibid., 231.
53. Ibid., 141.
54. Ibid., 226.
55. Ibid., 228. This entire passage is in boldface in Rohrbach's original German text.
56. Rohrbach, *Deutschland unter den Weltvölkern. Materialien zur auswärtigen Politik 1899–1918* (Stuttgart: Engelhorn, 1921), 28. All translations are mine.
57. *The New Encyclopaedia Britannica* (1990), 15th ed., vol. 14, 579.
58. Rohrbach, *World Policies,* 224.
59. Feroz Ahmad, "Ottoman Armed Neutrality and Intervention, August—November 1914," in *Studies on Ottoman Diplomatic History,* ed. Sinan Kuneralp, vol. IV (Istanbul: Isis, 1990), 41.
60. Ibid., 44.
61. Ibid., 68.
62. Bernard Lewis, *The Emergence of Modern Turkey* (London; Oxford; New York: Oxford University Press, 1961), 343.
63. Rohrbach, *Deutschland unter den Weltvölkern,* 105–6. Translation is mine.
64. Bilâl N. Simsir, "*The Genesis of the Armenian Question,*" *Publications of the Turkish Historical Society* July, 1984, 6–9.
65. Djemal Pasha, *Memories of a Turkish Statesman, 1913–1919* (New York: Doran, 1922), 99.
66. Simsir, "*Armenian Question,*" 22–23.
67. Wolfgang Iser, *The Act of Reading. A Theory of Aesthetic Response*

(1976; reprint, Baltimore and London: Johns Hopkins University Press, 1978), 35.

68. Schulz-Behrend, "Sources and Background," 123, mentions the harisa celebration but apparently was not aware of Werfel's source for this custom. One can find it described in great detail in C. F. Lehmann-Haupt's *Armenien einst und jetzt,* (Berlin: B. Behr, 1910), (vol. I) and 1926 (vol. II), 178–79. This passage is followed immediately by a description of the Widjak celebration, which Werfel also considered including in his novel: notes in the Vienna manuscript read, "*Das Widjakfest. Lehmann.*" In addition, two sketches in his UCLA notebook were copied from this work: the Armenian at the bazaar (L-H., vol. I, 153) and what he calls the "Dorf am Musa Dagh" (L-H., vol. II).

69. Schulz-Behrend, "Sources and Background," 118.

70. Johannes Lepsius, *Der Todesgang des Armenischen Volkes* (1916; reprint, Potsdam: Tempel, 1927), XII–XIX.

71. Questionnaire prepared by W. Paulsen, 1938, located in Franz Werfel Collection, Special Collections, University of California at Los Angeles. Translation is mine.

72. Djemal Pasha, *Memories of a Turkish Statesman, 1913–1919* (New York: Doran, 1922). The German translation, *Erinnerungen eines türkischen Staatsmannes,* has not been located for direct perusal.

73. *Meyers Lexikon,* vol. 12, 7th ed. (Leipzig: Bibliographisches Institut, 1930).

74. Djemal Pasha, *Memories of a Turkish Statesman,* 167.

75. Henry Morgenthau, *Ambassador Morgenthau's Story* (Garden City & New York: Doubleday, Page & Co., 1919).

76. Djemal Pasha, *Memories of a Turkish Statesman,* 203.

77. Morgenthau, *Morgenthau's Story,* 333–34.

78. Lützeler, "Fictionality," 36.

79. Ibid., 34.

80. Manuscript, 12.

81. James Davidheiser, "The Quest for Cultural and National Identity in the Works of Franz Werfel," *Perspectives on Contemporary Literature* 8 (1982): 62.

82. Manuscript, 425.

83. Jungk, *Lebensgeschichte,* 147.

Chapter 4. *Musa Dagh* as a Participant in Dominant Discourses

1. Stephen Greenblatt, "Towards a Poetics of Culture," in *The New Historicism,* ed. Aram H. Veeser (New York: Routledge, 1989), 12.

2. Franz Werfel, "Can We Live Without Faith in God?" in *Between Heaven and Earth,* trans. Maxim Newmark, (1932; reprint, New York: The Philosophical Library, 1944). All parenthetical indications of page numbers refer to this edition.

3. Ernst Haeckel, *Riddles of the Universe,* trans. Joseph McCabe (1899; reprint, New York, London: Harper and Brothers, 1905).

4. Franz Werfel, "Heimkehr ins Reich," *Die Österreichische Post* (*Courrier Autrichien*), 1 February 1939. All translations are mine.

5. Julien Benda, *La Trahison des Clercs,* trans. Richard Aldington (1927;

reprint, Boston: Beacon, 1959). Aldington translates "clercs" as "intellectuals" only in the title; in the text itself, it is translated as "clerks."

6. Ibid., 21.
7. Ibid., 31.
8. Ibid., 22.
9. Nancy Leys Stepan, and Sander L. Gilman, "Appropriating the Idioms of Science: The Rejection of Scientific Racism," in *The Bounds of Race. Perspectives on Hegemony and Resistance,* ed. Dominick LaCapra (Ithaca: Cornell University Press, 1991), 80.
10. Michael D. Biddiss, ed., *Images of Race* (New York: Holmes & Meier, 1979), 13.
11. Sander and Gilman, "Rejection of Scientific Racism," 81.
12. John William Jackson, "Race in Legislation and Political Economy," in *Images of Race* (New York: Holmes & Meier, 1979), 119.
13. Ibid., 137.
14. Ibid., 122.
15. George Mosse, *Toward the Final Solution* (New York: Fertig, 1978), 24.
16. Ibid., 28.
17. Ibid., 83.
18. Francis Galton, "Hereditary Talent and Character," in *Images of Race,* ed. Michael D. Biddis (New York: Holmes & Meier, 1979), 59.
19. Mosse, *Final Solution,* 85.
20. Ibid., 5.
21. Ibid., 26–27.
22. Benda, *La Trahison des Clercs,* 54.
23. Arthur de Gobineau, in *Gobineau. Selected Political Writings,* ed. Michael D. Biddis (New York; Evanston: Harper & Row, 1970), 41.
24. Robert Knox, *The Races of Men. A Philosophical Enquiry into the Influence of Race over the Destinies of Nations* (London, 1862), in *The Aryan Myth. A History of Racist and Nationalist Ideas in Europe,* ed. Léon Poliakov, trans. Edmund Howard (1971; reprint, London: Sussex University Press, 1974), 232.
25. Poliakov, *Aryan Myth,* 224.
26. Biddiss, *Images,* 27.
27. Thomas H. Huxley, *Man's Place in Nature and Other Anthropological Essays* (New York: D. Appleton, 1898), 240.
28. Herbert H. Odom, "Generalizations on Race in Nineteenth-Century Physical Anthropology," *Isis* 58 (1967): 8.
29. Benda, *La Trahison des Clercs,* 1–2.
30. Mosse, *Final Solution,* xi.
31. Biddiss, *Images,* 11.
32. LaCapra, *Bounds of Race,* 7.
33. Sander and Gilman, "Rejection of Scientifc Racism," 73.
34. Ibid., 100–101.
35. See Mary Louise Pratt, *Imperial Eyes. Travel Writing and Transculturation* (London; New York: Routledge, 1992).
36. Odom, "Generalizations on Race," 7.
37. Pratt, *Imperial Eyes,* 63–64.
38. Paul Rohrbach, *Armenien* (Stuttgart: Engelhorns, 1919), 69.
39. Ibid., 101–2.
40. Reverend Edwin Munsell Bliss, ed., *Encyclopedia of the Missions. De-*

scriptive, Historical, Biographical, Statistical, vol. I (New York; London; Toronto: Funk & Wagnalls, 1891), 100.

41. Henry Morgenthau, *Ambassador Morgenthau's Story* (Garden City; New York: Doubleday, Page & Co, 1919), 328.

42. Ibid., 337.

43. Samuel S. Cox, *Diversions of a Diplomat in Turkey* (New York: Charles L. Webster & Co., 1887).

44. Ibid., 178.

45. Ibid., 183.

46. Ibid., 184.

47. Ibid., 186.

48. Ibid., 181.

49. Mother Spalding Young, letter to Franz Werfel, 11 October 1947, Franz Werfel Collection, Special Collections, University of California at Los Angeles.

50. "Deutschnationaler Literaturmaßstab," *Prager Presse,* 20 March 1928. Translation is mine.

51. Karton MZV–VA 4112, folders labeled "Werfel, Frantisek," Prague.

52. "Werfel von den Tschechen preisgekrönt," *DÖ Tageszeitung* 11 February 1928. Translation is mine. This article was among the clippings in Prague, cropped down to its borders. I have been unable to identify the full name of the newspaper, which was indicated only in its abbreviated form as above.

53. Quoted in Odom, "Generalization on Race," 16.

54. Haeckel, "Heimkehr ins Reich," 380.

55. Mosse, *Final Solution,* 86.

56. Haeckel, "Heimkehr ins Reich," 269–70.

57. Ibid., vi.

58. Mosse, *Final Solution,* 87.

59. Haeckel, "Heimkehr ins Reich," 380–81.

60. Franza Werfel, "Realism and Inwardness," in *Between Heaven and Earth,* trans. Maxim Newmark, (1932; reprint, New York: The Philosophical Library, 1944), 45–76.

61. Ibid., 63.

62. Ibid., 47.

63. Ibid., 48–49.

64. Ibid., 62.

65. Werfel, "Faith in God," 89.

66. Ibid., 40.

67. Werfel, "Realism," 68.

68. Ibid., 64.

69. Many have pointed out the religious number imagery of *Musa Dagh.* See esp. Carl Steiner, "Religious Symbolism in Werfel's *Die vierzig Tage des Musa Dagh,"* in *Unser Fahrplan geht von Stern zu Stern. Zu Franz Werfels Stellung und Werk,* ed. Joseph P. Strelka and Robert Weigel (Bern; Berlin; Frankfurt: Peter Lang, 1992), 271–88.

70. Steiner, "Religious Symbolism," 276.

71. *Vierzig Tage,* 657.

72. Compare with Isaiah 63:3.

73. Steiner, "Religious Symbolism," 276.

74. UCLA notebook, 46. Translation mine.

75. Steiner, "Religious Symbolism," 286.

76. This is actually page 5 in the manuscript, however the main body of the text begins on page 2 here.

77. Manuscript, 3.
78. Ibid., 3.
79. Ibid., 3–4.
80. Ibid., 115.
81. Ibid., facing page 623.
82. Peter Stephan Jungk, *A Life Torn by History. Franz Werfel 1890–1945*, trans. Anselm Hollo (London: Weidenfeld and Nicolson, 1990), 139–40. Jungk also cites the preceding manuscript note in part. However, since his book is primarily a biography, he does not elaborate what sort of literary revisions Werfel made.
83. *Vierzig Tage*, 393.
84. Lionel Abel, "A Poet's Defense of Nationalism," *The Nation* 39 (December 12, 1934): 684.
85. Sander and Gilman, "Rejection of Scientific Racism," 76.
86. Ibid., 89.
87. Ibid., 101.
88. *Vierzig Tage*, 351
89. Ibid., 348.
90. Ritchie Robertson, "Leadership and Community in Werfel's *Die vierzig Tage des Musa Dagh*," in *Unser Fahrplan, geht von Stern zu Stern. Zu Frans Werfels Stellung und Werk*, ed. Joseph P. Strelka and Robert Weigel (Bern; Berlin, Frankfurt: Peter Lang, 1992), 262.
91. Werfel, "Heimkehr."
92. Werfel, "Realism," 64.
93. Werfel, "Faith in God," 140.
94. Steiner, "Religious Symbolism," 286–87. The poem was first published in *Hymnarium neuer Gedichte*, 1934. Translation is mine.
95. Ibid., 276.
96. *The Interpreter's Bible*, Vol. XII (New York; Nashville: Abingdon, 1957), 386–87, italics are mine.
97. Robertson, "Leadership and Community," 266–67.
98. Charles Taylor, *Multiculturalism and "The Politics of Recognition"* (Princeton: Princeton University Press, 1992), 68.
99. Jürgen Habermas, "Struggles for Recognition in the Democratic Constitutional State," in *Multiculturalism. Examining the Politics of Recognition*, ed. Amy Gutmann (Princeton: Princeton University Press, 1994), 148.
100. Paul Michael Lützeler, "Europäische Identität in der Postmoderne: Vom Nationalismus zur Multikulturalität," *Jahrbuch Deutsch als Fremdsprache* 19 (1993): 101. Translation is mine.

CHAPTER 5. RECEPTION AND LITERARY RESPONSE

1. Hans A. Joachim, "Ausgewählte Romane," *Die neue Rundschau der Freien Bühne* XLIV, no. I (1933): 133. All translations are mine.
2. Hermann Hesse, "Notiz zu neuen Büchern," (review of Gudmundur Kamban's *Jungfrau auf Skalholt*), *Die neue Rundschau der Freien Bühne* XLV, no. I (1935): 333–34. Translation is mine.
3. Paul von Zsolnay, letter of 20 November 1933, cited in Artem Ohandjanian, "'Diese Sucht, zu erniedrigen . . . ' Über Franz Werfel und seinen Roman 'The Forty Days of Musa Dagh,'" *Die Horen. Zeitschrift für Literatur, Grafik und Kritik* 35, no. 4 (1990): 161. Translation is mine.

4. Peter Stephan Jungk, *A Life Torn by History. Franz Werfel 1890–1945*, trans. Anselm Hollo (London: Weidenfeld and Nicolson, 1990), 144.

5. Ibid.

6. Joachim, "Ausgewählte Romane," 133.

7. O. M. F., "Franz Werfels neuer Roman," *Der Querschnitt* 13, no. 9 (December 1933): 636. All translations are mine.

8. M. R., "Die mißglückte Heimkehr. Franz Werfel: The Forty Days of Musa Dagh," *Vossische Zeitung* 10 December 1933, no. 555. All translations are mine.

9. Bertha Badt-Strauß, "Kampf der Schwachen. Zu Werfels neuem Roman," *Jüdische Rundschau* 98 (December 1933).

10. Herbert Friedenthal, "Franz Werfels neuer Roman," *Der Morgen* 9, no. 8 (1934): 479–80. All translations are mine.

11. Heinz Warschauer, "Der 'Bund deutsch-jüdischer Jugend,'" *Der Morgen* 9, no. 8 (1934): 480.

12. Annemarie Rheinländer-Möhl, *Umbruch des Geistes in seiner Auswirkung auf die literarische Situation der Gegenwart nachgewiesen an der zeitbedingten und artfremden Romankunst Franz Werfels* (Bochum-Langendreer: Pöppinghaus, 1936). All translations are mine. Though not published in book form until 1936, the writing of this thesis was finished in September 1933, two months prior to the publication of *Musa Dagh*.

13. Ibid., 7.

14. Robert Weninger, "Ästhetik versus Moral. Oder: Der Nutzen einer komparatistischen Rezeptionsästhetik," *German Life and Letters* 40, no. 1 (October 1986): 71–91.

15. Rheinländer-Möhl, *Umbruch des Geistes,* 49 (footnote).

16. Ibid., 71.

17. Hans Wagener, "Franz Werfel in der amerikanischen Literaturkritik," in *Franz Werfel im Exil,* ed. Wolfgang Nehring, Hans Wagener (Bonn; Berlin: Bouvier, 1992), 1–20.

18. Ibid.

19. Ibid., 9. Since this article treats the reception of all Werfel works in America, the section on *Musa Dagh* is necessarily restricted to only two pages.

20. Lewis Gannet, review of *Musa Dagh,* by Franz Werfel, *New York Herald Tribune,* 30 November 1934.

21. R. M. Gay, "The Man of the Month. Franz Werfel. The Forty Days of Musa Dagh," *The Atlantic* (undated article clipping from Franz Werfel Collection, Special Collections, Unviersity of California at Los Angeles).

22. Review of *Musa Dagh,* by Franz Werfel, *The Moslem World* 25, no. 3 (July 1935): 312–13.

23. Harry Hansen, review of *Musa Dagh,* by Franz Werfel, *New York World-Telegram,* undated (Franz Werfel Collection, Special Collections, University of California at Los Angeles).

24. Louis Kronenberger, review of *Musa Dagh,* by Franz Werfel, *New York Times,* 2 December 1934.

25. F. B., review of *Musa Dagh,* by Franz Werfel, *Chicago Daily Tribune,* 29 December 1934.

26. Review of *Musa Dagh,* by Franz Werfel, *Time,* 3 December 1934.

27. R. H. Phelps, review of *Musa Dagh,* by Franz Werfel, *Springfield Sunday Union and Republican,* 9 December 1934.

28. William Saroyan, review of *Musa Dagh,* by Franz Werfel, *Saturday Review of Literature,* 8 December 1934 (Vol. XI/21).

29. Geoffrey West, "A German Novel," *London Mercury,* January 1935, 300.
30. *Chicago Daily Tribune,* 29 December 1934.
31. *New York Herald Tribune,* 30 November, 1934.
32. G. T., review of *Musa Dagh,* by Franz Werfel, *The Catholic World* 140, no. 840 (March 1935): 753.
33. Robert Cantwell, "Outlook Book Choice of the Month," review of *Musa Dagh,* by Franz Werfel, *New Outlook* 164, no. 6 (December 1934): 54–5.
34. Review of *Musa Dagh,* by Franz Werfel, *Times Literary Supplement,* 27 December 1934.
35. Lionel Abel, "A Poet's Defense of Nationalism," *The Nation* 139, no. 3623 (12 December 1934): 684.
36. Robert Cantwell, "Book Choice," 54.
37. Harry Hansen, "Review."
38. Herschel Brickell, "Werfel and the Armenians," *New York Post,* 1 December 1934.
39. Robert Cantwell, "Book Choice," 54.
40. Harry Hansen, "Review."
41. F. R. Stern, letter to Franz Werfel, 3 July 1942, Franz Werfel Collection, Special Collections, University of California at Los Angeles.
42. Dr. Max Edwin Bircher, letter to Franz Werfel, 19 February 1943, Franz Werfel Collection, Special Collections, University of California at Los Angeles.
43. *Chicago Daily Tribune.*
44. Review of *Musa Dagh,* by Franz Werfel, *Golden Book,* December 1934.
45. *The Atlantic.*
46. Thomas Anz, "Der Mensch kann Ungeheures. Zum hunderststen Geburtstag des Expressionisten und Erfolgsschriftstellers Franz Werfel," *Frankfurter Allgemeine Zeitung,* 8 September 1990.
47. Ulrich Weinzierl, "Ich war ein Andrer! Umstritten bis heute / Ein Symposion diskutiert Franz Werfel," *Frankfurter Allgemeine Zeitung,* 30 April 1990.
48. Elisabeth Endres, "Der Weltfreund. Zum 100. Geburtstag von Franz Werfel," *Süddeutsche Zeitung,* 8/9 September 1990.
49. Artem Ohandjanian, "'Diese Sucht, zu erniedrigen . . . ' Über Franz Werfel und seinen Roman 'Die vierzig Tage des Musa Dagh,'" *Die Horen. Zeitschrift für Literatur, Grafik und Kritik* 35, no. 4 (1990): 159. Ohandjanian is also the author of *Armenien. Der verschwiegene Völkermord* (Wien; Köln; Graz: Böhlau, 1989).
50. Jungk tells us that the first version of *Musa Dagh* was not completed until late May, 1933, at which time Werfel immediately began the first of several revisions.
51. Hans Wagener, *Understanding Franz Werfel* (Columbia, S. C.: University of South Carolina, 1993), 121–23.
52. Lionel B. Steiman, "Werfel's Identity as Jew and Christian," in *Unser Fahrplan geht von Stern zu Stern. Zu Franz Werfels Stellung und Werk,* ed. Joseph P. Strelka and Robert Weigel (Bern: Peter Lang, 1992), 103.
53. Franz Werfel, letter to Alma Mahler, 1933, Franz Werfel Collection, Special Collections, University of California at Los Angeles. Translation is mine.
54. Hans Christoph Buch, "Ein Genozid, der offiziell nie stattgefunden hat. Über Franz Werfels Roman *Die vierzig Tage des Musa Dagh,*" in Buch, *Waldspaziergang* (Frankfurt: Suhrkamp, 1987): 107–17. All translations are mine.
55. Ibid., 108.
56. Ibid., 108–9.

57. Ibid., 109.
58. Ibid., 113.
59. Edgar Hilsenrath, *The Story of the Last Thought*, trans. Hugh Young (1989; reprint, Scribners, London: 1990), henceforth referred to as *Story*.
60. Peter Stenberg, "Memories of the Holocaust. Edgar Hilsenrath and the Fiction of Genocide," *Deutsche Vierteljahresschrift* 56, no. 2 (1982): 282.
61. Frances Spalding, review of *The Story of the Last Thought*, by Edgar Hilsenrath, *Times Educational Supplement*, 4 January 1991.
62. *Story*, 174.
63. Sidney Rosenfeld, review of *The Story of the Last Thought*, by Edgar Hilsenrath, *World Literature Today* 64, no. 2 (1990): 299.
64. Martin Hielscher, "Das Flüstern des Todes. Edgar Hilsenraths 'Märchen vom letzten Gedanken'—ein Roman über den Völkermord an den Armeniern," *Die Zeit*, 6 October 1989. All translations are mine.
65. *Story*, 13.
66. Hielscher, "Das Flüstern des Todes.".
67. *Story*, 66.
68. Ibid., 361.
69. Ibid., 415.
70. Ibid., 327.
71. Ibid., 415.
72. Ibid., 155–156.
73. Ibid., 102.
74. Leo Hamalian, *As Others See Us. The Armenian Image in Literature* (New York: Ararat, 1980).
75. *Story*, 70.
76. Ohandjanian, "Diese Sucht" 159. Translation is mine.
77. *Story*, 32.
78. Ibid., 40, 114.
79. Ibid., 187.
80. Ibid., 237.
81. Ibid., 193.
82. Ibid., 63.

Bibliography

Abel, Lionel. "A Poet's Defense of Nationalism." *The Nation* 139, no. 3623 (12 December 1934): 684.

Aust, Hugo. *Der historische Roman.* Stuttgart: Metzler, 1994.

Baumgarten, Murray. "The Historical Novel: Some Postulates." *Clio* IV, no. 2 (1975): 173–82.

Benda, Julien, *La Trahison des Clercs.* Translated by Richard Aldington. Boston: Beacon, 1959.

Berger, Peter L. "Identity as a Problem in the Sociology of Knowledge." *European Journal of Sociology* 7, no. 1 (1966): 105–15.

Bhabha, Homi K. *The Location of Culture.* London: Routledge, 1994.

Biddiss, Michael. *Images of Race.* New York: Holmes & Meier, 1979.

———, ed. *Gobineau. Selected Political Writings.* New York: Harper & Row, 1970.

Binger, Norman H., and A. Wayne Wonderley. *Studies in Nineteenth and Early Twentieth Century German Literature: Essays in Honor of Paul K. Whitaker.* Lexington: APRA Press, 1974.

Bliss, Reverend Edwin Munsell, ed. *Encyclopedia of the Missions. Descriptive, Historical, Biographical, Statistical.* New York: Funk & Wagnalls, 1891.

Bogdal, Michael, ed. *Neue Literaturtheorien. Eine Einführung.* Opladen: Westdeutscher Verlag, 1990.

Bracher, Karl Dietrich. *The German Dictatorship.* Translated by Jean Steinberg. New York: Holt, Rinehart & Winston, 1970.

Brunner, Franz. *Franz Werfel als Erzähler.* Zurich: Buchdruckerei neue Zürcher Zeitung, 1955.

Buber, Martin. *On Judaism.* Edited by Nahum N. Glatzer. Translated by Eva Jospe. Frankfurt a.M.: Rütten & Loening, 1916.

Buch, Hans Christoph. *Waldspaziergang.* Frankfurt: Suhrkamp, 1987.

Cohen, Gary. *The Politics of Ethnic Survival: Germans in Prague, 1861–1914.* Princeton: Princeton University Press, 1981.

Coles, Robert. *Erik H. Erikson. The Growth of His Work.* Boston: Little, Brown & Co., 1970.

Cox, Samuel S. *Diversions of a Diplomat in Turkey.* New York: Charles L. Webster & Co., 1887.

Davidheiser, James C. "The Quest for Cultural and National Identity in the Works of Franz Werfel." *Perspectives on Contemporary Literature* 8 (1982): 59–66.

Djemal Pasha. *Memories of a Turkish Statesman, 1913–1919.* New York: Doran, 1922.

Early, Gerald. "American Education and the Postmodernist Impulse." *American Quarterly* 45, no. 2 (1993): 220–29.

Eggert, Hartmut et al., ed. *Geschichte als Literatur. Formen und Grenzen der Repräsentation von Vergangenheit.* Stuttgart: Metzler, 1990.

Eisner, Pavel. *Franz Kafka and Prague.* New York: Golden Griffin, 1950.

Fehn, Ann et al., ed. *Neverending Stories. Toward a Critical Narratology.* Princeton: Princeton University Press, 1992.

Feuchtwanger, Lion. *The House of Desdemona or The Laurels and Limitations of Historical Fiction.* Translated by Harold A. Basilius. Detroit: Wayne State University Press, 1963.

Fletcher, Angus, ed. *The Literature of Fact.* New York: Columbia University Press, 1976.

Foley, Barbara. *Telling the Truth. The Theory and Practice of Documentary Fiction.* Ithaca: Cornell University Press,1986.

Fuhrmann, Manfred, and Hans Robert Jauß, ed. *Text und Application. Theologie, Jurisprudenz und Literaturwissenschaft im hermeneutischen Gespräch.* München: Fink, 1981.

Geertz, Clifford. *The Interpretation of Cultures.* New York: Basic Books, 1973.

Glatzer, Nahum N., and Paul Mendes-Flohr, ed. *The Letters of Martin Buber.* New York: Shocken, 1991.

Gleason, Philip. "Identifying Identity: A Semantic History." *The Journal of American History* 69, no. 4 (1983): 910–31.

Grimm, Gunter E., ed. *Im Zeichen Hiobs: Jüdische Schriftsteller und deutsche Literatur im 20. Jahrhundert.* Königstein: Athenäum, 1985.

Grossberg, Lawrence et al., ed. *Cultural Studies.* New York: Routledge, 1992.

Haeckel, Ernst. *The Riddle of the Universe.* Translated by Joseph McCabe. New York, London: Harper and Brothers, 1905.

Haley, Alex. *Roots.* Garden City: Doubleday, 1976.

Hamalian, Leo. *As Others See Us. The Armenian Image in Literature.* New York: Ararat, 1980.

Helbig, Jörg. "Thema und Variation. Kingsley Amis' *The Alteration* als postmoderne Spielart des historischen Romans." *Germanisch-Romanische Monatsschrift* 42, no. 4 (1992): 444–50.

Hesse, Hermann. "Notiz zu neuen Büchern." *Die neue Rundschau der Freien Bühne* XLV, no. I (1935): 333–334.

Hilsenrath, Edgar. *The Story of the Last Thought.* Translated by Hugh Young. London: Abacus, 1990.

Hirsch, Rudolf, and Ingeborg Schnack, ed. *Hugo von Hofmannsthal. Rainer Maria Rilke. Briefwechsel 1899–1925.* Frankfurt: Insel, 1978.

Holub, Robert C. "Trends in Literary Theory: The American Reception of Reception Theory." *German Quarterly* 55, no. 1 (January 1982): 80–96.

Horwath, Peter. "The Erosion of *Gemeinschaft*: German Writers of Prague, 1890–1924." *German Studies Review* 4, no. 1 (1981): 9–37.

Howard, Jean E. "The New Historicism in Renaissance Studies." *English Literary Renaissance* 16, no.1 (1986): 13–43.

Howard, Jean E., and Marion F. O'Connor, ed. *Shakespeare Reproduced: The Text in History and Ideology.* New York: Methuen, 1987.

Huxley, Thomas H. *Man's Place in Nature and Other Anthropological Essays.* New York: D. Appleton, 1898.

Hyršlová, K. "Zur Frage der Heimat im Werke Franz Werfels." *Zeitschrift für Slawistik* III, no. 5 (1958): 727–36.

Iser, Wolfgang. *The Act of Reading. A Theory of Aesthetic Response.* Baltimore: Johns Hopkins University Press, 1978.

———. *Prospecting: From Reader Response to Literary Anthropology.* Baltimore: Johns Hopkins, 1993.

Jacobson, Anna. "Franz Werfel: Eine Würdigung." *Journal of English and Germanic Philology* XXVI, no. 3 (1927): 337–49.

Jauß, Hans Robert. *Literaturgeschichte als Provokation.* Frankfurt: Suhrkamp, 1970.

———. *Question and Answer. Forms of Dialogic Understanding.* Minneapolis: University of Minnesota Press, 1989.

———. *Toward an Aesthetic of Reception.* Minneapolis: University of Minnesota Press, 1982.

Joachim, Hans A. "Ausgewählte Romane." *Die neue Rundschau der Freien Bühne* XLIV, no. I (1933): 133–34.

Jungk, Peter Stephan. *Franz Werfel. Eine Lebensgeschichte.* Frankfurt a.M.: Fischer, 1987.

———. *A Life Torn by History. Franz Werfel 1890–1945.* Translated by Anselm Hollo. London: Weidenfeld and Nicolson, 1990.

Kaes, Anton. "New Historicism: Writing Literary History in the Postmodern Era." *Monatshefte* 84, no. 2 (1992): 148–58.

———. "New Historicism and the Study of German Literature." *German Quarterly* 62, no. 2 (1989): 210–19.

Kieval, Hillel. *The Making of Czech Jewry. National Conflict and Jewish Society in Bohemia, 1870–1918.* New York: Oxford University Press, 1988.

Krolop, Kurt. "Das 'Prager Erbe' und 'das Österreichische.'" *Zeitschrift für Germanistik* (1983): 166–78.

Kuneralp, Sinan, ed. *Studies on Ottoman Diplomatic History.* Istanbul: Isis, 1990.

LaCapra, Dominick, ed. *The Bounds of Race. Perspectives on Hegemony and Resistance.* Ithaca: Cornell University Press, 1991.

Lämmert, Eberhard. "Der Autor und sein Held im Roman des 19. und 20. Jahrhunderts." *German Quarterly* 66, no. 4 (1993): 415–30.

———. "Geschichten von der Geschichte. Geschichtsschreibung und Geschichtsdarstellung im Roman." *Poetica* 17, no. 3–4 (1985): 228–54.

Lehmann-Haupt, C. F. *Armenien einst und jetzt.* Vol. I. Berlin: B. Behr, 1910. Vol. II, 1926.

Lepsius, Johannes. *Der Todesgang des Armenischen Volkes.* 1916. Reprint, Potsdam: Tempel, 1927.

Lewis, Bernard. *The Emergence of Modern Turkey.* London: Oxford University Press, 1961.

Lukács, Georg. *The Historical Novel.* Translated by Hanna and Stanley Mitchell. London: Merlin, 1978.

Lützeler, Paul Michael. "Europäische Identität in der Postmoderne: Vom Nationalismus zur Multikulturalität." *Jahrbuch Deutsch als Fremdsprache* 19 (1993).

Lyotard, Jean-François. *The Postmodern Condition: A Report on Knowledge.* Translated by Geoff Bennington and Brian Massumi. Minneapolis: University of Minnesota Press, 1989.

Matthews, Fred. "Cultural Pluralism in Context: External History, Philosophic Premise, and Theories of Ethnicity in Modern America." *Journal of Ethnic Studies* 12, no. 2 (1984): 63–79.

Morgenthau, Henry. *Ambassador Morgenthau's Story.* Garden City: Doubleday, Page & Co., 1919.

Mosse, George. *Toward the Final Solution.* New York: Fertig, 1978.

Nahirny, Vladimir C., and Joshua A. Fishman. "American Immigrant Groups: Ethnic Identification and the Problem of Generations." *Sociological Review* 13 (1965): 311.

Nehring, Wolfgang, and Hans Wagener, ed. *Franz Werfel im Exil.* Bonn: Bouvier, 1992.

Odom, Herbert H. "Generalizations on Race in Nineteenth-Century Physical Anthropology." *Isis* 58 (1967): 5–18.

Ohandjanian, Artem. *Armenien. Der verschwiegene Völkermord.* Wien: Böhlau, 1989.

―――. "'Diese Sucht, zu erniedrigen . . .' Über Franz Werfel und seinen Roman 'Die vierzig Tage des Musa Dagh.'" *Die Horen. Zeitschrift für Literatur, Grafik und Kritik* 35, no. 4 (1990): 158–63.

Okamura, Jonathan Y. "Situational Identity." *Ethnic and Racial Studies* 4, no. 4 (October 1981): 453–65.

Paulsen, Wolfgang. *Franz Werfel. Sein Weg in den Roman.* Tübingen; Basel: Francke, 1995.

Pechter, Edward. "The New Historicism and Its Discontents: Politicizing Renaissance Drama." *PMLA* 102, no. 3 (1987): 292–302.

Poliakov, Léon, ed. *The Aryan Myth. A History of Racist and Nationalist Ideas in Europe.* Translated by Edmund Howard. London: Sussex University Press, 1974.

Politzer, Heinz. "Prague and the Origins of Rainer Maria Rilke, Franz Kafka, and Franz Werfel." *Modern Language Quarterly* 16 (1955): 49–62.

Poster, Mark. "Postmodernity and the Politics of Multiculturalism: The Lyotard-Habermas Debate Over Social Theory." *Modern Fiction Studies* 38, no. 3 (1992): 567–80.

Pratt, Mary Louise. *Imperial Eyes. Travel Writing and Transculturation.* London: Routledge, 1992.

Puckett, Hugh. "Franz Werfel's Mission." *Germanic Review* 2 (1947): 117–25.

von Puttkamer, Annemarie. *Franz Werfel. Wort und Antwort.* Würzburg: Werkbund Verlag, 1952.

Reffet, Michel. "Franz Werfel und die Tschechoslowakei." *Österreich in Geschichte und Literatur (mit Geographie)* 27, no. 2 (1983): 84–90.

Rheinländer-Möhl, Annemarie. *Umbruch des Geistes in seiner Auswirkung auf die literarische Situation der Gegenwart nachgewiesen an der zeitbedingten und artfremden Romankunst Franz Werfels.* Bochum-Langendreer: Pöppinghaus, 1936.

Rigney, Ann. "Adapting History to the Novel." *New Comparisons* 8 (1989): 127–43.
Roberts, David, and Philip Thomson, ed. *The Modern German Historical Novel. Paradigms, Problems, Perspectives.* New York: Berg, 1991.
Rohrbach, Paul. *Armenien. Beiträge zur armenischen Landes-und Volkskunde.* Stuttgart: Engelhorns, 1919.
———. *Deutschland unter den Weltvölkern. Materialien zur auswärtigen Politik 1899–1918.* Stuttgart: Engelhorn, 1921.
———. *German World Policies.* Translated by Dr. Edmund von Mach. New York: Macmillan, 1915.
Rorty, Richard. *Consequences of Pragmatism. (Essays: 1972–1980).* Minneapolis: University of Minnesota Press, 1982.
Royce, Anna Peterson. *Ethnic Identity. Strategies of Diversity.* Bloomington: Indiana University Press, 1982.
Ruitenbeek, Hendrik M., ed. *Varieties of Modern Social Theory.* New York: Dutton, 1963.
Said, Edward. *Culture and Imperialism.* New York: Knopf, 1993.
Schaeder, Grete, ed. *Martin Buber. Briefwechsel aus sieben Jahrzehnten. Band I: 1897–1918.* Heidelberg: Lambert Schneider, 1972.
Schnitzler, Gunter et al., ed. *Bild und Gedanke: Festschrift für Gerhart Baumann zum 60. Geburtstag.* München: Fink, 1980.
Schulz-Behrend, George. "Sources and Background of Werfel's Novel *Die vierzig Tage des Musa Dagh*." *Germanic Review* XXVI (1951): 111–23.
Schwarz, Egon. "'Ich war also Jude! Ich war ein anderer!' Franz Werfels Darstellung der soziopsychologischen Judenproblematik." *Literaria Pragensia* 3, no. 6 (1983): 47–58.
Serke, Jürgen. *Böhmische Dörfer. Wanderungen durch eine verlassene literarische Landschaft.* Wien: Paul Zsolnay, 1987.
Simpson, David. "Literary Criticism and the Return to 'History.'" *Critical Inquiry* 14, no. 4 (1988): 721–47.
Sollers, Werner. *Consent and Descent in American Culture.* New York: Oxford University Press, 1986.
Stamm, Israel S. "Religious Experience in Werfel's *Barbara*." *Publications of the Modern Language Association* 54 (1939): 332–47.
Stenberg, Peter. "Memories of the Holocaust. Edgar Hilsenrath and the Fiction of Genocide." *Deutsche Vierteljahresschrift* 56, no. 2 (1982): 277–89.
Stephan, Alexander, and Hans Wagener. *Schreiben im Exil: Zur Ästhetik der deutschen Exilliteratur 1933–1945.* Bonn: Bouvier, 1985.
Strelka, Joseph P., and Robert Weigel, ed. *Unser Fahrplan geht von Stern zu Stern. Zu Franz Werfels Stellung und Werk.* Bern: Peter Lang, 1992.
Taylor, Charles. *Multiculturalism. Examining the Politics of Recognition.* Edited by Amy Gutmann. 1994. Reprint, Princeton: Princeton University Press, 1992.
Turner, Joseph. "The Kinds of Historical Fiction: An Essay in Definition and Methodology." *Genre* XII (1979): 333–55.
Veeser, H. Aram, ed. *The New Historicism.* New York: Routledge, 1989.
Wagener, Hans. *Understanding Franz Werfel.* Columbia, S.C.: University of South Carolina, 1993.

Weninger, Robert. "Ästhetik versus Moral. Oder: Der Nutzen einer komparatistischen Rezeptionsästhetik." *German Life and Letters* 40, no. 1 (October 1986): 71–91.

Werfel, Franz. *Barbara oder Die Frömmigkeit.* 1929. Reprint, Frankfurt a.M: Fischer, 1988.

———. *Between Heaven and Earth.* Translated by Maxim Newmark. 1932. Reprint, New York: The Philosophical Library, 1944.

———*The Forty Days of Musa Dagh.* Translated by Geoffrey Dunlop. New York: Viking, 1934.

———. "Heimkehr ins Reich." *Die Österreichische Post (Courrier Autrichien),* 1 February 1939.

———. *Poems.* Translated by Edith Abercrombie Snow. Princeton: Princeton University Press, 1945.

———. *The Pure in Heart.* Translated by Geoffrey Dunlop. New York: Simon and Schuster, 1931.

———. *Können wir ohne Gottesglauben leben?* Berlin: Paul Zsolnay, 1932.

———. *Das Lyrische Werk.* Edited by Adolf D. Klarmann. Frankfurt a.M.: Fischer, 1967.

———. *Pogrom.* 1926; Frankfurt a.M.: Fischer, 1989.

———. *Realismus und Innerlichkeit.* Berlin: Paul Zsolnay, 1931.

———. *Twilight of a World.* Translated by H. T. Lowe-Porter. New York: Viking, 1937.

———. *Verdi.* Translated by Helen Jessiman. London, New York, Melbourne: Jarrolds, 1945.

———. *Die vierzig Tage des Musa Dagh.* 1933; Frankfurt a.M.: Fischer, 1988.

———. *Zwischen Oben und Unten.* 1944. Reprint, München: Langen Müller, 1975.

Wetherill, P. M. "The Novel and Historical Discourse: Notes on a Nineteenth-Century Perspective." *Journal of European Studies* XV (1985): 117–30.

White, Hayden. *Metahistory. The Historical Imagination in Nineteenth-Century Europe.* 1973. Reprint, Baltimore: Johns Hopkins University Press, 1990.

Index

Abdul Hamid, 70, 95, 106
Ambassador Morgenthau's Story (Morgenthau), 104, 121
anti-Semitism, 52, 82; Alma Mahler Werfel's, 59, 62; in *Pogrom*, 33, 35; in Prague, 43–45; Rilke and, 47
Armenians, biases against, 56, 60, 68, 84, 165, 178; literary portrayal of, 177–78
Armenian National Party, 55
Armenien (Rohrbach), 121–22
assimilation: in *The Forty Days of Musa Dagh*, 54–55, 64, 108, 110, 156–57; in *Pogrom*, 35–36; of Prague Jews, 40, 43, 49, 51; in *The Pure of Heart*, 30

Baghdad Railway, 93, 97
Balkan War, 56, 94–95, 107, 129
Benda, Julien: *Betrayal of the Intellectuals*, 114–15
Betrayal of the Intellectuals (Benda), 114–15
Bezruč, Petr, 45; *Silesian Songs*, 45
Bhabha, Homi, 84
blood, 35, 50, 138, 141–42; as concept of community, 50, 65, 155. *See also* Race, discourse of
Brod, Max, 44.
Buber, Martin, 48–52, 58, 66, 69–70, 74; correspondence with Werfel, 49; "On Judaism", 49–51.

Carus, Carl Gustav: *Symbolism of the Human Form*, 117
Catholicism, 30
Christianity, 114
colonialism, 84, 92–98, 176
community, Armenian, 67, 73, 108, 141–42
community: lack of, 18; loss of, 19, 27, 30–31

community, history of, 14; bearing on individual identity, 14, 51, 105; in *The Forty Days of Musa Dagh*, 66, 69, 74, 108–9; in *Pogrom*, 39; in *The Pure of Heart*, 34
community, Jewish, 33–35, 39. *See* Prague: Jewish population of
community, narratives of, 84–85
counternarrative, 85–86
cultural studies, 83–84
customs, knowledge of, 68–69, 105
Czechs: minority status of, 25; national movement of, 43–45, 48; Werfel's portrayal of, 22–25, 27

Darwinism, 111, 114, 124
Degeneration (Nordau), 117
discourses: dominant, 111–49; religious, 113, 116, 135; scientific, 113–15, 118–19, 136, 139
Djemal Pasha, 101–4; *Memories of a Turkish Statesman, 1913–1919*, 102–4

Edict of Tolerance, 42
Emin, Mehmed, 84
enlighteners, Jewish. *See* maskilim
Enver Pasha, 85, 90–91, 98, 101–5, 130, 174
"*Essai sur l'inégalité des races humaines*" (Gobineau), 118
Essai sur la Physiognomie (Lavater), 116–17
ethnic groups, 22; traditions of, 22, 34

family: as community, 36–39, 58; father-son relationship in, 36–39
First World War, 16, 94, 153, 165, 167; in *Musa Dagh*, 53, 58, 99, 106, 173; in *Pogrom*, 32; in *The Pure of*

Heart, 28; Werfel's reaction to, 18, 20
Fuchs, Rudolf, 44

Gobineau, Arthur de: "*Essai sur l'inégalité des races humaines*", 118
God, 126–27; individual relationship with, 29, 144–46. *See also* intervention, divine
Good Soldier Schweik (Hašek), 44

Habermas, Jürgen, 148
Haeckel, Ernst, 112, 123–26, 149; *Natural History of Creation*, 124; *Riddles of the Universe*, 112–13, 125
Hanka, Václav, 44.
Hašek, Jaroslav, *Good Soldier Schweik*, 44
Heimat, 20, 22, 28–30, 40, 65
Herrmann, Leo, 48–49.
Hilsenrath, Edgar: *The Story of the Last Thought*, 172–80; style of, 172–73
historical novel. *See* novel, historical
historiography, 76–77, 81, 99–100, 105; use of pseudoscience in, 117
Hofmannsthal, Hugo von, 35, 40, 46–47; "*Where is . . .*", 40
human community, 17, 20

identity: "authentic"and "inauthentic", 31, 34, 36, 51, 65, 67, 112, 141; childhood experiences and, 57, 67; and community, 13–14, 16, 28, 33–34, 50–51, 54, 140–41; in crisis, 16, 32–33, 36, 39; defined, 13–14; education and, 43, 48; ethnicity and, 22, 34, 39, 58, 64, 66, 106, 136, 143–144; family and, 36–39; history and, 17, 20, 30, 34, 42, 51, 74, 79, 105–110; language and, 14, 30, 34, 42–43, 51, 62, 64, 74, 105; minority, 15, 84, 86, 141; nationality and, 15; "objective" and "subjective", 42; rejection of, 73; religion as component of, 30–31, 34, 42, 105, 144; theme in Werfel's works, 13; traditions and, 58, 64, 68, 71, 105; "universal", questioned, 15; *Volk* as component of, 20, 26, 30

identity markers: physical appearance as, 56, 63
individual, 57, 59, 73, 145–146, 155; relationship to community, 14, 19, 50, 74, 82, 154, 157
intervention, divine, 126–27, 129–30, 132, 134–35, 142

Joseph II, 42
Judaism, cultural heritage of, 30

Kafka, Franz, 41, 170
Kraus, Karl, 151

language: as identity component, 14, 30, 34, 42–43, 64, 74
Lavater, Johann Kaspar: *Essai sur la Physiognomie*, 116–17
Lepsius, Johannes, 73, 84, 90, 97–99, 101–2, 104, 128, 130–31, 147, 153, 176
Lukàcs, Georg, 78, 80, 90, 101, 107

Magic Mountain, The (Mann), 163
Mann, Thomas: *The Magic Mountain*, 163
marginalization, 71
maskilim, 42–43
minorities, 15, 23, 27, 53–54, 71, 82–86, 109–10, 111, 119, 139, 141, 155–56, 162, 168
modernity, principles of, 15, and Werfel, 16
monism, 124–25
Morgenthau, Henry, 176, 178; *Ambassador Morgenthau's Story*, 104, 121
multiculturalism, 15–16, 147–48

nationalism, 16, 18, 26, 43–45, 48, 53–54, 95, 97, 111, 114, 123, 132, 140, 143, 149
nationality, 51; Czech, 22; Slovak, 22; as identity component, 15, 39, 126, 140; and national traits, 22–23, 25–26, 32, 139
Natural History of Creation (Haeckel), 124
Nietzsche, Friedrich, 113, 131
nihilism, 113
Nordau, Max: *Degeneration*, 117
novel, historical, 76–110, 153, 171, 174; exile authors' use of: 77–78,

82, 98; goals of: 88–89; historical characters in: 101–5, 174–75; historical sources of: 87, 102–5; historical "truth" and: 80–81, 83, 87, 174; invented characters in: 88; narration in: 79; protagonist's role in: 78, 98; relationship to contemporary issues, 79, 107; reputation of, 151

Ost und West, 44

Palacký, František, 44
physiognomy, 116–17, 136–38
Pick, Otto, 44.
postmodernism, 15
Prague, 22, 82; Martin Buber and, 48–52; Czech population of,25; Jewish population of, 40–52; University of, 44, 48; Zionist movement in, 48–52
pseudoscience, 117; as replacement for religion, 114, 116, 126

race, discourse of, 116, 119–23; in *The Forty Days of Musa Dagh*, 111, 114, 135–36, 138, 148–49, 164; in *Story of the Last Thought*, 176
reception of *The Forty Days of Musa Dagh*: American and British, 158–65; Armenian, 169; German, 151–58; Jewish-German, 155–56; scholarly, 168
religion: Armenian (Gregorian), 60, 64; as identity component, 30–31, 34, 64
Riddles of the Universe (Haeckel), 112–13, 125
Rilke, Rainer Maria, 46–47
Rohrbach, Paul, 92–93, 121–22; *Armenien*, 121–22; *World Policies*, 92–93
Roth, Joseph, 144

Schönerer, Georg von, 43–44
Scott, Sir Walter, 80, 90, 117
secularization, 112–14, 123, 130, 132, 148
Silesian Songs (Bezruc), 45
Slovaks, Werfel's portrayal of: 25
stereotypes, of Jews, 35

Story of the Last Thought (Hilsenrath), 172–80
Symbolism of the Human Form (Carus), 117

Talaat Bey, 97, 103–4, 128, 175
Taylor, Charles, 19, 147
travel literature, racial assumptions and: 120–21
Turkish identity, 84–86

Viking Press, advertising strategies for *Musa Dagh*: 166–67
Volk, 17, 23, 30; heritage of, 21–22; ideology of, 20, 25

Werfel, Alma Mahler, 52, 59, 61
Werfel, Franz: Bohemia as *Heimat* and, 22; translator of Czech literature, 45; and Zionism, 49. Works: *Can We Live Without Faith In God?*, 112, 126; *Class Reunion*, 159; *Conjurations*, 25; "*Father and Son*", 37; "For I have done a good and kindly deed", 17; *The Forty Days of Musa Dagh*, 26–27, 53–75, 81–110, 111–12, 159–80; "*I am a Czechoslovakian*", 22; "*Inscription*", 18, 27; *The Man Who Conquered Death*, 159; "*The Mishap*", 23, 25; *Not the Murderer*, 37–39; *One Another*, 18; *The Pascarella Family*, 164; "*Permanence*", 21–22, 27, 51; *The Philanthropist*, 18; *Pogrom*, 32–36, 46; *The Pure in Heart*, 27–31, 33–34, 164; *Sleep and Awakening*, 21; "*The Slovak*", 25; *The Song of Bernadette*, 159; "*To the reader*", 17; "*Tempora mea in manibus tuis*", 145; *Verdi*, 80–81, 159; *We Are*, 18; *The World Friend*, 127
Werfel, Mizi, 62
"*Where is . . .*" (Hofmannsthal), 40
White, Hayden, 76–77
World Policies (Rohrbach), 92–93
World War I. *See* First World War

Young Turks, 55

Zionism, 48–52
Zsolnay, Paul von, 151–52